Fountas & Pinnell

Leveled Literacy Intervention

Program Guide

Green
SYSTEM

Irene C. Fountas

Gay Su Pinnell

Heinemann, Portsmouth, NH

Heinemann

361 Hanover Street
Portsmouth, NH 03801–3912
www.heinemann.com

Offices and agents throughout the world

ISBN-0-325-01950-9

ISBN-978-0-325-01950-5

0411/11002395

Printed in Dongguan, China
16   15   14   13   12   11   RRD   5   6   7   8   9

Program Guide, Green System

We use *Program Guide* synonymously with *System Guide* to indicate the systematic design of LLI. References in this guide are to the LLI System.

Section 4	Assessment and Record-Keeping	77

| Section 5 | Professional Development for LLI | 93 |

| Appendix | | 105 |

The Leveled Literacy Intervention System

▶ LLI: 15 Keys to a Successful Intervention Design

Powerful early intervention can change the path of a child's journey to literacy. Children who experience difficulty in the early grades fall further and further behind their peers (Stanovich, 1986). Research shows that children who read below grade level at the end of Grade 1 are likely to continue to read below grade level (Juel, 1988). Many are retained at grade level or receive supplementary help throughout schooling. Others drop out of school as soon as they qualify. A growing body of research shows that reading difficulties are preventable with effective intervention programs (Clay, 2005; Goldenberg, 1994; Hiebert and Taylor, 1994; Schmidt, Askew, Fountas, Lyons, and Pinnell, 2005; What Works Clearinghouse, http://ies.ed.gov/ncee/wwc/reports/beginningreading/).

Leveled Literacy Intervention is a scientifically-based system that is designed to prevent literacy difficulties rather than correct long-term failure. It has been highly successful in achieving its goal of cutting across the path of literacy failure and bringing children to grade level performance in hundreds of schools. Leveled Literacy Intervention has the following key characteristics:

- ❑ LLI is designed to **supplement**, not substitute for, the small-group instruction that children receive in the classroom.

- ❑ LLI lessons are provided **daily** and are of sufficient length to assure reinforcement of new learning and to support accelerated progress. The thirty-minute lesson provides instruction in reading, writing, and phonics/word study.

- ❑ LLI lessons are provided to a small group, with a strong recommendation for **three children in the group.** The size of the group assures close observation and the intensive teaching interactions that promote individual learning and allow children to make faster progress.

- ❑ LLI is a **short-term intervention**. The System is designed to bring children to grade level performance in about twelve to twenty weeks. The Green System provides up to twenty weeks of lessons. The number of lessons can be extended to more weeks if necessary by using more lessons from the Orange or Blue System. As one group exits, a new group enters the teaching slot, allowing for six or more children to be served in each thirty-minute teaching slot for the year.

- ❑ LLI provides a well-defined **framework for lessons** within which teachers make decisions specific to observations of the children's needs. The lessons include reading texts, writing, and phonics. Children learn the routines for each of the regular elements of the lesson so lessons are efficient.

- Lessons are **fast paced**. The lessons are designed to move quickly with suggested time frames for each segment. Instead of "slowed down" teaching, children are highly engaged in experiences in which they find success.

- The focus of reading is deep **comprehending of texts**. Children read several books in every lesson. The teacher supports comprehension throughout the reading of the text and is provided a list of key understandings for each book.

- The focus of writing is the building of **early writing strategies**. Children learn how to compose, construct, and develop essential strategies for writing in the classroom. They learn how to use sound analysis, important spelling skills, and early writing conventions.

- Fluency is an important goal of LLI instruction. Lessons include **attention to fluent, phrased reading,** as well as fluency in writing. In order to be perceived as successful by classroom peers (as well as to process print effectively), readers and writers need to read smoothly and write quickly. It is especially important for low-achieving children to become fluent in literacy—before they become discouraged and perpetuate slow processing.

- Three collections of **high-quality texts** have been created specifically for LLI. Written by children's authors and illustrated by well-known illustrators, the texts are designed to engage young readers with high-quality fiction and nonfiction selections. They have been systematically crafted to build phonics and word analysis skills and arranged along a careful gradient of text characteristics (see Fountas and Pinnell, 2007). Across a series of texts at each level of LLI, readers have the advantage of processing a new text every day. Every other day the reader is given a book that is easier than the instructional level (generally one or two levels below) to support confidence and fluency. Children have the opportunity to read texts that are challenging, which stretch the processing system, and easy texts that build confidence. In the Appendix, starting on page 108, you can read a detailed analysis of the phonics, word analyses, decoding, and vocabulary challenges for each book.

- The lessons include **systematic phonics**. They focus on key aspects of phonics learning—phonological awareness, letter formation and knowledge, letter-sound relationships, word structure, spelling patterns, high-frequency words, and word-solving actions.

- LLI includes initial and ongoing **assessments, progress-monitoring,** and **record-keeping instruments** that are practical and that continuously inform teaching. The assessments will help you determine appropriate reading levels for grouping and provide useful information for daily teaching. Forms are provided for taking Reading Records on each child about once per week.

- LLI provides a high level of **professional development** within and outside lessons. You will notice the professional understandings provided in each lesson, including the analysis of book characteristics, support for teaching English language learners, assessment suggestions, and references to professional resources. The professional book *When Readers Struggle: Teaching that Works* is designed to provide strong support for teacher knowledge and decision-making in the lessons. In addition, *Professional Development and Tutorial DVDs* are included and the lessons also suggest other resources.

- LLI provides a strong **classroom connection**. Each lesson provides a link to the classroom. Children take books to read, word activities to review, and writing to reread. LLI teachers have efficient record-keeping documents that can be shared with the classroom teacher.

- LLI provides a strong **home connection**. When children have more opportunities to share their successes in the home, their self-esteem is enhanced. In addition, they gain valuable reading and writing practice. Children have many opportunities to take home phonics materials and writing. Take-Home Books and Parent Letters are provided to the children at the end of every lesson.

Finally, in any effective teaching, attention must be paid to children's language and its relation to literacy. Each LLI lesson provides a list of lesson-specific suggestions that will help teachers adjust instruction to make it more powerful for **English language learners.**

▶ What Is Leveled Literacy Intervention?

Leveled Literacy Intervention, or LLI, is a small group, supplementary intervention designed for children who find reading and writing difficult. These children are the lowest achievers in literacy in their grade level and are not receiving another intervention. The goal of the intervention is to bring the children to grade level achievement. The LLI Systems have been designed to bring children from the earliest Level A (kindergarten level) to Level N, which is about early Grade 3 level. Typically, LLI is used with kindergarten, Grade 1, or Grade 2 children reading below grade level, though many teachers have used it very successfully to bring children in other grades to a Level N goal.

Leveled Literacy Intervention is based on the Fountas and Pinnell gradient of text difficulty. Each level of text makes increasing demands on the reader, but the change is gradual. By engaging in intensively supportive lessons on each level, young readers have the opportunity to expand their reading and writing abilities. With the support of instruction, they stretch themselves to read more complex texts with accuracy, fluency, and comprehension and to write more complex messages. With these goals in mind, children are effectively engaging in the reading and writing process every day.

We use the term *leveled* because leveled books are a key component in helping children become competent readers. Each book is carefully analyzed and selected to provide enough support and a small amount of challenge so the reader can learn on the text and make small steps toward grade level goals.

FIGURE 1 LLI lessons are designed for children who find reading and writing difficult.

The Gradient of Text

The Fountas and Pinnell leveling system, created and refined as a teaching and assessment tool over the past twenty years, consists of twenty-six points on a gradient of reading difficulty (Figure 2). Each point on that gradient, from the easiest at Level A to the

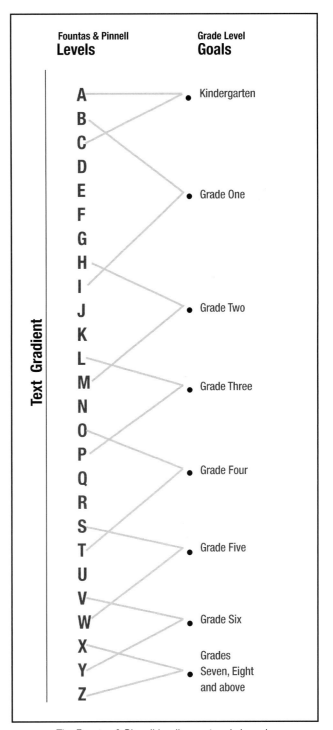

FIGURE 2 The Fountas & Pinnell leveling system is based on a gradient of text difficulty.

most challenging at Level Z, represents a small but significant increase in difficulty over the previous level. In the LLI Green System, the small books begin at Level A and continue through Level J, with a total of 110 lessons.

LLI is a **literacy** intervention. Through systematically designed lessons, you support both reading and writing development and help children expand their knowledge of words and how they work. Over a span of two lessons, the child reads several books, writes about reading, and receives explicit teaching in phonics and word study. In the writing segment, you help the child develop critical writing strategies that can be applied in classroom writing contexts. Also, children learn how to write about their reading.

LLI is an **early intervention**. When you intervene early, the chances of closing the gap between below-level and on-level performance are far greater. Before the child falls behind and develops poor self-esteem, you can help her get back on track and benefit fully from the reading and writing instruction that is being provided by the classroom teacher. Using LLI in Grade 1 means intervening early to get children on track with their peers who are developing effective processing systems.

When the reader is not struggling, you can provide scaffolds that allow him to progress. In LLI, the child receives many opportunities to process texts that are not too difficult and not too easy, allowing the reader to learn on the text.

While they are progressing along the text gradient, you are also providing specific instruction in phonics and word work; but it is the daily opportunity to apply what they know to reading and writing continuous text that enables children to make accelerated progress. Additionally, you provide specific instruction in comprehension as the children discuss the texts, and you intentionally draw their attention to aspects of a text that they need to understand.

Key understandings are indicated on the Recording Forms used for conducting Reading Records in even-numbered lessons. You can check closely on children's comprehension as you engage them in responding to texts. These Reading Records make it possible to monitor progress over time. Assessment of phonics and word analysis, writing, reading, and comprehending are built into each lesson.

The gradient of text is the foundation for *The Continuum of Literacy Learning*, which provides a level by level description of the demands of the texts on readers at each level as well as the corresponding competencies to teach for, assess, and reinforce. You will find the specific competencies on a Continuum at the end of each level in the *Lesson Guide.*

▶ Who Is LLI For?

LLI is designed to be used with small groups of children who need intensive support to achieve grade level competencies. It is designed to serve the lowest achieving children in the classroom who are not receiving another supplementary intervention (for example, individual tutoring). It also provides strong support for children who are acquiring English as an additional language and are receiving classroom reading instruction in English. You may also decide to include children who are identified as having special needs if the content of the LLI intervention meets the educational program specifications for the child.

LLI in Grade 1

LLI is particularly important for the lowest achieving children in Grade 1. It serves as an important prevention program for literacy difficulties in subsequent years of schooling. We suggest that classroom teachers engage first grade children in rich literacy opportunities including interactive read-aloud, shared reading, guided reading, interactive writing, and writing workshop as part of the classroom instructional program. The Green System may be used with older children who need support in reading Levels A to J.

Even with many high-quality literacy opportunities, some children show extreme difficulty in early literacy learning. An early intervention program will get them on track so they can benefit fully from classroom instruction. LLI can give these children a boost so they can begin Grade 2 (P3)* at the same level as their peers. The child's success in first grade will be a strong predictor of literacy success throughout schooling.

---

*In many countries outside the United States, grade levels are designated as Primary 1 (Kindergarten), Primary 2 (Grade 1), Primary 3 (Grade 2), and Primary 4 (Grade 3).

In Grade 1, Reading Recovery is a one-to-one tutorial that provides the most effective early intervention for the lowest achieving children. (See the What Works Clearinghouse Website at www.whatworks.ed.gov.) Leveled Literacy Intervention can serve as a powerful complement to Reading Recovery (see Appendix, page 273). In addition, LLI is an important intervention component in any complete literacy program in a school (see Leveled Literacy Intervention Within Comprehensive Educational Systems, Appendix, p. 274).

LLI for English Language Learners

Each lesson in the LLI program provides specific suggestions for supporting English language learners who are selected for the program (also see *When Readers Struggle: Teaching that Works*). You will want to use your district criteria for language proficiency to determine eligibility for reading instruction in English. English language learners will benefit greatly from conversation with an adult and interaction with a very small group of children. They will also benefit from reading the large amount of continuous text provided in LLI. Through reading, talking, and writing about reading, they extend their knowledge of the structure of English and expand their vocabulary. The LLI lesson is ideal for these children because of the opportunities for increased language modeling. Oral language surrounds every element of the lesson. In addition, the group size and instructional approaches allow for decision making based on the specific strengths and needs of the children.

If children can not follow your instructions or participate fully in the activities of the group, you may want to give them whatever language support your district offers before placing them in an LLI group. Each lesson in the LLI program provides specific suggestions for supporting English language learners who are selected for the program. In addition, you can keep some general suggestions in mind as you work across lessons. Below we list suggestions in four categories: oral language, reading, writing, and phonics. These ideas will be helpful as you work with ELL children as well as with other children who can benefit from extra support. You will also find specific suggestions in every lesson and a comprehensive chapter in *When Readers Struggle: Teaching that Works.*

SUPPORTING ORAL LANGUAGE

❑ Make instruction highly interactive, with a great deal of oral language surrounding everything children are learning.

❑ At the same time, use short, simple (although natural sounding) sentences instead of long and involved ones that children will find hard to follow.

❑ Have the children repeat sentences, if needed.

❑ When introducing books, use the language of the text in a conversational way and have children repeat the language several times to help them remember the syntax.

❑ Show children what you mean when you give directions. You may need to act out certain sequences of action and have children repeat those actions while you coach them. Have them repeat directions to each other or say them aloud as they engage in the activity. Support them during their first attempts rather than expecting independence immediately.

❑ Give English language learners more "wait and think" time. You could say, "let's think about that for a minute" before calling for an answer. Demonstrate to children how you think about what you are going to say.

❑ Paraphrase and summarize for children. Repeat the directions or instructions several different ways, watching for feedback that they understand you.

❑ Remember that typical English language learners understand more than they can say. Ask children if they understand and repeat, if needed.

❑ Expand children's sentences in a conversational way during discussion rather than correcting them.

SUPPORTING READING

❑ Understand that shared reading involves children in a great deal of language repetition, often language that is different from or more complex than the language they can currently use in speech. This experience gives children a chance to practice language, learn the meaning of the words, and use the sentence structures of English. Several repetitions of a new language structure, within a meaningful and enjoyable activity, will enable a child to add the new structure to her repertoire. The Lap Books and poetry in LLI are very beneficial to children.

❑ Check understanding to see if you need to explain a concept or vocabulary word that would be familiar to most English speakers but might not be for ELLs.

❑ Direct attention to pictures and use understandable oral language when you introduce texts to children.

❑ Help learners relate new words to words they already know. During and after reading, check with children to be sure they understand vocabulary and concepts. Allow time within the lessons for children to bring up any words they do not know.

❑ Be sure children understand the prompts you are using before you ask them to demonstrate what they have learned. English language learners might need support for their understanding of the concepts, such as, *first, last, beginning,* and *ending.* For example, they need to understand the concept of "beginning," if they are to respond to a question like, "What letter would you expect at the beginning of. . .?"

❑ For a Home/School Connection, encourage children to read aloud to a parent or sibling at home, even if that parent or sibling is not yet fluent in English. If children have siblings at school, request that a sibling support the younger child at home by listening to him read.

SUPPORTING WRITING

❑ Value and encourage children's drawing. Through drawing, they can represent thinking and connect their ideas to the writing.

❑ Have children repeat several times the sentence they are going to write so that they will be able to remember it. If the sentence is difficult for children to remember, you may need to reduce the complexity.

❑ Guide children to produce some repetitive texts that use the same sentence structure and phrases over and over again, so that children can internalize them.

❑ Once a text has been successfully produced in interactive writing, dictation, or independent

writing and children can easily read it, you can use the text as a resource for talking about language—locating specific words, noticing beginning and ending sounds, noticing rhymes, and so on.

❑ Make time to have children reread their writing and poetry books (called *My Writing Book, My Poetry Book).*

❑ Demonstrate how to say words slowly, providing more individual help and demonstration, if needed.

❑ Surround children's independent writing with a great deal of oral language. Talk with children and help them express their ideas in oral language before they write.

❑ Learn something about the sound system of the children's first language. That knowledge will give you valuable insights into the way they "invent" or "approximate" their first spellings. For example, notice whether they are using letter/sound associations from the first language or whether they are actually thinking of a word in the first language and trying to spell it.

❑ Help the children use standard pronunciation and spelling of words. Work toward helping children develop knowledge of the visual features of words.

❑ Notice how English pronunciation improves as children experience reading and talking.

❑ Be sure children understand the meaning of the words in the Verbal Path (see *Fountas and Pinnell,* 2009, *Prompting Guide 1)* you are using for the writing/recognition of letters. If they do not understand, demonstrate the motions and have them follow.

SUPPORTING PHONICS AND WORD STUDY

❑ Providing the "hands on" activities in LLI lessons will be very helpful to your English language learners. It will give them a chance to manipulate magnetic letters, move pictures around, and work with word and letter cards. Repeat activities that you find most beneficial for your learners.

❑ Build quick recognition of the set of picture cards provided on the LLI *Lesson Resources CD.* These will form a core vocabulary that children in the group share.

- ❏ Support children in naming the pictures on each card, on the Alphabet Linking Chart, and in *My ABC Book.*

- ❏ Be sure the print for all charts is clear and consistent so that children who are working in another language do not also have to deal with varying forms of letters.

- ❏ Make sure your English language learners are not sitting where it is hard for them to see the charts. (For poems, for example, sitting at the far side of a chart means that their view is distorted.)

- ❏ When needed, use a real object to help children learn a concept.

- ❏ Be sure to enunciate your own words clearly and accept children's approximations. If they are feeling their own mouths as they say (or approximate) the sounds, they will be able to make the connections. Sounds and letters are abstract concepts and the relationships are arbitrary. Building understanding of letter-sound correspondence will be especially complex for children whose sound systems do not exactly match that of English. They may have trouble saying the sounds that are related to letters and letter clusters.

- ❏ Accept alternative pronunciations of words with the hard-to-say sounds and present the written form to help learners distinguish between them. Sounds that are like each other, have similar tongue positions, and are easily confused, such as *s* and *z*, *r* and *l*, *sh* and *ch*, *f* and *v*, can be quite difficult for English language learners to differentiate. They often have difficulty with inflected endings (*s*, *ed*) because they have not yet achieved control of the language structure.

- ❏ Speak clearly and slowly when working with children on distinguishing phonemes and hearing sounds in words, but do not distort the word so much that it is unrecognizable. Distortion may confuse English language learners in that it may sound like another word that they do not know.

- ❏ When discussing concepts such as *beginning, ending, first,* and *last,* be sure children understand these concepts.

▶ The LLI Systems

Three systems of materials are available for LLI:

- • Orange System: Levels A through C
- • Green System: Levels A through J
- • Blue System: Levels C through N

Lessons across the three systems progress from beginning reading in kindergarten or Grade 1 (Level A) to beginning reading for Grade 3 (Level N). Characteristics of lessons at all levels include the following:

- ❏ Combination of reading, writing, and phonics/ word study.

- ❏ Emphasis on teaching for comprehending strategies.

- ❏ Explicit attention to the features of nonfiction and fiction texts.

- ❏ Specific work on sounds, letters, and words in activities designed to help children notice the details of written language and learn how words "work."

- ❏ Explicit teaching of effective and efficient strategies for expanding vocabulary.

Approximate Grade Level Equivalence	Orange	Green	Blue
Kindergarten	A	A	
Kindergarten	B	B	
Kind./Grade 1	C	C	C
Grade 1		D	D
Grade 1		E	E
Grade 1		F	F
Grade 1		G	G
Grade 1		H	H
Grade 1/2		I	I
Grade 2		J	J
Grade 2			K
Grade 2			L
Grade 2/3			M
Grade 3			N

FIGURE 3 Grade Level Equivalence Chart

- ❏ Explicit teaching for fluent and phrased reading.
- ❏ Use of writing about reading for the purpose of communicating and learning how to construct a message using a variety of writing strategies.

The LLI systems are coordinated with the grade levels at which they will most likely be used; however, educators may make other decisions as they work to match the program to the needs of particular readers. *The books and lessons for each system are unique, with no overlap of texts.* You may choose to extend the number of lessons at a level on the gradient by using a set of lessons and titles from another system. For example, after ten days of teaching at Level E in the Green System, you may decide that the children need a few more lessons at the level. You can use Level E books and lessons from the Blue System to meet your children's needs. The need to work for more than ten days at a level is rare. You may also decide to spend fewer than ten days at a level when you have evidence that the children control all the competencies.

The Orange System and the Green System begin with ten days of lessons for "Getting Started." These lessons utilize Lap Books in shared reading scenarios to provide a rich foundation for emergent readers. Getting Started lessons start at Level A and progress to Level C. Very high support is provided in the form of shared reading. Teachers read texts *to* and *with* children. After reading Level A texts in a shared way several times, children can read them independently. If children do not control voice-print match, the support of shared reading is provided for texts at Levels B and C. The ten days of Getting Started are designed to help children learn how print works, start to monitor reading, use information from pictures, and learn some high-frequency words. After these ten days, they start at Level A for instructional and independent reading.

All systems have organized lessons around the following quantities of small books:

- Orange Collection: 70 titles
- Green Collection: 110 titles
- Blue Collection: 120 titles

There is a specific *Lesson Guide* for each collection.

Orange System

The books and lessons in the Orange System provide a large amount of easy reading for children who are having difficulty becoming oriented to print and learning the function of letters and sounds. Ten days of lessons in the Getting Started format provide maximum support for children for whom the world of print is very new. The seventy lessons on Levels A through C include systematic and intensive work in phonological awareness, letters, and phonics to help young children learn how to look at print, hear sounds, and use letter-sound relationships in flexible and powerful ways. At the same time, they are reading and writing continuous text every day as well as engaging in conversation to help them expand their comprehension of texts.

LLI Orange System will be useful in helping kindergarten children who are identified as having difficulties after the first few months of their first year of school. The Orange System will also be helpful to children who are learning English because it provides easy reading and plenty of opportunities to talk about texts. You can also use the collection with special education children for whom the program meets the educational specifications or children beyond the kindergarten level who need to develop competencies at Levels A–C.

Green System

The books and lessons in the Green System also begin with ten days of Getting Started, which supports children with shared reading and interactive writing as they become oriented to print and begin to develop early reading behaviors. The independent reading begins with Level A, and ten days of lessons are provided for every level, A through J.

The Green System will be helpful to first graders who are identified as reading below expected grade level. It may also be used to help children in higher grade levels who are reading below Level J. It can also be used for special education children for whom the program meets the educational program specifications.

Blue System

The books and lessons in the Blue System begin with Level C and continue, with ten titles per level, to Level N. As in the Orange and Green Systems, lessons in the Blue System provide specific instruction in phonics, word work, comprehension, and writing.

The Blue System will be helpful to second and third graders who are reading below grade level. The Blue System may also be used to help children at higher grade levels who are reading below Level N. It has also been effectively used with special education children for whom the activities meet the educational program specifications.

Leveled Literacy Intervention System

System	Levels	Description	Students
Orange *70 books*	Getting Started, plus A – C	• 10 Getting Started Lessons (with Lap Books and small books for readers) • 20 Level A Lessons • 20 Level B Lessons • 20 Level C Lessons	Kindergarten Special education students ELL students, as appropriate Before- or after-school students Summer school students Grade 1 (LLI students for extra work on a level)
Green *110 books*	Getting Started, plus A – J	• 10 Getting Started Lessons (with Lap Books and small books for readers) • 10 Level A Lessons • 10 Level B Lessons • 10 Level C Lessons • 10 Level D Lessons • 10 Level E Lessons • 10 Level F Lessons • 10 Level G Lessons • 10 Level H Lessons • 10 Level I Lessons • 10 Level J Lessons	Grade 1 students Grade 3 students reading below grade level Special education students ELL students, as appropriate Before- or after-school students Summer school students Grade 2 LLI students (for extra work on a level)
Blue *120 books*	C – N	• 10 Level C Lessons • 10 Level D Lessons • 10 Level E Lessons • 10 Level F Lessons • 10 Level G Lessons • 10 Level H Lessons • 10 Level I Lessons • 10 Level J Lessons • 10 Level K Lessons • 10 Level L Lessons • 10 Level M Lessons • 10 Level N Lessons	Grade 2 students Special education students ELL students, as appropriate Before- or after-school students Summer school students Upper elementary students reading below Grade 3 level Grade 1 LLI students (needing extra work at a level) Grade 3 students or students at other grades reading below grade level

FIGURE 4 Overview of the LLI System

▶ LLI System Components

In Figure 5, you can see the key components provided for implementing Leveled Literacy Intervention, Green System.

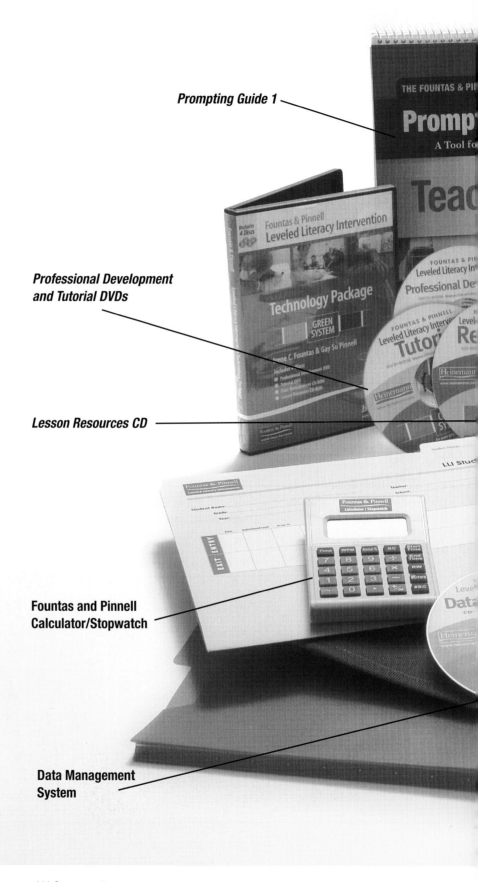

Prompting Guide 1

Professional Development and Tutorial DVDs

Lesson Resources CD

Fountas and Pinnell Calculator/Stopwatch

Data Management System

FIGURE 5 LLI Components

Professional Book

**Teaching Guides
for the System**

FIGURE 6 *Program (System) Guide*

FIGURE 7 *Lesson Guide*

Program (System) Guide

A copy of the Leveled Literacy Intervention *Program (System) Guide* is included in the Green System. *Program Guide* is used synonymously with *System Guide* to indicate the systematic design of LLI.

Lesson Guide

The teacher's Leveled Literacy Intervention Lesson Guide for the Green System includes 110 thirty-minute lessons for teaching children in small groups.

At the end of each set of lessons at a level, you will find the Continuum that specifies the important behaviors and understandings to notice, teach, and support at the level.

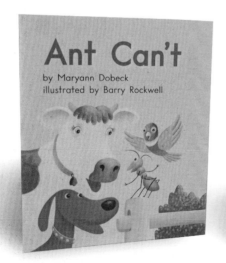

FIGURE 8 Small Book

Genre

Lesson Number

Book Level

Small Books

In the Leveled Literacy Intervention, Green System, learning takes place with the foundational support of 110 small books. The first ten titles are part of the Getting Started feature. An 11-by-13 inch Lap Book is provided to facilitate shared reading of a text. In addition, matching small books are provided to help children move to independence.

FIGURE 9 Getting Started Lap Books and small books

For LLI lessons from Levels A to J, Green System includes twenty different titles for Level A, ten for Level B lessons, ten for Level C lessons, ten for level D lessons, ten for Level E lessons, ten for Level F lessons, ten for Level G lessons, ten for Level H lessons, ten for Level I lessons, and ten for Level J lessons. The books can be kept in the LLI plastic folders that can be slipped into the hanging folders provided.

Within each level, an easier text is provided as the new book every other day. On the back cover of each book, you will find the genre, level, book/lesson number, and number of running words. The configuration of texts is shown in a chart in the Appendix, page 105.

FIGURE 10 Small books

Writing Books

You have consumable writing books, called *My Writing Book,* in various colors for child choice. On the cover you will find room for the child's photograph or illustration. The writing books are filled as children write in LLI lessons. When all pages of a book are completed, the child takes it home and begins a new one. Completed pages of the writing books are excellent for reading practice. Additional writing books can be ordered from Heinemann.

Take-Home Bags

These brightly colored bags provide a plastic pocket in which you can place a card with the child's name. Children take home items such as word bags, sentence strips, Take-Home Books, Parent Letters, or other materials for classroom and home connection activities in these bags. They learn the importance of daily responsibilities and the colorful bag helps them keep track of materials and remember their assigned tasks. They bring back the bag each day. Replacement bags are available from Heinemann.

Take-Home Books

In every lesson, you send home a Take-Home Book for rereading. Take-Home Books are black and white versions of the books children read in their lessons. There is a place on the back cover for children to write their names. The children can keep the Take-Home Books in a basket or box at home for rereading and build a home library of books. Replacement Take-Home Books are inexpensive and can be ordered from Heinemann.

Student Folders

You will receive a set of folders to keep Reading Records and other data for each child. These folders can be passed on each year as part of children's records. The inside of the folder includes a graph for tracking a child's entry level, progress throughout LLI, and exit level information.

Fountas and Pinnell Prompting Guide 1: A Tool for Literacy Teachers

Prompting Guide 1 is a tool you will use in each lesson. It provides a quick reference for specific language you can use to teach for, prompt for, or reinforce effective reading and writing behaviors. The Guide is organized in categories and color coded so that you can turn quickly to the area needed and refer to it as you teach.

Professional Book: *When Readers Struggle: Teaching that Works, K–3*

When Readers Struggle: Teaching that Works is a rich guide to support effective teaching in the lessons. Each lesson will refer you to chapters that will be helpful in developing your professional expertise in working with classroom children who find literacy learning difficult.

Lesson Resources CD

The *Lesson Resources CD* provides instructional materials in a printable PDF format. There are General Resources that are used in multiple lessons, as well as Lesson Resources that are tied to specific lessons. Those include Recording Forms for taking reading records, word and picture cards, Letter Minibooks, *My ABC Book,* Alphabet Linking Chart, *My Poetry Book,* Parent Letters, and other record-keeping and observation forms and resources used in LLI. In addition, you can also go to the tabbed section on the screen called Custom Card/Game Maker to create some of your own materials and customize games to meet your individual instructional needs.

Data Management CD

Also included in the Green System is a *Data Management CD* that enables you to track and print

FIGURE 11 Lesson Resources CD and forms

reports on entry/exit data and progress monitoring data for individuals or groups of children.

Professional Development and Tutorial DVDs

You can use the *Professional Development and Tutorial DVDs* to support your work individually or with a study group of professionals. There are two disks for each system (Orange, Green, and Blue). The first provides an overview of the system and presents model lessons. The second DVD contains a tutorial on coding, scoring, and analyzing Reading Records and information on how to use the information to inform your teaching.

FIGURE 13 Professional Development and Tutorial DVDs

Fountas and Pinnell Calculator/ Stopwatch

The F&P Calculator/Stopwatch performs highly specific functions related to taking Reading Records. With the push of a button, you will be able to see children's reading rate, percentage of accuracy, and self-correction ratio. The F&P Calculator/Stopwatch can be used by any teacher who uses running records to assess children. The calculator is included in the Green System to make your work more time efficient. We do not recommend assessing reading rate until about Level J. Extra calculators may be ordered from Heinemann.

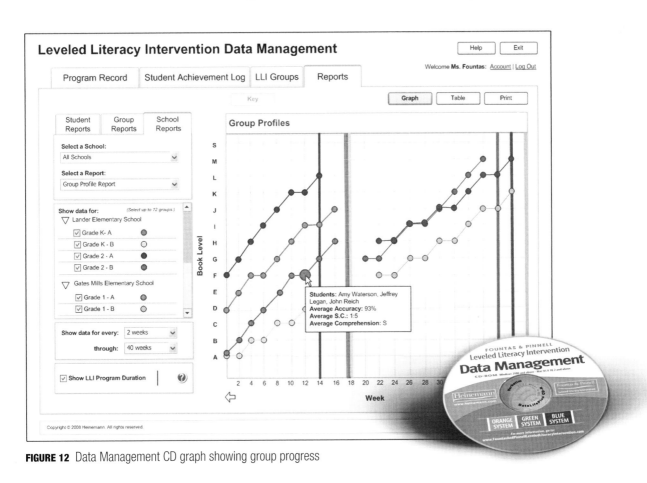

FIGURE 12 Data Management CD graph showing group progress

Implementing the LLI System

Systematic assessment is very helpful because the more precise you are in your assessment, the more effective you will be in your teaching. Many children in Grade 1 will not be reading at all, so begin at Level A, but you still need information as described below.

▶ Initial Assessment of Children

Your goal is to identify the lowest achieving children in Grade 1 (or other selected grade) and find the instructional reading level for each of them. As a source of information, you will have the observations of the classroom teacher who has worked with the children for the first weeks of school and has had the opportunity to notice the strengths and needs of the children. The classroom teacher may be able to recommend several children for systematic assessment of reading levels and other competencies. In the fall, many of the lowest achieving children in Grade 1 will begin at Level A and will benefit from the Getting Started lessons at the beginning of LLI. (See pages 26–31.)

▶ Finding the Instructional Reading Levels of the Lowest Achieving Children

For entry to LLI, it will be necessary to assess the child's instructional and independent reading levels.

Using the Fountas and Pinnell *Benchmark Assessment System 1*

If possible, we recommend that you use the Fountas and Pinnell *Benchmark Assessment System 1* to determine the instructional level of your children because the levels will correlate precisely to LLI levels. You will be able to identify each child's specific reading level according to the levels used in this intervention. The Fountas and Pinnell *Benchmark Assessment System* will also provide critical information on the child's reading strengths and needs in processing strategies, comprehension, and fluency and will link them directly to instruction. In addition, you will be able to select specific assessments from the section called Optional Assessments for diagnostic purposes. For example, at the Grade 1 level, you may want to use any of the following:

❑ Letter Identification—Children say the letters of the alphabet by recognizing the shapes of uppercase and lowercase letters.

❑ Early Literacy Behaviors—Children demonstrate that they know and can use the following conventions related to print: finding specific words within a text, matching words they hear with words they read.

❑ Reading High-Frequency Words (50)—Children read fifty high-frequency words while the observer notes correct responses and attempts.

❑ Phonological Awareness—Initial Sounds—Children identify pictures with the same initial sound as a spoken word.

❑ Phonological Awareness—Blending—Children hear and say the individual sounds in a word and then blend the sounds to say the word.

❑ Writing Picture Names—Children say words slowly and write the sounds they hear in response to a picture.

Many of the assessments are quick and some, like Phonological Awareness: Initial Sounds, and Writing Picture Names, may be administered in a small group. All of the assessments will provide a wealth of information to inform instruction.

Using Other Benchmark Assessment Systems

If you do not have access to the Fountas and Pinnell *Benchmark Assessment System*, you can use any other benchmark assessments you have in your school or district. Many publishers provide correlation charts to connect their assessment systems with the Fountas and Pinnell levels. You may find the following correlation chart (Figure 14) helpful, although the Fountas and Pinnell Assessment Levels and the Reading Recovery levels are the most reliable and closely match this intervention.

Grade-Level Equivalence Chart

Grade	Fountas & Pinnell Level	Basal Level	Reading Recovery Level	Rigby Level	DRA Level
Kindergarten	A	Readiness	1	1–2	A, 1, 2
Kindergarten	B		2	3–4	
Kindergarten Grade 1	C	PP1	3, 4	5	3
Grade 1	D	PP2	5, 6	6	4
Grade 1	E	PP3	7, 8	7	6, 7, 8
Grade 1	F	Primer	9, 10	8	10
Grade 1	G		11, 12	9	12
Grade 1	H	Grade 1	13, 14	10	14
Grade 1 Grade 2	I		15, 16	11	16
Grade 2	J	Grade 2	17, 18	12	18, 20
Grade 2	K		19, 20	13–14	
Grade 2	L			15	24–28
Grade 2 Grade 3	M			16–17	
Grade 3	N	Grade 3		18	30
Grade 3	O			19	
Grade 3 Grade 4	P			20	34–38
Grade 4	Q	Grade 4			40
Grade 4	R				
Grade 4 Grade 5	S				44
Grade 5	T	Grade 5			
Grade 5	U				
Grade 5 Grade 6	V				
Grade 6	W	Grade 6			
Grade 6	X				
Grade 6	Y				
Grade 7, 8 and Above	Z	Grade 7, 8			

FIGURE 14 Grade-Level Equivalence Chart

Alternative Assessments

If you do not have access to a benchmark assessment, you can use the information from any assessments in the district (e.g., Letter Identification, Phoneme Awareness) and select the lowest performers. Once you have identified these children, you may want to use a quick informal assessment of reading level using leveled books as described in the next section. If you are using a basal system, the chart on page 18 may be helpful in selecting children reading below level.

Assessment Using Leveled Books

A quick and informal way to select children is to have an individual child read aloud one or two books at a particular level. If you have some leveled books in your school, select from that collection. Notice the child's ability to point under each word at Levels A and B. Assess the percentage of words read accurately and note specific errors (substitutions, omissions, insertions). The level at which the child reads with 90-94% accuracy and satisfactory comprehension (as well as accurate pointing on Levels A and B) is the child's instructional level.

You will have an assessment of accuracy and also insights into the kind of information the child is using when errors are made (for example, words that look like other words or words that are inaccurate but make sense). Errors can sometimes illustrate a child's strengths and give you insights into how to help him.

Following the oral reading, involve the child in a conversation that will help you know what he understood from the text. You can ask several questions but the assessment should not feel like an interrogation.

If the level of the text is too difficult, move down the levels until you find something the child can read with 90–94% accuracy and good understanding. If the level seems easy, move up the levels until you find books that are too hard. Start your instruction with the level a child can read with 90-94% accuracy and adequate understanding. Your introduction and teaching will support the child in taking on books at this level.

For children who can not read books as high as Level B, assess letter knowledge using a set of letter cards and ask them to write their names and any other words or letters they know. This will give you an idea of the extent to which they are aware of print.

You might want to read a Level A book to a child twice and then ask him or her to point and "read" it to you. You will learn the extent to which the child can remember language patterns (cued by pictures) and the degree to which he can track print. Children at this level would start the intervention lessons at Level A.

▶ Selecting Children for the Intervention

If children are reading below the level indicated for Grade 1 at the time of the school year, you may select them for LLI. You will want to adjust the chart below to coincide with the months of your particular school year. For Grade 1, we suggest beginning LLI as soon as possible at the start of the year. In addition, the chart shows the criteria for selecting children from other grades using the Orange or Blue System.

Criteria for Selecting Children

Grade	Month 1	Month 2	Month 3	Month 4	Month 5	Month 6	7	8	9	10
K Orange	Rich classroom literacy opportunities			A	A	B	B	C	C	C
1 Green	C	D	E	E	F	G	G	H	I	I
2 Blue	I	J	J	K	K	K	L	L	M	M
3 and higher	M	N	N	N	O	O	O	P	P	P

FIGURE 15 Criteria for Selecting Children

Progress Monitoring

You can monitor the progress of the children through your weekly use of Reading Records with one child from each group and use of the graph in the *Data Management CD*. You should expect the trajectory of the graph to go up. You can also find a progress monitoring chart for reading levels on the Leveled Literacy Intervention Website for Fountas and Pinnell, www.FountasAndPinnellLeveledLiteracyIntervention.com.

Criteria for Selecting Children

In your school, you may have many children who do not meet expectations for grade level reading—many more than can be served in the intervention. In this case, begin with the children who need the most help and serve all you can. On the other hand, you may have higher grade level expectations in your school than are indicated on the chart. If children can not fully participate and learn from the level of instruction in the classroom, they can benefit from the LLI intervention. You can adjust the levels accordingly.

Forming LLI Groups

Any form of grouping requires some compromise. Ideally, you would teach each reader individually so you could meet individual needs and provide the very specific instruction that helps that particular reader move forward. We recommend intensive individual tutoring (e.g., Reading Recovery) for readers who are struggling the most in Grade 1. Additional children who also need extra help can be served in intervention groups.

Once you determine the instructional levels of the children, create small groups of readers who are similar enough that you can begin lessons at a particular level. In the Green System, we strongly recommend that you work with three children at a time for up to about eighteen weeks. Then work with another group of three in the thirty-minute teaching slot. You will serve at least six children in the teaching slot across the year. In this way, you will work with six children, but only three at a time to achieve better results. From time to time, you may make other decisions; however, we recommend a group of three so that you can:

❑ Observe closely and provide strong individual support.

❑ Keep all children in the group highly engaged throughout the 30-minute lesson.

❑ Use precise language to prompt for effective reading strategies while listening in to individual readers.

❑ Observe closely and interact with children as they write to support the development of writing strategies.

❑ Maintain efficiency in time management.

Children do not always fall neatly into just the right number of groups! After all, they are individuals who can not be defined by "reading level." You will probably have to do some problem-solving when you begin to group children. Your goal is to group the children so that the level of instruction is appropriate for them all. Our guideline is to start the group at a text level that allows every child to begin with success. Here are some suggestions:

❑ Make some "one level" compromises. Three children whose instructional levels are D, D, and E, for example, may be able to read together and benefit from the intervention lessons starting at Level D.

❑ If you are working alongside a teacher in a classroom, make arrangements for a child from the "next door" classroom to join the group you are teaching.

❑ Take children at the same level from different classrooms (but be sure that it doesn't take too much time to assemble them in the space where you are teaching).

Your priority should be to group children efficiently and effectively so that you can teach them at the appropriate level. (See Frequently Asked Questions, page 97.)

Regrouping Children

Any time you work with a group of children, you will notice that they develop differently from each other. You may want to provide extra challenge to a particular child by expecting more writing or placing a basket of extra books for him to read in the center of the table. Of course, if the child makes enough progress to reach grade level competencies, you may want to exit the child from the group.

You may move a child from one group to another at any time. Sometimes, after a few weeks, teachers look at their data on all the children and reform their groups. In LLI, it is not usually a problem if a child experiences a few lessons for the second time or skips a few books and lessons, depending on the child's strengths and needs.

▶ Management of LLI Groups

Scheduling LLI Groups

The LLI system is designed to provide intensive, short-term support. Children need daily lessons so that what they learned yesterday can be reinforced and built on today. It is important that the daily lessons are a supplement to, not a substitute for, classroom small-group reading instruction. The supplementary teaching will allow the children to make faster progress and catch up with their peers.

If you provide lessons fewer than five times per week, your children will make progress, though not as quickly. Our research shows the importance of daily lessons in helping children make accelerated progress and catch up with their peers. Good, consistent small-group teaching in the classroom is a key factor in supporting ongoing learning. *Additional* intensive small group instruction is the key to intervention that will bring children to grade level. Readers who struggle need to participate in both classroom reading instruction and LLI to close the achievement gap.

For each thirty-minute teaching slot in your schedule, you will be able to work with one group. As children reach grade level performance in a period of up to about eighteen weeks, you will be able to enter another group in the teaching slot. If you have three thirty-minute teaching slots per day, you will be able to work with at least six groups in the school year. If you have four teaching slots in the day, you will be able to work with at least eight groups in the school year. If you have six teaching slots, you will

be able to teach at least twelve groups per year! This means that you can serve from eighteen to thirty-six of the lowest achieving children in a school year.

The length of time spent in the LLI program will vary by the progress of the groups. The Green System provides lessons for up to twenty-two weeks (assuming daily instruction, five days per week), but most children will not need the program for that long. In our experience, most children can be brought to grade level in less than eighteen weeks, with some needing more time. Also, programs may sometimes last longer because of holidays and other interruptions, although all teachers try to keep these to a minimum.

Remember that if you are using the LLI Green System, you may add more lessons at particular levels from the Blue System. But if you find that children have reached grade level and are exhibiting strong reading and writing behaviors, you can move them out of the LLI groups. Some children may participate for as few as eight to twelve weeks.

You can begin the teaching year working with first grade children using the LLI Green System or with Grade 2 children using the LLI Blue System and, as groups exit, you can initiate kindergarten groups, if your schedule allows, using the Orange System. Figure 16 below shows four teaching slots across the year. This teacher worked half a day with children who needed extra literacy support.

This chart shows the teacher began with two Grade 1 groups and two Grade 2 groups. As the Grade 1 children reached grade level, the teacher entered

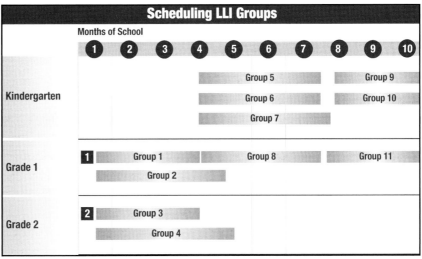

FIGURE 16 Scheduling LLI Groups

three kindergarten groups and another Grade 1 group in the four teaching slots. As the kindergarten and Grade 1 children reached grade level goals, the teacher initiated two more kindergarten groups and a new Grade 1 group.

Each group had three children. The twenty-four children in the first four slots achieved grade level performance. The nine additional children made significant progress, with six of them reaching grade level. A total of thirty children were served and reached grade level. Three more children made progress but did not yet reach grade level.

Entering the System

Use your assessments to determine a starting point for the system (see pages 17–19). This means that you may start with the intervention at the beginning of any level. It is important to start at a level where you are confident the children will find success. So if you are wavering, decide to start on the lower level. You can always decide not to spend all ten days at a level.

Coordinating LLI Lessons with Classroom Instruction

Once the children have entered the LLI system, your partnership with the classroom teacher will be critical in helping the child make fast progress and catch up with peers. The following suggestions may be helpful, but you will have many more ideas. Talk together about the importance and benefits of daily LLI lessons and frequent small-group instruction in the classroom.

- ❑ Invite the classroom teacher to observe an LLI lesson.
- ❑ Share the Lesson Record or other record-keeping charts, such as the Letter-Word Record or Reading Graph, on a regular basis so you both have the same information on the child's progress.
- ❑ Ask for any information the classroom teacher may have that will inform your teaching (for example, Writing Folder, Reading List).
- ❑ Send Classroom Connection suggestions with the child so the teacher can observe the child's reading and writing. Discuss the whole idea of

classroom connections with the child's teacher at the beginning of this program. It will help to show some examples of the activities and to talk about how you will explain the task so the children can be independent.

- ❑ Share the child's writing book, *My Writing Book*, frequently and discuss with the classroom teacher the writing that shows evidence of learning.
- ❑ Show the classroom teacher the Parent Letter (in English and Spanish), Take-Home Books, fold sheets, and other materials so they can be aware of what is expected at home. Though you cannot count on home practice for the child's success in the intervention, any extra practice will be a bonus.

Amount of Time in the System

The amount of time in the program will be related to the entry level and the distance to grade level performance. In our experience, children reading up to one year or slightly more below grade level in Grades 1 and 2 were able to reach grade level performance in between eighteen and twenty-two weeks with daily lessons and strong teaching.

You may decide to keep the children a few weeks longer if they are approaching grade level performance, but this will keep out other children needing the intervention and will shorten their time in it.

If children enter one or more years below grade level, you should expect significant progress, but they may not reach grade level in eighteen weeks. If teaching resources permit, you could keep them in the intervention longer, even a full school year.

Exiting the System

When you and the classroom teacher feel the children are reading well at the end of a series of lessons that are at least on grade level, you can use your final Reading Record as an indicator of the children's competencies. Ideally, you will have the Fountas and Pinnell *Benchmark Assessment System* so you can re-administer the leveled assessments to confirm your observational notes, the classroom performance, and your final Reading Record. Figure 17 on page 23 can be used to identify grade level goals or competencies. Adjust it to fit your school or district expectations.

Grade Level Goals			
G	Beginning	Mid-year	End
K		A	C

FIGURE 17 Grade Level Goals

▶ Getting Organized for Teaching

A Space for Teaching

LLI lessons can be taught just about anywhere that you can accommodate yourself and the group of three children. You can use a section of the classroom or a space outside the classroom. The materials are not bulky, and at any one time, it takes only a folder of materials to teach a group of children. You will need a small space in which you can place children so that they are facing you and will not be distracted (for example, in a corner of the classroom or in a small room).

Selecting a Table

You will want to use a table that allows children to face you directly and also allows them to see clearly when you write on a chart or hold up the whiteboard. A horseshoe table or a rectangular table will work well so that you can look directly at children all the time. Notice the height of the table and have the legs adjusted if needed. The table should come just above the children's waists so they can hold the book and look down at it. It is not a good idea to place children on either side of you at a rectangular table because it will be very hard for them to see the visual displays.

Planning and Organizing for LLI Lessons

The intervention lessons are designed to require a minimum of planning time for teachers, but you will need to review and think about the week's lessons and print out the corresponding materials from the *Lesson Resources CD*. If you choose not to use some materials, you can decide not to print them. The first section of your *Lesson Guide*, called Getting Organized for Teaching, will be helpful in the process because it shows what you will print from the CD and what other supplies you will need prior to starting the teaching.

Some suggestions for planning are listed below:

❑ Review the *Lesson Guide* for the appropriate lessons. Notice the "You Will Need" list at the top of the first lesson page. The first materials listed are supplied in the program. These are followed by the supplies you should have at your school. Next are the items that you can print out from the *Lesson Resources CD*. Those items that you may want to print out once at the beginning of the intervention have a check mark.

❑ Print from the *Lesson Resources CD* and organize the other materials, for example, Recording Forms, word cards, picture cards, sentence strips, markers, and *My Writing Books*, so you can access them efficiently during the lesson.

❑ Have all the materials for a group in a plastic tub or basket (e.g., *My Writing Books*, new books for the lesson, word bags, *My ABC Books*).

❑ Read the lessons and note any lesson variations needed.

❑ Have books organized to use with the group.

❑ Have your *Prompting Guide 1* ready to use. You may want to quickly review a section of the guide that you know you will need to use.

❑ Note the writing children will be doing, and put the lesson number on the writing book pages.

❑ Take note of transitions and think about how to save time.

❑ Have record-keeping forms, such as the Recording Form and the Lesson Record, ready on a clipboard with the children's names on them, as needed.

❑ Have your calculator ready to use.

❑ Consider placing the magnetic letters for the lesson in separate sealable bags or small plastic containers so they are ready for use. Some teachers use small metal trays (stove burner covers), cookie sheets, or tackle boxes to presort the letters. You can also place letters on a small magnetic whiteboard that you can just hand to each child.

- ❏ Consider a rolling cart next to your table to place markers, your whiteboard, and so on.

- ❏ If you move from classroom to classroom, consider a special container to organize your materials or a rolling cart.

MATERIALS AND SUPPLIES FROM YOUR SCHOOL

You will need to gather some basic supplies for your lessons:

- ❏ A whiteboard and dry-erase marker for group phonics and writing

- ❏ Small individual whiteboard and dry-erase marker for each child to use for word study

- ❏ Thin, dark-colored markers for the children to use to write in their *My Writing Books*

- ❏ Chart paper for phonics and writing

- ❏ Three sets of small, multicolor lowercase magnetic letters for letter and word work

- ❏ One set of multicolor uppercase magnetic letters for letter and word work

- ❏ Cardstock for printing games and some charts

- ❏ One-inch sentence strips cut from card stock

- ❏ One-inch white correction tape to cover errors in children's writing books or interactive writing

- ❏ Pocket chart for word work (tabletop or regular)

- ❏ Highlighter marker, which is a light yellow marker used to show a letter or word you or the child mark

- ❏ Highlighter tape, which is a type of removable colored tape to place over letters, words, or phrases

GROUP MATERIALS

Managing small group work will be much easier if you keep all lesson materials for a group together in one hanging folder or accordion folder. For a lesson, you will need:

1. the plastic folders for the particular lessons, in which you can place the new books and the Take-Home Books.

2. the plastic folder for the previous day's lesson, in which you have placed the books that children will reread.

3. the *Lesson Guide.*

4. word cards, picture cards, and games you have pre-prepared (in clear, sealable bags).

5. a folder for the group with Lesson Records and completed Recording Forms for children as well as Recording Forms for the week.

6. *My Writing Book* for each child.

7. *My Poetry Book* (if using) for each child.

8. *My ABC Book* (if using) for each child.

9. *My Vowel Book* (if using) for each child.

10. Alphabet Linking Chart for each child.

11. Consonant Cluster Linking Chart (if using) for each child.

12. group-made Table Charts.

(See Instructional Routines, page 62.)

Teaching With the Leveled Literacy Intervention System

▶ The Essential Elements of LLI Lessons

LLI lessons include reading, writing, phonics and word study, and the extensive use of oral language throughout. There are three types of lesson structures in the system: (1) Getting Started lessons; (2) odd-numbered lessons; (3) even-numbered lessons.

The first ten lessons in the Green System are called Getting Started. The following is an overview of the information on each page of Lessons 1–10, Getting Started. These Getting Started lessons follow the same format and engage children in five instructional activities: (1) rereading, (2) phonics, (3) reading a new book with several levels of support, (4) writing about reading, and (5) letter/word work.

▶ Getting Started Lessons

Here you will find a list of materials beginning with those that are included in the LLI package, followed by more generic materials available from your school. Many of the listed materials provided in the LLI package can be printed out from the *Lesson Resources CD*, as indicated. Multi-use resources that can be printed out once at the beginning of the program have a check mark.

You will find that the lesson numbers correspond to the book numbers on the small books. The system, new book title, and genre of the new book are also provided.

These are the specific teaching goals for the lesson. These goals will help you think about how the lesson activities are supporting the development of the reading and writing processes.

Each new book is analyzed to show the specific demands on the reader for each characteristic.

YOU WILL NEED

- Take-Home Book, *The New Puppy*
- "Pease Porridge Hot," enlarged poem
- Alphabet Linking Chart, enlarged version
- magnetic letter set
- highlighter tape

From the CD:
- Alphabet Linking Chart pictures: *j, k, l (jack-in-the-box, kite, leaf)* ✓
- Letter Minibooks ✓
- Verbal Path ✓

- picture cards: *tree, cat, car, fish, fan, snake, bee, hat, star, dish, van, rake*
- word cards: *is, big, little, has*
- fold sheet
- Parent Letter

GETTING STARTED

LESSON **4** · SYSTEM **Green**

NEW BOOK *Friends*

GENRE **Fiction**

NEW BOOK
Friends, Level A,
Lap Book and small books

REREADING
The New Puppy, Level A,
Lap Book and small books

Frog Food, Level A,
small books

Goals

- Learn to identify words that sound alike at the end (rhyme).
- Learn to identify the number of syllables in a word by clapping.
- Understand the Alphabet Linking Chart as a tool for learning about letters.
- Understand that there is a relationship between a letter and a sound.
- Look closely at names, letter by letter, left to right.
- Notice distinctive features of letters.
- Use the Verbal Path to gain control of directionality in writing letters.
- Recognize a few high-frequency words by looking closely at them.
- Read with voice-print match across one line of text.
- Say words slowly to identify the first sound and letter.
- Read with crisp pointing under each word.
- Understand the comparison of big and little.
- Understand that even if dogs are different, they need the same things.
- Understand and discuss the idea of friendship.

Analysis of New Book Characteristics   *Friends*, Level A

GENRE/FORM
- Fiction
- Series (#1 in *Orson and Taco Series*)

TEXT STRUCTURE
- Sentences about Orson on left page
- Sentences about Taco on right page
- Comparisons always on opposite pages until the end

CONTENT
- Familiar accessories for children who have experience with pets
- Dogs' needs

THEMES AND IDEAS
- Pets
- Friends
- Big and little

LANGUAGE AND LITERARY FEATURES
- NA

SENTENCE COMPLEXITY
- One five-word simple sentence on every page, with two five-word sentences on the last page
- Present tense
- Repeating pattern on each page, with variation in the adjectives *big* and *little* and the dog accessories

VOCABULARY
- Names of items: *collar, bone, ball, bark, bowl, bed*
- Content words: *dog, friend*
- Adjectives: *little, big*

WORDS
- High-frequency words: *is, a, big, little, has*
- One- and two-syllable words
- See the Word Analysis Charts in the *Program Guide* for specific words in each category.

ILLUSTRATIONS
- Drawings and print on every right page
- Close match between pictures and text

BOOK AND PRINT FEATURES
- Large font
- Ample space between words
- One line on each page of print, except the last page, which has two lines
- Periods

19

26

Approximately 5 minutes
This is the first part of the lesson. You will find a visual
showing the cover of yesterday's new book and the new
book from the previous day, and suggestions for
rereading them, if time allows.

Approximately 5 minutes
This is the second part
of the lesson. The focus
is on developing strong
control of letter and
sound knowledge.

This is an example of
the visual or chart you
will create with the
children.

Here you see a concise
statement of the phonics
principle children need
to understand.

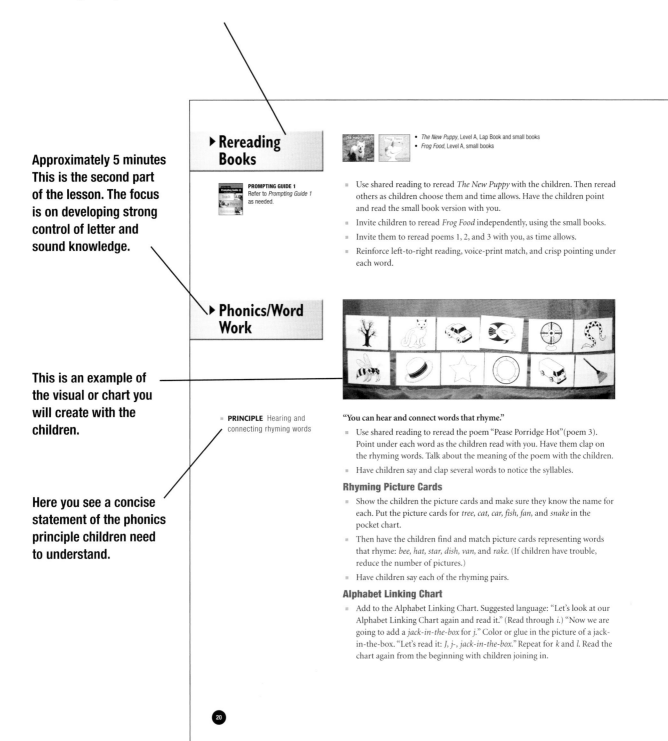

▶ **Rereading
Books**

PROMPTING GUIDE 1
Refer to *Prompting Guide 1*
as needed.

- *The New Puppy*, Level A, Lap Book and small books
- *Frog Food*, Level A, small books

▪ Use shared reading to reread *The New Puppy* with the children. Then reread
others as children choose them and time allows. Have the children point
and read the small book version with you.
▪ Invite children to reread *Frog Food* independently, using the small books.
▪ Invite them to reread poems 1, 2, and 3 with you, as time allows.
▪ Reinforce left-to-right reading, voice-print match, and crisp pointing under
each word.

▶ **Phonics/Word
Work**

▪ **PRINCIPLE** Hearing and
connecting rhyming words

"You can hear and connect words that rhyme."

▪ Use shared reading to reread the poem "Pease Porridge Hot"(poem 3).
Point under each word as the children read with you. Have them clap on
the rhyming words. Talk about the meaning of the poem with the children.
▪ Have children say and clap several words to notice the syllables.

Rhyming Picture Cards

▪ Show the children the picture cards and make sure they know the name for
each. Put the picture cards for *tree, cat, car, fish, fan,* and *snake* in the
pocket chart.
▪ Then have the children find and match picture cards representing words
that rhyme: *bee, hat, star, dish, van,* and *rake*. (If children have trouble,
reduce the number of pictures.)
▪ Have children say each of the rhyming pairs.

Alphabet Linking Chart

▪ Add to the Alphabet Linking Chart. Suggested language: "Let's look at our
Alphabet Linking Chart again and read it." (Read through *i*.) "Now we are
going to add a *jack-in-the-box* for *j*." Color or glue in the picture of a jack-
in-the-box. "Let's read it: *J, j-, jack-in-the-box*." Repeat for *k* and *l*. Read the
chart again from the beginning with children joining in.

20

Approximately 15 minutes
The third part of the lesson provides instructions for teaching using the new book.

Here you introduce the new Lap Book to the children, encouraging them to use information from the pictures, as well as their own experiences, to talk about the text.

▶ New Book

Friends,
Level A, Lap Book and small books

PROMPTING GUIDE 1
Refer to *Prompting Guide 1* as needed.

Here you find specific suggestions to scaffold the child's use of the meaning, language, and visual information in print as you read the Lap Book with the children.

In this section, you give the children the small book version of the new book and use shared reading to have children read the book with you.

Read To

- As you introduce the children to the Lap Book, encourage them to notice and use information in pictures, and invite conversation around the text. Build on their comments to expand the amount of language used.
- Suggested language: "This book is called *Friends*. These two dogs are friends. The big dog is Orson (point to tag on collar) and the little dog is Taco (point to tag)." Invite the children to talk about the dogs and how they look. Explain that they are going to read many books about these dogs. Point and read the *Orson and Taco Series* banner on the cover.
- Have children say and clap the names Orson and Taco.
- Turn to pages 2 and 3. Point and read. Invite talk about the illustrations.
- As you turn to pages 4 and 5, ask what they notice about Orson's collar. Point and read. Then ask about Taco's collar. Point and read. Repeat the process through page 15.
- Turn to page 16. "And the two dogs are very good friends." Point and read page 16.

Read With

- Reread the text with the children as you point crisply under each word.
- Turn to a few different pages, and have the children say a particular high-frequency word (*has, a, little, big*). Ask, "What letter would you expect to see first?"
- Then have the children find the word using a masking card, a flag, or highlighter tape. Notice how quickly and easily they can find the word.
- As you read with the children, you may find opportunities to help them notice the sound at the beginning of the name of the item and its first letter. Show them they can see the item in the picture and check it with the word.

Read By

- Give the children the small book version of the book.
- Ask them to point under each word and read the book with you.

21

Approximately 10 minutes
In this section in Getting Started, you engage the children in composing sentences to write about the new book using interactive writing. During interactive writing, share the pen with the children at selected points.

▶ **Writing About Reading**
Interactive Writing

Orson has a big ball.
Taco has a little ball.
Orson has a big bark.
Taco has a little bark.

PROMPTING GUIDE 1
Refer to *Prompting Guide 1* as needed.

- Talk with the children about Orson and Taco, the two dog friends, and all the things they have.
- Engage the children in composing two to four sentences about things the dogs have, e.g.,

     Orson has a big ball.
     Taco has a little ball.
     Orson has a big bark.
     Taco has a little bark.

- Use interactive writing, sharing the pen with the children at selected points. It is important to prioritize your teaching points so you don't bog down the writing. Try to get it written quickly.
- Write the names of the dogs. Emphasize using a capital letter for names and to start a sentence. Emphasize good spacing and end punctuation.
- Engage children in writing *has* and *a*. Work for quick writing of *has*. You may need to model it on the whiteboard.
- You may want to have the children say *big* slowly to listen for each sound, and show them how to form the letters using the Verbal Path. If this is too difficult, have them listen for the first sound and write the first letter only, then complete the word for them.
- Involve children in listening for the first sound and writing the first letter of the last word.
- As you finish each sentence, point and read it with the children. Reread all the sentences at the end.
- If time permits, have the children make a quick sketch of the two friends.

22

You will find specific suggestions for children to practice and extend their learning in the classroom, including rereading the Take-Home Book. This is optional. Some classroom teachers pair an LLI child with an older "buddy" from another class to reread the Take-Home Book and complete the activity. If there is no opportunity for extra classroom practice, you may eliminate these suggestions.

You will find specific suggestions for children to practice and extend their learning at home. You can find necessary materials and a Parent Letter explaining the task to parents in English and Spanish on the *Lesson Resources CD.* Home support may involve a parent, guardian, or sibling. This is also optional. Reading the Take-Home Book, fold sheets, and many other suggested activities can be done as independent work at home or at school.

Approximately 5 minutes
Here you guide children in some quick "hands on" word work. You will find a visual showing the materials used in the teaching. You will also find suggestions for teaching the children about letters and words.

▶ Letter/Word Work

- Place the magnetic letters *b, g, o, j, n, m,* and *r* on the whiteboard. Suggested language: "Some letters have tall sticks. The letter *b* has a tall stick. And *l* has a tall stick." Tell children some letters have tails, circles, tunnels, and a dot. Demonstrate with magnetic letters. Put them on the table, and have children find and trace over letters that have these features.

Word Bags
- Show *is, big, little,* and *has* with magnetic letters. Have the children make each word two or three times.
- Give children the word cards *is, big, little,* and *has.*
- Have children read all the word cards, including their own names.

Letter Minibooks
- Give children the Letter Minibook for *b.* Have them use the Verbal Path: "*b*–pull down, up, around" and read each page.

Classroom Connection

- Give children the fold sheet with Meli's picture at the top and the sentence written twice at the bottom: *I got a little puppy.*
- Have children cut up the bottom sentence and mix it up.
- Have them match the cut-up words below the sentence. Put the words in an envelope.
- Have children take the fold sheet back to the classroom to draw things the puppy needs. They may glue on the cut-up sentence.
- Give children the Take-Home Book *The New Puppy* to reread.

- Have children take home their fold sheets to read to family members.
- Have them take the Take-Home Book *The New Puppy.*

Home/School Connection

23

This section provides suggestions for observational assessment across the lesson or additional assessment tips if you find they are needed.

Assessing Reading and Writing Behaviors

Observe to find evidence that children can:

- identify words that sound alike at the end (rhyme).
- look at their names and see letters in sequence.
- identify some letter names.
- read with voice-print match across one line of text.
- use voice-print match to self-monitor reading.
- notice and identify the first sound and letter of some words.
- talk about the contrast of big and little.
- understand that Orson and Taco are friends and have things in common even though they are different.

You find specific lesson suggestions for supporting the literacy learning of children who do not speak English as a first language and who are learning to read and write in English.

Supporting English Language Learners

To support English language learners, you can:

- **demonstrate** what you mean by "pointing under each word."
- **demonstrate** what you mean by "You can hear and connect words that rhyme." Be explicit that they sound the same at the *end*, and say the part that rhymes.
- **monitor** for understanding of the number of parts when you clap syllables.
- **demonstrate** what you mean by "stick," "circle," "tunnel," and "dot" when talking about features of letters.
- **provide** background knowledge to understand pets and what they need.
- **be sure** children understand the meaning of the words *big* and *little*.
- **have** children point to the items in the pictures and say the labels.
- **use** the language of the text in a conversational way, and have children repeat the language several times to help them remember the syntax.
- **demonstrate** and check for understanding of "What letter would you see *first?*"
- **be sure** children understand their class/homework.

You find references to sections of the *Professional Development and Tutorial DVDs* as well as professional reading in *When Readers Struggle: Teaching that Works,* which has been written to accompany the *Lesson Guide.* In addition, we refer to other key professional readings to support your teaching in the lessons. A bibliography is provided at the end of this guide.

Professional Development Links

When Readers Struggle: Teaching that Works
Chapter 4: Reading Behavior: What Does It Tell Us? Use this chapter to understand how children build processing systems.

Professional Development and Tutorial DVD, Green System
View Getting Started lessons to notice how the teacher is organized for teaching. Think about your space and materials.

Interactive Writing: How Language and Literacy Come Together
Chapter 1 (pp. 3–14). Use this chapter to explore how interactive writing supports emergent writers and to understand the key features of interactive writing.

24

Lessons 11–110 each include six pages of teaching support. As you will see in the following pages, there are two structures. One structure is used in the odd-numbered lessons. The other is used in the even-numbered lessons. In both structures, the first and sixth pages provide important information for preparation, planning, understanding of the new text, supporting English language learners, connections to the classroom and home, as well as professional development. The second through fifth pages are for your use as you teach the thirty-minute lesson.

▶ Odd-Numbered Lessons

This tells the instructional level you are working on for ten days and the lesson number. You will find the same number on the books for the children. The system or grade indication, new book title, and genre of the new book are also stated here.

Here you will find a list of materials beginning with those that are included in the LLI package, followed by more generic materials available from your school. Many of the listed materials provided in the LLI package can be printed out from the *Lesson Resources CD*, as indicated. Multi-use resources that can be printed out once at the beginning of the program have a check mark.

These are the specific teaching goals for the lesson. These goals will help you think about how the lesson activities are supporting the development of the reading and writing processes.

Each new book is analyzed to show the specific demands on the reader.

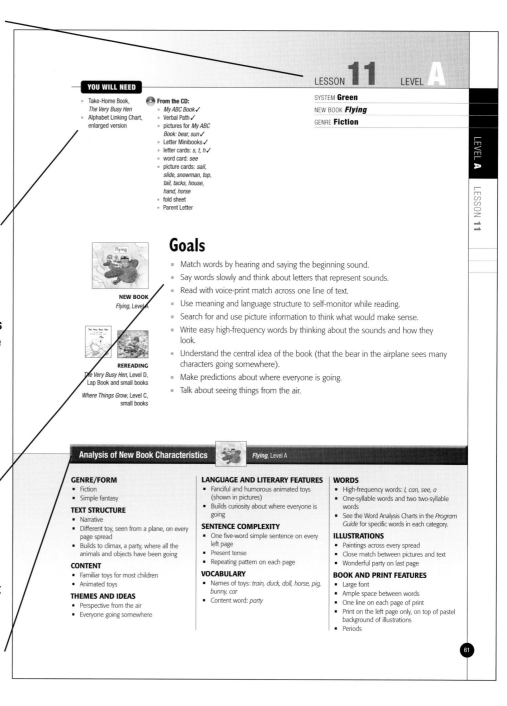

LESSON **11**   LEVEL **A**

SYSTEM **Green**
NEW BOOK *Flying*
GENRE **Fiction**

LEVEL A

LESSON 11

YOU WILL NEED

- Take-Home Book, *The Very Busy Hen*
- Alphabet Linking Chart, enlarged version

From the CD:
- *My ABC Book* ✓
- Verbal Path ✓
- pictures for *My ABC Book: bear, sun* ✓
- Letter Minibooks ✓
- letter cards: *s, t, h* ✓
- word card: *see*
- picture cards: *sail, slide, snowman, top, tail, tacks, house, hand, horse*
- fold sheet
- Parent Letter

NEW BOOK
Flying, Level A

REREADING
The Very Busy Hen, Level D, Lap Book and small books
Where Things Grow, Level C, small books

Goals

- Match words by hearing and saying the beginning sound.
- Say words slowly and think about letters that represent sounds.
- Read with voice-print match across one line of text.
- Use meaning and language structure to self-monitor while reading.
- Search for and use picture information to think what would make sense.
- Write easy high-frequency words by thinking about the sounds and how they look.
- Understand the central idea of the book (that the bear in the airplane sees many characters going somewhere).
- Make predictions about where everyone is going.
- Talk about seeing things from the air.

Analysis of New Book Characteristics   *Flying*, Level A

GENRE/FORM
- Fiction
- Simple fantasy

TEXT STRUCTURE
- Narrative
- Different toy, seen from a plane, on every page spread
- Builds to climax, a party, where all the animals and objects have been going

CONTENT
- Familiar toys for most children
- Animated toys

THEMES AND IDEAS
- Perspective from the air
- Everyone going somewhere

LANGUAGE AND LITERARY FEATURES
- Fanciful and humorous animated toys (shown in pictures)
- Builds curiosity about where everyone is going

SENTENCE COMPLEXITY
- One five-word simple sentence on every left page
- Present tense
- Repeating pattern on each page

VOCABULARY
- Names of toys: *train, duck, doll, horse, pig, bunny, car*
- Content word: *party*

WORDS
- High-frequency words: *I, can, see, a*
- One-syllable words and two two-syllable words
- See the Word Analysis Charts in the *Program Guide* for specific words in each category.

ILLUSTRATIONS
- Paintings across every spread
- Close match between pictures and text
- Wonderful party on last page

BOOK AND PRINT FEATURES
- Large font
- Ample space between words
- One line on each page of print
- Print on the left page only, on top of pastel background of illustrations
- Periods

61

Approximately 5 minutes
This is the first part of the lesson. You will find a visual showing yesterday's new book and the new book from the previous day, and suggestions for rereading them, if time allows.

▶ **Rereading Books**

• *The Very Busy Hen*, Level D
• *Where Things Grow*, Level C

PROMPTING GUIDE 1
Refer to *Prompting Guide 1* as needed.

■ Invite children to reread *The Very Busy Hen* and *Where Things Grow*.

■ Reinforce use of voice-print match and first letters of words to self-monitor and self-correct reading as needed, e.g., "Did it match? Try that again and make it match. Try that again and think of what would look right."

Approximately 5 minutes
This is the second part of the lesson. The focus is on developing strong control of letter and sound knowledge.

▶ **Phonics/Word Work**

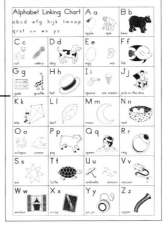

This is an example of the visual or chart you will use and/or create with the children. You may want to write the phonics principle at the top of your chart.

Here you see a concise statement of the phonics principle children need to understand.

■ **PRINCIPLE** Recognizing and using beginning consonant sounds and the letters that represent them: *s, m, t, b, f, r, n, p, d, h, c, g, j, l, k, v, w, z, qu, y, x*

"You can hear the sound at the beginning of a word."
"You can match letters and sounds at the beginning of a word."
"When you see a letter at the beginning of a word, you can make its sound."
"When you know the sound, you can find the letter."
"You can find a word by saying it and thinking about the first sound."

■ Have children quickly read the Alphabet Linking Chart in order: letter name, letter sound, word, e.g., *B /b/ bear*.

■ Place the letter cards *s, t,* and *h* on the pocket chart. Hold up picture cards, one at a time, and ask children to place them under the appropriate letter, using the Alphabet Linking Chart to make connections. Suggested language: "*Sail* sounds like *sun* at the beginning." Picture cards: *sail, slide, snowman; top, tail, tacks; house, hand, horse.*

My ABC Book

■ Introduce *My ABC Book*. Have children find the page for *B* and color in a picture of a *bear*. Have them say the letter, the sound, and then the word *bear*.

■ Have them write the word *big* on the page, first saying it slowly to hear the sounds. Have them check it by pointing as they read.

62

Approximately 15 minutes
The third part of the lesson provides instructions for teaching using the new book.

Here you find specific suggestions to scaffold the child's use of the meaning, language, and visual information in print.

▶ New Book

Flying,
Level A

Introducing the Text

- Introduce children to the book by talking about the bear and what he can see. Suggested language: "This book is called *Flying.* The bear is flying, and he tells all the things he can see. What do you notice about him? Let's look at some of the things he can see."
- "Turn to pages 2 and 3. What can he see? Yes, he sees a train, so he says, 'I can see a train.' Can you say that? Watch me point under each word and read. Now read it again with me."
- "Turn the page. What can he see now? Yes, so what does he say? Yes, he says, 'I can see a duck.' Say *can.* What letter comes first in *can?* Yes, the letter *c.* Find <u>can</u>. Run your finger under it and say *can.*"
- "Turn to pages 10 and 11. What does he say he can see? Say the word *see.* What letter do you expect to see first? Find the word <u>see</u>."
- "The bear can see lots of things below him, and they are all going somewhere. Turn back to the beginning, and read about all the things he can see when he is flying and where they go. Point and read softly."

PROMPTING GUIDE 1
Refer to *Prompting Guide 1*
as needed.

Reading the Text

- As the children read, prompt for or reinforce self-monitoring of voice-print match. For example, ask, "Were you right?" or "Did it match?" Be sure to ask both when they are right and when they are not.
- Reinforce crisp pointing, e.g., "You pointed under each word."

You find suggestions for using the *Fountas and Pinnell Prompting Guide 1* to support the children's effective problem-solving strategies as they read the text.

Discussing and Revisiting the Text

Invite children to talk about the party and all the guests. Some key understandings children may express are:

- As the bear is flying his airplane, he sees many things on the ground. [Extend by asking for examples of what he sees—train, duck, doll, etc.]
- They all seem to be toys. [Extend by asking for evidence from pictures.]
- The toys are all going to a party. [Extend by asking what kind of party they think it is, and why.]
- It seems to be a birthday party because there is a cake with candles, presents, and balloons. [Extend by asking whose party they think it is, and why. Invite them to share reasonable connections to the story.]

You will find suggestions for having a comprehension conversation with the children and key understandings about the text.

PROMPTING GUIDE 1
Refer to *Prompting Guide 1*
as needed.

Teaching Points

- Based on your observations, use *Prompting Guide 1* to select a teaching point that will be most helpful to the readers.
- You may want children to quickly locate *I, can,* or *see* on different pages.
- Reinforce careful pointing and noticing when something didn't look right, e.g., "You noticed something was wrong."

Based on your observations, you select key teaching points that will help the children. You will use *Prompting Guide 1* to teach for, prompt for, or reinforce effective behavior. We provide some suggestions for you to consider.

LEVEL A

LESSON 11

63

Approximately 5 minutes
This is the fourth part of the lesson. Here you guide children in some quick "hands on" word work. You will find a visual showing the materials used in the teaching. You will also find suggestions for teaching the children about letters and words.

▶ **Letter/Word Work**

- Write the word *see* on the whiteboard, and ask children to read it.
- Give children the word card *see*.
- Have them lay out all their word cards face-up. Ask them to find the word *see* in their word cards.

My ABC Book
- Have children open *My ABC Book* and write *see* on the page for *S*.
- Have them color in the picture of the *sun*. They will now have two pages completed.

Letter Minibooks
- Have children read the Letter Minibooks for *n* and *p*. Have them trace a finger over the letter on the front, using the Verbal Path, and then say the name of each picture slowly.
- Have children reread Letter Minibooks for *s, t, h, c,* or other letters that continue to need attention.

64

You will find specific suggestions for children to practice and extend their learning in the classroom, including rereading the Take-Home Book. This is optional. Some classroom teachers pair an LLI child with an older "buddy" from another class to reread the Take-Home Book and complete the activity. If there is no opportunity for extra classroom practice, you may eliminate these suggestions.

Classroom Connection

Green #11   Name: Maria

s	t

see   to

- Give the children the two-column fold sheet with *s* and *t* at the top.
- Give each child the fold sheet with pictures *sun, slide, snowman, top, tail, tacks* and word cards *to* and *see*.
- Have children take the sheets back to the classroom to cut up the pictures and words and sort them in the columns.
- Give children an envelope for their pictures and word cards. Alternatively, they may glue the cards to the fold sheet.
- Give children the Take-Home Book *The Very Busy Hen* to reread.

You will find specific suggestions for children to practice and extend their learning at home. You can find necessary materials and a Parent Letter explaining the task to parents in English and Spanish on the *Lesson Resources CD.* Home support may involve a parent, guardian, or sibling. This is also optional. Reading the Take-Home Book, fold sheets, and many other suggestions can be done as independent work at home or at school.

Home/School Connection

- Have the children take home their fold sheets and cards to read or sort again.
- Have them take the Take-Home Book *The Very Busy Hen* to read to family members.

65

This section provides suggestions for observational assessment across the lesson or additional assessment tips if you find they are needed.

Assessing Reading and Writing Behaviors

Observe to find evidence that children can:
- associate letters with sounds at the beginning of words.
- read with voice-print match across one line of text.
- use meaning and language structure to monitor while reading.
- search for information in the pictures to think what would make sense.
- write high-frequency words by thinking about the sounds and how they look (letters in the right sequence).
- say words slowly and write some letters to represent beginning sounds.
- understand the central idea of the book (that the bear in the airplane sees many characters going somewhere).
- make predictions and draw conclusions about where everyone is going.
- talk about the perspective of seeing things from the air.

You will find specific lesson suggestions for supporting the literacy learning of children who do not speak English as their home language and who are learning to read and write in English.

Supporting English Language Learners

To support English language learners, you can:
- **monitor** for understanding of prompts, such as, "Did it match? Try that again and make it match," and "Were you right?"
- **make sure** children can recognize and name all the pictures and words used in Phonics and Letter/Word Work.
- **help** children understand that the bear sees things while flying above them.
- **use** the pictures to help children recognize and name the objects bear sees.
- **use** the language of the text in a conversational way, and have children repeat the language several times to help them remember the syntax.
- **use** the pictures to support children in discussing what the bear sees and what the objects he sees have to do with the party at the end of the book.
- **remind** children to read at home even if their listener doesn't speak English.

You will find references to sections of the *Professional Development and Tutorial DVDs* as well as professional reading in *When Readers Struggle: Teaching that Works,* which has been written to accompany the *Lesson Guide.* In addition, we refer to other key professional readings to support your teaching in the lessons. A bibliography is provided at the end of this guide.

Professional Development Links

When Readers Struggle: Teaching that Works
Chapter 7: Language Matters: Talking, Reading, and Writing. Use this chapter to help children use language structure as a source of information in reading.

Professional Development and Tutorial DVD, Green System
View Getting Organized for Teaching to help you think about working efficiently in your lessons.

Word Matters: Teaching Phonics and Spelling in the Reading/Writing Classroom.
Chapter 12 (pp. 139–142). Use this chapter to explore ways to use the Alphabet Linking Chart and the Letter Minibooks.

66

▶ Even-Numbered Lessons

The other lesson structure (even-numbered lessons) also includes four parts and an option for additional letter and word work.

This tells the instructional level you are working on for ten days and the lesson number. You will find that the lesson numbers correspond with the book numbers on the small books. The system or grade indication, new book title, and genre of the new book are also stated here.

Here you will find a list of materials beginning with those that are included in the LLI package, followed by more generic materials available from your school. Many of the listed materials provided in the LLI package can be printed out from the *Lesson Resources CD,* as indicated. Multi-use resources that can be printed out once at the beginning of the program have a check mark.

These are the specific teaching goals for the lesson. These goals will help you think about how the lesson activities are supporting the development of the reading and writing processes.

Each new book is analyzed to show the specific demands on the reader.

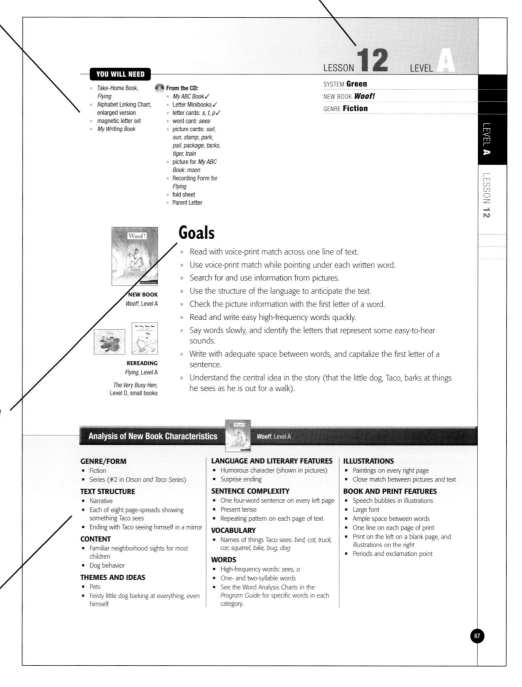

YOU WILL NEED

- Take-Home Book, *Flying*
- Alphabet Linking Chart, enlarged version
- magnetic letter set
- *My Writing Book*

From the CD:
- *My ABC Book* ✓
- Letter Minibooks ✓
- letter cards: *s, t, p* ✓
- word card: *sees*
- picture cards: *sail, sun, stamp, park, pail, package, tacks, tiger, train*
- picture for *My ABC Book: moon*
- Recording Form for *Flying*
- fold sheet
- Parent Letter

LESSON **12** LEVEL **A**

SYSTEM **Green**
NEW BOOK ***Woof!***
GENRE **Fiction**

LEVEL A

LESSON 12

NEW BOOK
Woof!, Level A

REREADING
Flying, Level A

The Very Busy Hen,
Level D, small books

Goals

- Read with voice-print match across one line of text.
- Use voice-print match while pointing under each written word.
- Search for and use information from pictures.
- Use the structure of the language to anticipate the text.
- Check the picture information with the first letter of a word.
- Read and write easy high-frequency words quickly.
- Say words slowly, and identify the letters that represent some easy-to-hear sounds.
- Write with adequate space between words, and capitalize the first letter of a sentence.
- Understand the central idea in the story (that the little dog, Taco, barks at things he sees as he is out for a walk).

Analysis of New Book Characteristics   *Woof!*, Level A

GENRE/FORM
- Fiction
- Series (#2 in *Orson and Taco Series*)

TEXT STRUCTURE
- Narrative
- Each of eight page-spreads showing something Taco sees
- Ending with Taco seeing himself in a mirror

CONTENT
- Familiar neighborhood sights for most children
- Dog behavior

THEMES AND IDEAS
- Pets
- Feisty little dog barking at everything, even himself

LANGUAGE AND LITERARY FEATURES
- Humorous character (shown in pictures)
- Surprise ending

SENTENCE COMPLEXITY
- One four-word sentence on every left page
- Present tense
- Repeating pattern on each page of text

VOCABULARY
- Names of things Taco sees: *bird, cat, truck, car, squirrel, bike, bug, dog*

WORDS
- High-frequency words: *sees, a*
- One- and two-syllable words
- See the Word Analysis Charts in the *Program Guide* for specific words in each category.

ILLUSTRATIONS
- Paintings on every right page
- Close match between pictures and text

BOOK AND PRINT FEATURES
- Speech bubbles in illustrations
- Large font
- Ample space between words
- One line on each page of print
- Print on the left on a blank page, and illustrations on the right
- Periods and exclamation point

67

Approximately 5 minutes
This is the first part of the lesson. You will find a list and suggestions for rereading yesterday's new books and the book from the previous day. As two children softly reread the previous day's new book, listen to one child read yesterday's new book, code the child's oral reading on the corresponding Recording Form, have a brief comprehension conversation, and make a teaching point that will be most helpful to the reader.

▶ Rereading Books and Assessment

• *Flying*, Level A
• *The Very Busy Hen*, Level D, small books

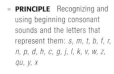

PROMPTING GUIDE 1
Refer to *Prompting Guide 1* as needed.

- Listen to one child read *Flying* as you code the reading behavior on the Recording Form, have a brief comprehension conversation, and make a teaching point that you think will be most helpful to the reader. Score and analyze the Reading Record following the lesson.

Take a Reading Record

- Have the other children reread *The Very Busy Hen* and then *Flying*.

- Prompt children to use picture information, voice-print match, and the first letters of words as appropriate, e.g., "What would make sense and look right?"

Place a stick-on note in this box to remind yourself of the name of the child you will assess.

▶ Phonics/Word Work

Here you see the visual or chart you provide to help children learn the principle.

- **PRINCIPLE** Recognizing and using beginning consonant sounds and the letters that represent them: *s, m, t, b, f, r, n, p, d, h, c, g, j, l, k, v, w, z, qu, y, x*

"You can hear the sound at the beginning of a word."
"You can match letters and sounds at the beginning of a word."
"When you see a letter at the beginning of a word, you can make its sound."
"When you know the sound, you can find the letter."

- Use the enlarged Alphabet Linking Chart on the easel.
- Have children quickly read the chart in order: Letter name, letter sound, word—e.g., *B /b/ bear*.
- Place the letters *s, t,* and *p* on the pocket chart. Hold up picture cards, one at a time, and ask children to place them under the appropriate letter, using the Alphabet Linking Chart to make connections. Suggested language: "*Tiger* sounds like *top* at the beginning." Picture cards: *sail, sun, stamp; park, pail, package; tacks, tiger, train*.

My ABC Book

- Have the children take out *My ABC Book*, find the page for *M*, and glue in a picture of a *moon*. Have them say the letter, the sound, and then the word *moon*.
- They can also write the high-frequency word *me* on the page.

Approximately 5 minutes
This is the second part of the lesson. You will engage children in learning a phonics principle. The focus is on developing strong control of letter and sound knowledge.

68

Approximately 10 minutes
This is the third part of the lesson. You will find one of three types of writing to use with the children: Interactive Writing, Dictated Writing, or Independent Writing.

You see an example of the writing the children will do.

▶ **Writing About Reading**

Dictated Writing

• **MY WRITING BOOK**
• **PROMPTING GUIDE 1**
Refer to *Prompting Guide 1* as needed.

I can See a duck.
I can See a doll.

- Introduce the children to *My Writing Book.*
- Dictate the following sentences for children to write in *My Writing Book:*

  I can see a duck.
  I can see a doll.

- Emphasize good spacing and end punctuation. The children should be able to write *I* and *a* easily. You may want to help them say *can* and *see* and think about the sounds they hear. You can support them by writing a word on the whiteboard.
- They should be able to hear the sound and write the first letter in the last word in each sentence independently.
- Have the children reread the sentences and illustrate them.
- If time allows, have them locate a word in the text quickly.

69

Approximately 10 minutes
This is the fourth part of the lesson in which you introduce the new book. The book is usually one or two levels below the level of the new book in the odd-numbered lesson. You will find specific instructions for teaching using the new book.

Here you find specific suggestions to scaffold the child's use of the meaning, language, and visual information in print.

Woof!,
Level A

▶ New Book

Introducing the Text

- Introduce the children to the book by talking about the dogs in the story. Suggested language: "This book is called *Woof*. Do you remember the two dog friends in this story? Yes, here is little Taco, and there is his friend, Orson. In this story, Taco sees lots of things, and he says 'Woof!' every time."
- "Turn to page 2 to see what Taco sees. Yes, Taco sees a bird. Say *Taco*. Clap *Taco* with me."
- "Turn the page to find out what he sees. Yes, Taco sees a cat. What does he do? Watch me point and read. 'Taco sees a cat.' What letter do you expect to see first in *sees?* Yes, it starts with *s*. Say *sees* and point under it."
- "Turn to pages 12 and 13. What does Taco see? Yes, Taco sees a bike. And what does he do?"
- "Turn to the end, page 16, and look at what Taco sees. Yes, Taco sees a dog! What does he do?"
- "Turn back to the beginning, and point and read softly."

PROMPTING GUIDE 1
Refer to *Prompting Guide 1* as needed.

Reading the Text

- As the children read, prompt for or reinforce self-monitoring of voice-print match as needed, e.g., "Were you right?" or "Try that again."
- Reinforce their use of picture information to solve new words, e.g., "Can the picture help you?"
- If they have voice-print match under control, help them think about what Taco sees in the picture and check it with the first letter of the word, e.g., *bike*.

You find suggestions for using the *Fountas and Pinnell Prompting Guide 1* to support the children's effective problem-solving strategies as they read the text.

Discussing and Revisiting the Text

Invite the children to talk about Taco and the things he sees. Have them tell what they notice. Some key understandings they might express are:

- Taco, the dog, barks at many different things. [Extend by asking for examples from the book.]
- Taco barks the most at himself in the mirror because he thinks it is another dog.
- Taco seems to bark when he is excited, surprised, or angry. [Extend by asking for evidence from the pictures.]

You will find suggestions for having a comprehension conversation with the children and key understandings about the text.

PROMPTING GUIDE 1
Refer to *Prompting Guide 1* as needed.

Teaching Points

- Based on your observations, use *Prompting Guide 1* to select a teaching point that will be most helpful to the readers.
- Have children locate *sees* on one or more pages.
- Help children understand how to check a word they said with the first letter of the word. Have them say the word after you, e.g., *cat, squirrel, bike,* and ask what letter they expect to see first.
- Ask them to check the picture with the word.

Based on your observations, you select key teaching points that will help the children. You will use *Prompting Guide 1* to teach for, prompt for, or reinforce effective behavior. We provide some suggestions for you to consider.

70

You will find additional suggestions for work with letters and words if time allows.

You will find specific suggestions for children to practice and extend their learning in the classroom. This includes rereading the Take-Home Book.

You will find specific suggestions for children to practice and extend their learning at home. You can find necessary materials and a Parent Letter explaining the task to parents in English and Spanish on the *Lesson Resources CD*. Home support may involve a parent, guardian, or sibling. These activities are also optional. Reading the Take-Home Book, fold sheets, and many other suggestions can be done as independent work at home or at school.

▶ **Optional Letter/ Word Work**

S s ☼
sees

- Have children lay out their word cards face-up.
- Write *see* on the whiteboard, and ask children to read the word.
- Have them find the word *see* in their word cards.
- Write the word *sees* on the whiteboard under the word *see*. Ask children what they notice (the words are the same except *sees* has an *s* at the end). Have them read the two words. Then have them write the word *sees* on the *S* page of *My ABC Book*.
- Give children the word card *sees* to add to their word bags.

Letter Minibooks
- Have children read the Letter Minibooks for *n* and *w*, using the routine.
- Have children reread other Letter Minibooks as needed.

Magnetic Letters
- If time allows, have the children sort magnetic letters two or three ways (see Instructional Routines, Ways to Sort and Match Letters, in the *Program Guide*).

Classroom Connection

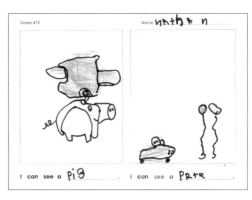

- Give children the fold sheet with a sentence on each half: *I can see a _____.*
- Have children quickly name things that the bear in *Flying* can see.
- Have them take the fold sheet back to the classroom to fill in the blank and draw a picture for each sentence.
- Give children the Take-Home Book *Flying* to reread.

Home/School Connection

- Have the children take home their fold sheets to read to family members.
- Have them take the Take-Home Book *Flying* to read to family members.

This section provides suggestions for observational assessment across the lesson or additional assessment tips if you find they are needed.

Assessing Reading and Writing Behaviors

Observe to find evidence that children can:

- read with voice-print match across one line of text.
- search for and use information from pictures.
- use language structure to solve words.
- check information from the pictures with the first letter of a word.
- read and write easy high-frequency words.
- write with adequate space between words and capitalize the first letter of a sentence.
- understand the central idea in the story (as Taco is out for a walk, he barks at everything he sees, including himself in the mirror).

You will find specific lesson suggestions for supporting the literacy learning of children who do not speak English as their home language and who are learning to read and write in English.

Supporting English Language Learners

To support English language learners, you can:

- **monitor** for understanding of "_____ sounds like _____ at the *beginning*."
- **make sure** children can recognize and name all the pictures and words used in Phonics and Letter/Word Work.
- **model** articulating the /s/ at the end of *sees*. Discuss how it changes the meaning of the word.
- **help** children say the names of the objects that Taco sees.
- **use** the language of the text in a conversational way, and have children repeat the language several times to help them remember the syntax.
- **use** the pictures to support children in discussing what Taco sees.
- **monitor** for understanding of "What letter would you see *first?*"
- **ask** children to repeat the dictated sentences several times so they begin to hold on to the language structure.

You will find references to sections of the *Professional Development and Tutorial DVDs* as well as professional reading in *When Readers Struggle: Teaching that Works,* which has been written to accompany the *Lesson Guide.* In addition, we refer to other key professional readings to support your teaching in the lessons. A bibliography can be found at the end of this guide.

Professional Development Links

When Readers Struggle: Teaching that Works
Chapter 7: Language Matters: Talking, Reading, and Writing. Use this chapter to help children use language structure as a source of information in reading.

Professional Development and Tutorial DVD, Green System
View the Tutorial, Coding Oral Reading, to review the coding conventions.

Word Matters: Teaching Phonics and Spelling in the Reading/Writing Classroom
Chapter 1: Eight Principles of Literacy Learning (pp. 3–11). Use this chapter to explore principles of literacy learning.

72

▶ The Continuum of Learning Literacy

This figure is an example of the Continuum that is included at the end of each level. You will want to refer to it as you teach the ten-lesson sequence at the level (see page 105 in this guide). It includes the behaviors and understandings to notice, teach, and support in your lessons on each level.

This designates the level of the lessons in this sequence.

This refers to the reader's ability to efficiently process the text to gain literal understanding.

This involves bringing thinking to the text to go beyond literal meaning.

Behaviors and Understandings to Notice, Teach, and Support

Thinking Within the Text

Solving Words
- Recognize most words quickly with the support of meaning and language structure
- Say a word and predict its first letter before locating it
- Say a word slowly to hear and identify the first sound and connect to a letter
- Recognize a few easy high-frequency words
- Locate familiar, easy high-frequency words by noticing anything about the word
- Locate easy high-frequency words in a text
- Slow down speech to assist in voice-print match

Monitoring and Correcting
- Reread the sentence to problem solve, self-correct, or confirm
- Reread to search for/use information from language or meaning
- Self-monitor and self-correct using language structure
- Use voice-print match to self-monitor and self-correct
- Show evidence of close attention to print
- Use known words to self-monitor and self-correct

Searching for and Using Information
- Read left to right across one line of print
- Match one spoken word with one printed word
- Search for and use information in the print
- Use oral language in combination with pointing, matching voice with words on the page (indicated by crisp pointing)
- Search for and use information from pictures
- Reread to search for information
- Use language structure and meaning to learn about print

Summarizing
- Remember what the story is about during reading
- Remember information to help in understanding the end of a story
- Remember important information

Maintaining Fluency
- Point crisply and read at a steady rate slow enough to match voice to print but without long pauses
- Notice and use end punctuation and reflect it in voice

Adjusting
- Slow down to problem solve words and resume reading with momentum

Thinking Beyond the Text

Predicting
- Use knowledge of language structure to anticipate the text
- Make predictions based on information in the pictures
- Predict the ending of a story based on reading the beginning and middle
- Make predictions based on personal experiences and knowledge

Making Connections
- Talk about own experiences in relation to the text
- Make connections between texts on the same topic or with the same content
- Identify recurring characters or settings when applicable

Synthesizing
- Talk about what the reader already knows relative to text information
- Identify new information in text or pictures

Inferring
- Talk about characters' feelings
- Talk about the pictures, revealing interpretation of a problem or of characters' feelings

181

LEVEL **A** **Behaviors** and **Understandings** to Notice, Teach, and Support

Thinking About the Text

Analyzing
- Understand how the ideas in a book are related to each other
- Understand how the ideas in a text are related to the title

Critiquing
- Share opinions about a text
- Share opinions about illustrations

This involves awareness of elements of the writer's craft as well as the ability to critique the text.

Additional Suggestions for Letter/Word Work

Use a chart or easel, whiteboard, magnetic letters, or pencil and paper to develop fluency and flexibility in visual processing, if needed.

- Recognize a few easy high-frequency words (for example, *the, a, I, and, is, can, in, it*) quickly
- Recognize a few easy CVC words (*can, get*) quickly
- Make a few easy CVC words (*cat, pin, sat, hot, can*)
- Make a few easy high-frequency words (*it, is, in, we, me, to, the*)
- Write a few easy CVC words (*can, I, run*)
- Write a few easy high-frequency words (*a, an, the, me, to*)
- Match/sort pictures by initial/final sounds
- Match or sort pictures by end rhyme

- Match or sort letters by a variety of features (uppercase or lowercase; tall or short; with and without sticks, circles, tails, dots, tunnels)
- Match lowercase letters with speed
- Clap the syllables in one- and two-syllable words (from pictures)
- Search for and locate letters by name quickly
- Read the Alphabet Linking Chart by letter names, pictures and words, and in different ways (all vowels, all consonants, letters only, backwards order, every other letter)

These suggestions are based on the kinds of word-solving strategies readers need at this text level.

 182

▶ Using the *Lesson Guide*

The *Lesson Guide*, Green System, includes an introduction to the system that will help you prepare materials you will use throughout; Lessons 1-110; and, at the end of each ten-lesson sequence, the Continuum for the level, or set of specific behaviors to notice, teach, and support in your lessons. An introductory Parent Letter and daily letters can be printed from the *Lesson Resources CD* and sent home. The letter offers suggestions to parents on how to support children with home activities.

In this section, we will provide a brief overview of the structure of the lessons and the information on the Continuum at the end of each section or level. You will find that the structure provides for a smooth, well-paced thirty-minute lesson that will become very comfortable for you. The children also benefit from the predictability of the lesson and learn the routines quickly.

Teaching Within the LLI Lessons

We have provided a brief overview of the information in the six-page lessons in the *Lesson Guide* and in the specific material for the level from *The Continuum of Literacy Learning*. Notice that we have suggested time frames. While these time frames may vary by a minute or two, keep in mind that you have a total of only 30 minutes, so try not to get bogged down on any one component. You will find that a timer will be helpful in pacing the lesson. We suggest getting a digital timer and starting it at thirty minutes, or you can use the F & P Calculator/Stopwatch to keep track of time. (Note that the Calculator/Stopwatch does not have an alarm.) If too much time is spent on any one component, it will not be possible to complete the combination of tasks, all of which are essential. You will also find that as you and the children get used to the lesson framework, the lessons will be smoother and more time efficient.

The instructional activities are designed to:

❑ Support children in reading a new text that has opportunities to extend comprehension, vocabulary, and processing strategies.

❑ Develop fluency and phrasing through rereading.

❑ Help children learn about letters, sounds, and words.

❑ Learn to apply knowledge of phonics to word solving while reading continuous text.

❑ Extend comprehension through discussion, teacher's instruction, and writing.

❑ Learn how to write about their reading.

❑ Display new understandings in classroom work.

❑ Develop the habit of home reading.

The following chart is a summary of the lesson structures.

Plan for Getting Started Lessons (Lessons 1–10)

Approximate Time: 30 minutes

5 minutes	Rereading Books*
5 minutes	Phonemic Awareness/Phonics
8 minutes	New Book (Lap Book and small books)
7 minutes	Writing About Reading
5 minutes	Letter/Word Work

In the first lesson, find any text children have read and can reread or skip this component.

Plan for Odd-Numbered Lessons

Approximate Time

5 minutes	Rereading Books
5 minutes	Phonics/Word Work
15 minutes	New Book (Instructional Level)
5 minutes	Letter/Word Work

Plan for Even-Numbered Lessons

Approximate Time

5 minutes	Rereading Books and Assessment
5 minutes	Phonics/Word Work
15 minutes	Writing About Reading
5 minutes	New Book (easier level)
If time allows	Optional Letter/Word Work

In this section, we will provide more detailed information about the lesson. We expect that you will use your knowledge and observations to modify the lesson suggestions as needed. No one lesson plan will fit all readers. Your decision making across the lesson is critical as you respond to the specific strengths and needs of the individual children you teach.

▶ Using Getting Started Lessons

The first ten lessons in the Green System are designed to engage children in highly supported reading and writing experiences. They learn how to read simple books and poems, write a message, and work with sounds and letters. Your goals are to help the children become active, engaged learners and to build a foundation of early reading and writing behaviors.

This is also a time for close observation of the children's strengths so you can build on them in lessons. Encourage the children to notice letters, sounds, words, and information in illustrations and to engage in conversation about texts.

1. Rereading Books

The children read Lap Books with you as you point to the words. You may want to have children say and find a few words in the text after reading. The children point and read the small books softly and independently (Level A). For Levels B, C, and D texts, have the children point and read the small books in unison with you to assure voice-print match. (The last Getting Started Lap Book in the Green System is Level D.)

2. Phonics/Word Work

You will engage the children in a variety of experiences in working with sounds and letters. They learn how to recognize their names, listen for sounds, and connect them with letters.

3. New Book

You introduce a new Lap Book by pointing under each word as you read aloud and engaging children in conversation about the text. Often, you introduce characters from the series books children will read later. Next, you invite the children to read *with* you as you point. Finally, the children point and read the text softly and independently (Level A). At Levels B, C, and D, have the children point and read the small books in unison with you to assure voice-print match. At Level

C in later lessons, however, you will want them to begin reading with their eyes without the aid of a finger so they begin to read with phrasing and fluency.

4. Writing About Reading

Talk and write about yesterday's new book. In this section, children engage in one of three kinds of writing: interactive, dictated, or independent. Children write their own messages only during independent writing; others are suggested by the teacher or co-constructed. During interactive writing, share the pen with the children at selected points. In dictated writing, you will dictate a word or sentence for children to write and follow up with work on the whiteboard or on chart paper to check what they have done.

5. Letter/Word Work

Engage the children in hands-on work to learn about how print works. Children will be working with name puzzles; letter, word, and picture cards; magnetic letters; Letter Minibooks; and other materials.

▶ Using Odd-Numbered Lessons

There are two kinds of lessons in LLI. The first day, an odd-numbered lesson—such as 11, 13, 15, 17, 19—is for the introduction of a new *instructional* level book. The focus is on reading, discussion of meaning, and phonics and word work.

1. Rereading Books (5 minutes)

In Part 1, children reread the new book from the previous lesson softly as you observe their processing. Rereading develops fluency and offers the child a chance to perform smooth processing. During and after reading, you may prompt for strategic actions and briefly discuss the meaning of the text. The emphasis is on engagement and enjoyment and reading the whole book.

2. Phonics/Word Work (5 minutes)

Part 2 provides some very explicit and systematic instruction to help children learn how written language "works." In lessons for Levels A, B, and C, you work with children to develop phonemic awareness, which means hearing the individual sounds in words. Hearing and identifying the sounds in words helps them to connect sounds to letters. In this section, you will find specific suggestions for teaching children how to connect sounds and letters. If several activities are suggested, be sure to teach the principle and have the children apply it. Skip the additional suggestions if time is a problem.

3. New Book (15 minutes)

In Part 3, you introduce the new book which will be the basis for the lesson for two days. The new book in this odd-numbered lesson is at the children's *instructional* level. That means they can read texts at the level *with* teacher support. You will find specific suggestions for:

- ❑ Providing an overview of the meaning of the whole text.

- ❑ Using in conversation some specific language structures that will help children read the text.

- ❑ Conversationally using specific vocabulary words that are important for the text.

- ❑ Helping children locate known and unknown words (thinking about the sounds and letters).

- ❑ Helping children notice particular features of the words or the print.

- ❑ Pointing out important features (such as text organization, punctuation, organization, and illustrations).

You will also find brief guidelines for observing and interacting with individuals during reading and for discussing the meaning of the text after reading. Refer to the *Fountas and Pinnell Prompting Guide 1* for specific language to use in teaching.

The new book reading includes some explicit teaching for processing strategies. At Levels A and B, the children need to point crisply under each word. At Level C, you will want to help them start to use their eyes without the aid of the finger so they can begin to read with phrasing and fluency.

While children are reading LLI texts, you will want to interact with each of them briefly. You can listen to one at a time. Ask them to read very softly. Observe and listen to them as they read, leaning in to interact briefly with individuals as needed. You can simply turn from one child to another and listen. If they are reading so softly you cannot hear them, just

lightly tap the child you want to hear and he can raise his voice a little. However, volume is not usually a problem with younger children. We recommend that you have the children read silently beginning at about Level H.

When you interact with individuals, you will want to teach for, prompt for, or reinforce effective reading behaviors. (See *Fountas and Pinnell Prompting Guide 1*.)

- ❑ *Teaching* involves demonstrating, or modeling, behaviors. It means intervening to show the child what you want him to do. For example, you could say, "Watch while I read the sentence again and get my mouth ready to say the word (by making the sound of the first letter). Now you do that." Or, "Watch while I point right under the words. Now you point and read."

- ❑ *Prompting* means using some precise language to get the child to engage in the behavior. Successful prompting depends on the child's understanding of what you mean, so the behavior must be demonstrated first. For example, you might say, "Try that again and get your mouth ready." Or, "Did it match?" Use consistent language in your prompting as you did in your demonstration.

- ❑ *Reinforcing* behaviors means giving some very quick and concise comments that just let the child know what she did that was effective. For example, you might say, "You got your mouth ready for the word." Or, "You pointed right under the words." Again, remember to use the same language you used in your prompting. Notice that we use purely descriptive language designed to communicate precisely what the child did (rather than "good" or "I like the way you..."). Evaluative remarks like "good boy" or "that's what good readers do" do not really help the reader. The best way to encourage children is to enable them to be successful in processing and to comment specifically on what they do.

4. Letter/Word Work (5 minutes)

Here in Part 4, you involve children in active exploration of letters and words in order to help them learn how words "work." They will break words apart using magnetic letters, write words, and acquire a core of high-frequency words.

▶ Using Even-Numbered Lessons

The second day in the sequence, an even-numbered lesson—such as 12, 14, 16, 18, 20—offers the introduction of a new independent level book for the child. The focus is on writing to extend the meaning of books (as well as to achieve a close look at print, letters, and sounds), on phonics and word work, and on fluency. The even-numbered lessons vary slightly in their structure from the odd-numbered lessons. The instruction is designed to

❑ Extend the children's understanding of the meaning of the new text through writing and sometimes drawing.

❑ Develop children's early writing skills.

❑ Help children notice and use features of the text.

❑ Develop fluency and processing strategies through rereading yesterday's new book and through encountering a new but easier book.

❑ Continue teaching children about letters, sounds, and words.

1. Rereading Books and Assessment (5 minutes)

In Part 1, children reread softly the new books that were read the day before. You will find some tips for observing and interacting briefly with the readers. Reading yesterday's new book for the second time helps children to process with greater ease the challenges that led to problem solving yesterday. Use this time to take a Reading Record on one child, using the Recording Form for the instructional level book that was introduced and read the day before. On the day of the even-numbered lesson, listen to one child read aloud while you code the reading, have a brief comprehension conversation, and make a teaching point. Based on your observation of the process, provide brief teaching points that will help the reader problem-solve more efficiently.

2. Phonics/Word Work (5 minutes)

In Part 2, continue to expand children's awareness of sounds and letters in words. You may examine the principle introduced the day before but add examples to expand children's knowledge; or, you may introduce

FIGURE 18 Listening to a child read

a new principle. If there are several activities, do only what time allows after working with the new principle.

3. Writing About Reading (15 minutes)

Part 3 involves children in extending understanding of the text through writing and develops early writing strategies. All writing is in conventional form, and we strongly suggest using unlined paper. You will also want to help the children use lowercase letters consistently, except where uppercase is needed. Sometimes the writing is interactive. You will compose a text with the children and then write it on a chart that all children can see. Children sometimes move quickly to the chart to write a letter or word. You will notice an example of what the interactive writing might look like in each lesson, but compose your own sentences with the children.

In some lessons, children write specific sentences that you *dictate*. Here, children have opportunities to consider a small piece of text in detail and to think about sounds and letters as they construct words with your support.

Sometimes children write independently. This means the children compose and write sentences of their own with your support to assure conventional form. The focus is on developing early writing strategies (see *When Readers Struggle: Teaching that Works*). Depending on your needs and on your children's abilities, you may decide to use any of the three kinds of writing in any given lesson. That means that although dictated writing might be specified for a particular lesson, you might decide that it is more useful for children to engage in interactive or independent writing.

Independent writing may take several different forms, according to the purposes of the lesson, for example:

- ❏ Lines from the text that children can illustrate (at home or in the classroom).
- ❏ Innovations on the text (using the same structure with ideas/words that children contribute).
- ❏ Summary statements.
- ❏ Interesting information from the text.
- ❏ A response or reaction to the text.

These written texts become texts for reading by the children, so they must be clear. All of the writing is scaffolded by the teacher so it is written conventionally. Show the children how to write in lowercase letters and allow uppercase letters only when needed. Help them use good spacing and capitals as appropriate. Use the Verbal Path (see also *Prompting Guide 1*, Verbal Path for Letter Formation, or the *Lesson Resources CD*) to guide letter formation, as needed. Help them use sound analysis and visual analysis to spell words correctly.

Remember that the writing is most beneficial to learners when it is surrounded by conversation. The children's dictated and independent writing will be in their personal writing books, *My Writing Book*. You may want to type the interactive writing pieces in a large font (about the size of the font in Level A texts) and have children glue them in their writing books to reread and illustrate. In addition, you may want children to glue their sentence strips on a page when they are used in a lesson. This blank book is used at your direction and is a good way to compile a collection of writing that can be reread and sent home at the end of a series of lessons.

In addition, you will find that children often write letters and words in their writing books as part of Word Study. In the process, they develop a network of knowledge about how words work.

As part of word study, they may

- ❏ practice letter formation (see *Prompting Guide 1* or the *Lesson Resources CD* for using the Verbal Path)
- ❏ write high-frequency words
- ❏ categorize words, noticing different features

- ❏ categorize pictures according to sound and/or match them with letters
- ❏ construct words letter by letter or part by part
- ❏ show connections between words
- ❏ use analogy to construct new words

Get to know the Instructional Routines for learning letters with a Verbal Path, Letter Minibooks, high-frequency word cards, magnetic letters, letter and word games, and letter sorting. Each is explained in Instructional Routines for LLI starting on page 62 and on the DVD. In addition, you can read about a wide variety of effective teaching practices for letter and word learning in *When Readers Struggle: Teaching that Works*, Chapter 11: Learning to Solve Words: Effective and Efficient Phonics.

Sometimes children's interactive, dictated, or independent writing will be reproduced to take home and share with family members. You can reproduce the sentence(s) and cut them up into individual words that children can put in order and glue onto a sheet of paper and illustrate at home. Place the pieces in an envelope and have the children put them in their Take-Home Bags.

4. New Book (5 minutes)

In Part 4, you introduce a new book to children by quickly pointing out some of the important ideas in the book. The book is usually two levels easier than the new book children read for instruction on the previous day, so it will be easy for them to read. In many cases, books have been selected to extend concepts, language, or vocabulary of the previous book or books in the series of lessons at the level. Children read through the whole book quickly in a soft voice and take it back to the classroom and home to read again. This book can also be used for rereading if there is time in the lesson.

Optional Letter/Word Work

The phonics/word study work in the LLI lesson is designed to supplement the classroom phonics program. If time allows, you may want to provide additional letter/word work for the children if they need it. Alternatively, you may suggest it to the classroom teacher.

Three Kinds of Writing in Leveled Literacy Intervention Lessons

Interactive Writing	You and the children compose and write a message together. ❑ You and the children write the message in large print on a chart that everyone can see. ❑ You and the children engage in conversation as you compose and write the message together. ❑ Use the *Prompting Guide 1* to support early writing strategies, letter formation, and to help the children construct a text in conventional form. ❑ Children take over the writing at particular points that have instructional value. For example, you may ask a child to contribute the writing of a letter or word. The children reread the message. Sometimes you invite them to revisit the text for letter or word study. ❑ You may provide a typed copy for children to glue in their writing books and illustrate. You may write the sentences on sentence strips to cut up and have the children assemble and glue on paper.	Interactive writing engages children in every aspect of the writing process in a highly supported way.
Dictated Writing	You read aloud a sentence. Then you reread it as children write it in their books with your support. ❑ Some of the words will be known. ❑ For unknown words, help children engage in word solving by using sound or letter boxes (see Instructional Routines) prompting them to use sound analysis or visual analysis, helping them think of words they know (see *Prompting Guide 1*). Or, you may write the word on a whiteboard for children either to check their attempt or to copy. The completed text is in conventional form. ❑ Use the Verbal Path (see Instructional Routines) and *Prompting Guide 1* to support letter formation. ❑ Children reread their sentences when finished and may draw a picture if there is time. ❑ You may have them highlight words or word parts of interest.	Children learn how to go from oral to written language. They experience word solving within a meaningful sentence. They reread and check their work.
Independent Writing	The children write a text independently. ❑ The text may be a list, a message or sentence, labels for pictures, or any other type of writing. ❑ As the text is for rereading, provide support as needed to help the children write in conventional form. ❑ Use the *Prompting Guide 1* to support the construction of the message. ❑ Use sound/letter boxes or the Verbal Path as appropriate (see Instructional Routines) *and Prompting Guide 1.* ❑ Use the *Prompting Guide 1* to support early writing strategies.	Children develop independent control of early writing strategies. They learn to represent ideas in different ways. They learn to self-monitor (check on themselves) in writing.

FIGURE 19 Three Kinds of Writing in LLI Lessons

▶ Key Aspects of Teaching in LLI Lessons

In LLI lessons, the teaching centers around four critical areas: Reading Texts, Writing Texts, Phonics/Word Study, and Oral Language Learning. The children read numerous books, write stories, learn phonics skills in a systematic way, and expand their oral language, including vocabulary.

Reading Texts in LLI Lessons

At the kindergarten and Grade 1 levels, children are developing early reading behaviors. They are learning the differences between the print and the pictures and are also learning to:

❏ read left to right across a word

❏ read left to right across a line of text

❏ return to the left after reading a line

❏ read the left side of the page before the right

❏ understand what a letter is

❏ understand what a word is

❏ understand that words are made of letters

❏ understand that letters in a word are always in the same order

❏ understand that there are spaces between words in a text

❏ understand that you can get information from pictures

❏ match one spoken word with one written word in print

❏ self-monitor and self-correct their errors

❏ stop at a period

❏ raise the voice at a question mark

❏ show excitement at an exclamation point

❏ use quotation marks to identify dialogue

❏ read a core of high-frequency words

❏ use letter/sound relationships

❏ use information from pictures

❏ use language structure to read

❏ use the meaning of the story to read

❏ read with phrasing and fluency

As they progress, the children will also learn to:

❏ notice mismatches in reading

❏ use meaning and language to solve new words

❏ recognize a large core of high-frequency words

❏ use word parts to solve new words

❏ check the first letter of the word with the meaning

❏ check the meaning and language with print

❏ self-correct using meaning, language, or visual information

When you use the Lap Books and the small books in the system, children have massive opportunities to read texts and develop these early reading behaviors. The *Fountas and Pinnell Prompting Guide1* will also help you to teach for, prompt for, and reinforce these behaviors and understandings. It is a key tool for your use while children are reading the text and for selecting Teaching Points.

At Level C, the children will begin to cease pointing at words and will learn to read with phrasing and fluency (see *When Readers Struggle: Teaching that Works*, Chapter 16: Teaching for Fluency in Processing Texts). You will find books that support their fluent reading—books with dialogue, plays for rereading, texts with repetition, texts with natural language, texts on familiar topics, texts with familiar vocabulary, texts with known high-frequency words, texts with words in bold type, and texts that have phrases laid out to support fluency.

FIGURE 20 Small books and *Prompting Guide 1*

You will find a large section of the *Fountas and Pinnell Prompting Guide1* dedicated to language that supports fluent reading. Key areas include stress, rate, pausing, phrasing, intonation, and integration. In addition, *Prompting Guide 1* provides language for other critical areas of teaching—solving words, searching for and using information, monitoring and correcting errors. You will want to refer to each of these sections as you determine areas of need for teaching during the reading of books.

As the children develop effective processing strategies at a level, the teacher increases the challenge by selecting books at the next level on the gradient. The children move up the ladder of support to grade level proficiency. In Grade 1, your goal is to bring children successfully to Level I or J by year end, depending on the school standard. If the child reaches expected grade level performance earlier, the exit level criteria will be lower.

Writing Texts in LLI Lessons

The children will have numerous opportunities to compose and construct sentences about their reading. Your goal is to help them develop early writing strategies (see *Prompting Guide 1* and *When Readers Struggle: Teaching that Works*, Chapter 13, Extending Reading Power: Writing to Read) using several different teaching approaches—Interactive Writing, Dictated Writing, and Independent Writing. Your role in each supports conventional writing of a text that will be reread.

In Interactive Writing, you and the children share the pen. You select teaching points to support new learning or reinforce partially controlled behaviors. When the children already control an understanding

or when it is too difficult, you write it for them. After you construct the text together, children reread it together as a shared reading text.

In Dictated Writing, you read aloud a sentence once and then read the words slowly. You support the children as they write each word as necessary. For unknown words, you may write on the whiteboard or help children think how to write it. You may use sound boxes to support sound analysis (Elkonin boxes) or letter boxes to support visual analysis. (See Instructional Routines, page 62.) You help them write high-frequency words quickly, say words slowly, form letters efficiently, and use what they know about words. The children reread and illustrate their sentences.

In Independent Writing, you invite the children to compose their own sentences. You scaffold the writing as needed in the same ways as you did in Dictated Writing. Children reread and illustrate their sentences.

You can use *Prompting Guide 1* as a tool for supporting early writing behaviors, as well as composing, constructing words, and forming letters.

Phonics and Word Study in LLI Lessons: Letters, Sounds, and Words

The effective reader demonstrates strong control of letter-sound relationships and word structure as part of the reading process. We have designed the lessons to provide explicit teaching and numerous opportunities for the application of principles in reading and writing. The making of words, using a variety of materials, provides numerous kinesthetic experiences for strong teaching. In addition, the children learn how to recognize and take words apart as they read text. The writing of texts is also designed to build phonics and word knowledge (see *When Readers Struggle: Teaching that Works*, Chapter 11, Learning to Solve Words: Effective and Efficient Phonics).

In the Green System, children develop several areas of phonics knowledge, early literacy concepts, phonological awareness, letter knowledge, letter-sound relationships, easy spelling patterns, word meanings, and a core of at least forty high-frequency words, which become a foundation for learning other words. In addition, they learn efficient letter formation. (See Appendix, page 108 for Word Analysis

FIGURE 21 Children working on sorting letters

Charts.) You will provide teaching for this knowledge in the specified lesson components and also in the reading and writing segments. Letter learning must be tidied up so that the child knows the letter names, sounds, and efficient formation. You will find numerous tools and explicit teaching suggestions in the lessons. (See *When Readers Struggle: Teaching that Works*, Chapter 9, Learning to Read and Write: the Phonological Base; Chapter 11, Learning to Solve Words: Effective and Efficient Phonics.)

Oral Language Learning in LLI Lessons

An important aspect of teaching in LLI lessons is the expansion of oral language, including vocabulary. Children have many opportunities in the lesson to converse with each other and with the teacher because the group is small, so the amount of opportunity for talk is increased.

In the lessons, you will provide explicit demonstrations of ways to use language. You can engage the children in conversation about their experiences and about texts, expanding their knowledge of language structure as they talk. You will introduce texts to them, giving them opportunities to say and hear new words, phrases, and sentences. In the writing segment, you engage them in talking about ideas and composing several sentences. Oral language surrounds their literacy learning. (See *When Readers Struggle: Teaching that Works*, Chapter 7, Language Matters: Talking, Reading, and Writing.)

▶ Working with Series Books in LLI Lessons

One of the features of LLI is the large collection of series books. Across all three systems, we have created a variety of series, as shown in Figure 22 on pages 55–61.

Some of the values of series books are:

❑ Children become interested in the topics, characters, or plots so that they are motivated to read more.

❑ As children move through a series, they experience the satisfaction of bringing a great deal of background knowledge to reading.

❑ Readers get to know characters so that they are better able to talk about their characteristics and infer their feelings and motivations.

❑ Children have the experience of reading connected text over time.

❑ Readers learn the process of making many connections between texts—typical situations, problems, settings, character traits, style of writing and illustrations.

We present the entire range of series books in Figure 22 because you may have all three systems of LLI in your school. If so, you can borrow from one system to use in another to develop interest in a series. If you do not have all three systems, you can take opportunities to connect the series books in the system you are using.

Since LLI is designed for flexible use, you may start your readers on any level appropriate to their current abilities. That means children may be reading a fiction series book without having read prior stories. That will not be a problem because every text stands alone; however, you may want to create chances for children to read and enjoy the easier books (on lower levels) in a series by adding them to the rereading segment or letting them take them to the classroom for independent reading.

When children have read one or more of the books in a series, it will be easy for them to form expectations when they are introduced to a new book in the same series. The following are some suggestions for using series books:

❑ In the introduction to a text, make explicit connections between texts by holding up previous books and reminding children of what a character was like or what happened in the story.

LLI Series Books

Series Title	Description	Book Titles	Level	System 0	G	B
Meli Nonfiction	Meli, an adorable little West Highland terrier, gets care, training, and lots of love from her owner, Ron.	 The New Puppy	A		X	
		 Meli on the Stairs	C		X	
		 A Walk with Meli	E		X	
		 Meli at the Pet Shop	E			X
		 Meli at the Vet	E			X
		 Taking Care of Meli	F			X
		 Meli at School	G			X
		 The Problem with Meli	J			X
Big Machines Nonfiction	Kids will love the dynamic photographs and interesting facts about cranes, fire trucks, bulldozers, road rollers, and more.	 Trucks	B		X	
		 Police Car	B			X
		 Fighting Fires	G			X
		 Road Builders	I			X
		 Cranes	I			X
Fun Club Fiction with a factual element	Miss Dimple takes the After School Fun Club on fun-filled field trips to a post office, an aquarium, a vet clinic, and a dairy farm. Photos bring readers up close as they learn lots of interesting facts about these destinations.	 The Fun Club Goes to a Dairy Farm	H			X
		 The Fun Club Goes to the Post Office	I			X
		 The Fun Club Goes to the Vet Clinic	I			X
		 The Fun Club Goes to the Aquarium	K			X

FIGURE 22 LLI Series Books

continues

Series Title	Description	Book Titles	Level	System		
				O	G	B
All About Nonfiction	Get ready to learn about everything from honey-bees to volcanoes. Stunning photographs, diagrams, and other nonfiction text features make these books accessible at every level.	*All About Animal Babies*	F		X	
		All About Chimps	H		X	
		All About Honeybees	I		X	
		All About Dolphins	J		X	
		All About Boats	H		X	
		All About Penguins	C			X
		All About Snakes	C			X
		All About Sharks	F			X
		All About Bugs	F			X
		All About Sled Dogs	H			X
		All About Spiders	H			X
		All About Dinosaurs	I			X
		All About Redwood Trees	I			X
		All About Bats	J			X
		All About the Sonoran Desert	J			X
		All About African Elephants	K			X
		All About Astronauts	N			X
		All About Volcanoes	N			X
		All About Robots	K			X

Series Title	Description	Book Titles	Level	System		
				O	G	B
Orson and Taco Fiction	Big, easy-going Orson and feisty little Taco are canine friends whose adventures will touch your heart and tickle your funny bone.	*Friends*	A		X	
		Oh No!	A		X	
		Woof!	A		X	
		Orson's Tummy Ache	B		X	
		Looking for Taco	C		X	
		The Good Dog	D		X	
		Brave Taco	E		X	
		The Big Storm	F		X	
		A Trip to the Laundromutt	H		X	
Fixit Family Fiction	The Fixit family doesn't have a lot of luxuries, but they do have a lot of know-how. And that's a good thing, because something always seems to need fixing around their place.	*The Drip*	D			X
		Billy's Pen	D			X
		The Broken Clock	E			X
		Pinky the Pig	C			X
		The New Roof	G			X
		The Bird Feeders	H			X

continues

section **3**

Teaching With the LLI System

Series Title	Description	Book Titles		Level	System		
					O	G	B
Froggy and Friends Fiction	Artistic and fun-loving Froggy likes nothing better than spending time with his friends—with the possible exception of eating bugs!		Frog Food	A		X	
			The Painter	A		X	
			Baby Pictures	E		X	
			The Cherries	H		X	
			The Red Pajamas	D			X
			The Trip	E			X
			Frog Songs	J			X
			Good Friends	L			X
Fox Family Fiction	This loving family of foxes includes a rambunctious big sister and a slightly less secure little brother. Children will relate to the familiar situations, including trying to play quietly in the house, being wide awake at bedtime, and not liking what's for dinner.		A Surprise for Roxy	D			X
			Andy Fox at School	E			X
			A Fast Fox	F			X
			Super Fox	G			X
			Wide Awake!	H			X
			The Perfect Picnic	G			X
			Puddle Play	K			X

Series Title	Description	Book Titles	Level	System O	System G	System B
Sam and Jesse Fiction	These realistic stories feature two cousins with very different interests. Still, the boys get along well most of the time, and they have one important thing in common—they both adore their grandfather.	*Jesse*	A		X	
		Sam and Papa	B		X	
		A Day at the Park	C		X	
		The Soccer Game	F		X	
		Papa's Birthday	G		X	
		At the Beach	G			X
		The Pirates	L			X
		The Hot Day	N			X
Bunny Rabbit Fiction	Bunny is a happy-go-lucky little rabbit from a big, extended family who finds fun in ordinary days—and manages to solve a couple of problems, too.	*My Family*	B	X		
		Hop, Hop, Hop	B	X		
		Out to Play	C	X		
		The Storm	E		X	
		Bunny and the Monster	F		X	
Meg and Hugs Fiction	These gentle stories tell of the relationship between Meg, a little girl who lives with her grandparents, and Hugs, her lovable but slightly contrary cat.	*Up in a Tree*	D		X	
		Pictures of Hugs	F		X	
		Fun for Hugs	I		X	
		The Missing Cat	I		X	

continues

section **3**

Teaching With the LLI System

Series Title	Description	Book Titles	Level	System		
				O	G	B
Moosling Fiction	The young moose hero of these books cannot be described as the brightest or most experienced animal in the forest. Still, his positive, helpful approach to life somehow always makes him a winner.	A Picnic in the Rain	D			X
		The Hug	E			X
		Moosling the Babysitter	G			X
		Footprints	H			X
		Hide and Seek	J			X
		Moosling in Winter	K			X
		Moosling the Hero	L			X
		The Costume Party	M			X
Family Fiction	Photographs lend realism to these simple stories of family members playing, working, going out to lunch, and planting a garden.	Playing Dress Up	A	X		
		My Big Brother	B	X		
		Family Pictures	A		X	
		Helping Mom	E		X	
		Out for Lunch	F		X	
		Grandma's Glasses	F		X	
Kim and Lizzy Fiction	Kim and Lizzy are best friends who live close to one another in the city and who share everything—even colds.	The Cold	D			X
		Kim's New Shoes	G			X
		The Play Date	G			X
		The Scream	K			X

Series Title	Description	Book Titles	Level	System O	System G	System B
Classic Tales Fiction	The Classic Tales are updated versions of the familiar stories and themes that children have been enjoying for decades. At the end of each story, there is a play based on the story for rereading or dramatization. The books are oversized to accommodate rich artwork.	The Hat	B	X		
		The Three Pigs	D		X	
		The Three Bears	E		X	
		Three Little Pigs and a Big Bad Wolf	F		X	
		Goldie and the Three Bears	G		X	
		The Goat in the Garden	G		X	
		The Gingerbread Man	H		X	
		Stone Soup	I		X	
		The Lion and the Mouse	J		X	
		The Three Billy Goats	J		X	
		The Little Red Hen	C			X
		The Mitten	D			X
		Chicken Little	E			X
		The Wind and the Sun	I			X
		The Great Big Enormous Turnip	H			X
		The Coyote and the Rabbit	H			X
		The Hare and the Tortoise	J			X
		The City Mouse and the Country Mouse	K			X
		Jack and the Beanstalk	L			X
		The Fox and the Gulls	M			X

section **3**

Teaching With the LLI System

- For nonfiction texts, remind children of the ways information is usually presented in the whole series. In this way, you set expectations for the way information is organized in the genre.

- Substitute previous books in a series for the Rereading portion of the lesson so that the texts are fresh in children's minds. They can always take the other books back to the classroom for independent reading.

- Take a day to reread all the books in a series and talk about the characters in fiction or the way nonfiction texts are organized. Do some writing about the series. Write about a character or create another story in the series. Use nonfiction series as a model for children to write about something they know.

- When working in one collection, borrow series books from other collections. Have children use them for extra reading in the classroom.

- As children become more advanced, have them try writing their own stories about a character. Or, create a group story using interactive writing.

Series books provide a strong scaffold for reading comprehension. Children have the experience of continuing meaningful reading over a longer period of time and extend their ability to remember important elements of texts.

▶ Using *Prompting Guide 1* in Leveled Literacy Intervention Lessons

The *Fountas and Pinnell Prompting Guide 1* is a tool for you to use to support the children as they read or write. You will find specific language to teach for strategies in reading and writing.

The first section provides language to develop early reading behaviors and keep systems of strategic actions evident in oral reading. There are three columns, one that provides language to teach, a second with language for prompting readers to engage problem-solving actions you have taught, and the third to reinforce effective behaviors that are newly emerging.

The second part of the guide provides language for supporting early writing behaviors; letter formation; and composing and constructing words in interactive, independent, and dictated writing.

▶ Instructional Routines for LLI

In this section we describe, in alphabetical order, some general Instructional Routines that may appear again and again across LLI lessons. Often, a particular routine will be very briefly described within a lesson, and sometimes the direction will be more open (for example, "children work with high-frequency words"). You can refer to this section to learn more about the routines. In addition, you will find more information on these routines in *When Readers Struggle: Teaching that Works*, Chapter 10, Learning About Print: Early Reading Behaviors and Chapter 12, Using Words: How to Build a Repertoire. You can also use these routines to enrich your instruction and make it more powerful.

Alphabet Linking Chart

The Alphabet Linking Chart is a tool for supporting children's learning of letter names in uppercase and lowercase forms, the related initial sounds, and letter formation. The chart is referred to for use in many of the early lessons. You may want to print out the chart on card stock for children to use in daily lessons and make extra copies so the children can take it home. This chart will help tidy up all the children's knowledge related to letters.

When you first introduce the Alphabet Linking Chart, you may want to make an enlarged version (about the size of the Table Charts) with the letters but no pictures. Children can then think about the beginning sound of each picture and match the sound to a letter. You can build the chart with the children in this way, helping them develop ownership of it, by gluing in one or more pictures each day. Have them read only the blocks with pictures glued in. When children receive their own copy of it, the chart will be more meaningful because they have participated in making it.

As an alternative to cutting apart the pictures and placing them in the appropriate boxes, you may want to start with the Alphabet Linking Chart that has the black and white pictures in the boxes and color in the pictures in the boxes that apply each day. Have the children read just the colored boxes. At the end of the cycle, all the boxes will be colored in. Also, each time a letter is colored or glued in on the Alphabet Linking Chart, you can have children do the same in their personal alphabet books, which are called *My ABC Book*.

You can have the children read the chart in a variety of ways:

❑ Read the whole chart in order (Aa apple).

❑ Read just the pictures.

❑ Read just the letters.

❑ Read just the uppercase letters.

❑ Read just the lowercase letters.

❑ Read the consonants only.

❑ Read the two sounds of the vowels only (or just the short vowel sounds or just the long vowel sounds).

❑ Sing the chart to the tune of the Alphabet Song.

❑ Read every other letter.

❑ Read randomly as you point to boxes.

You will find that the lessons are designed to support the buildup of the chart. If you find the children read a different sequence or some letters are already known, you should make adjustments to meet your children's needs.

Consonant Cluster Linking Chart

This chart includes pictures that begin with two consonant letters, including the consonant digraphs. It is designed to help children develop quick recognition and blending of initial consonant clusters and digraphs. Once again, you may want to use an enlarged version. You can have the children

❑ Read it in order [e.g., *bl blanket, br bridge*].

❑ Read randomly as you point to various boxes.

❑ Read every other box.

❑ Read it backwards.

Fold Sheet

You will see references to a fold sheet in many lessons as a suggestion for classroom and home practice. You can print fold sheets from the *Lesson Resources*

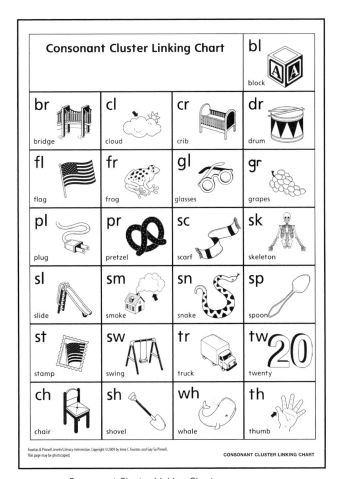

FIGURE 23 Consonant Cluster Linking Chart

CD. The fold sheet involves having the children write their names and sometimes do a little writing or illustrating in the classroom or at home to reinforce learning. If the sheet has more than one section, fold it on the line and have children write their names on the cover. It will fit nicely in the Take-Home Bag.

Introducing New Words to Learn

As you help children learn new words, you may want to use some of the following teaching suggestions:

❑ Use language that makes it clear you are talking about a *word* (not a letter): "This word is [word]." (Some children confuse letters and words and may be focusing on only a *part*.)

❑ Tell children to look at the beginning of the word and show them what that means (first letter on the left).

❑ Read the word to children as you run your finger under the word, left to right.

FIGURE 24 Child writing on whiteboard and using magnetic letters

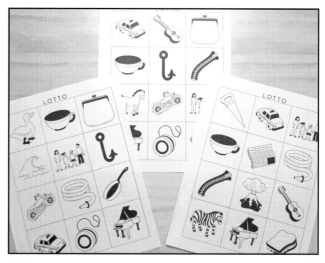

FIGURE 25 Lotto game

❏ Ask children to look closely at the word and say what they notice at the beginning.

❏ Ask them to look at the word and then read it as they run a finger under it, left to right.

❏ Sometimes another word will help children remember a new word: *an, and; the, then.*

❏ Help children notice the first letter and then look across the word left to right to notice more.

❏ Give children magnetic letters in order to build the word left to right.

❏ Using magnetic letters, have the children break the word by pulling down the first letter and then the rest of the letters. The have them put it together again.

Letter and Word Games

Word, letter, and phonics games are a way to help children learn some very basic foundational understanding. The game is interesting and requires the children to look carefully at words, letters, and parts of words. They have many exposures to the same units.

In addition to the engaging ways of working with words and letters (listed above), we have included three basic games:

1. Lotto, which is like Bingo.
2. Follow the Path.
3. Concentration.

Directions for Lotto

Making the Game You will need enough Lotto game boards made of card stock for the number of children who will participate. You can print the game from the *Lesson Resources CD*. The players' boards are different from one another. You may want to create sets of colored boards and then make sure each person in the group has a different color.

Playing the Game Give each player a game card. Place the letter, picture, or word cards and the plastic chips or other markers in the middle of the table. Players take turns drawing a card and saying what it is. All players search their game cards for a corresponding letter, picture, or word. They can mark any spaces that correspond. The first player to cover the entire board wins the game. The game can then continue, if desirable, until others fill their cards.

Directions for Follow the Path

In Follow the Path, players throw a die or draw a card to move a marker along a curved "path." Follow the Path games may also have names like Going to the Zoo, Trip to Outer Space, Race to the Finish, or Trip to the Ice Cream Store. The objective is to reach the destination (or end of the path) first.

Making the Game Print the game from the *Lesson Resources CD.* You can also customize the game by using the Custom Card Maker and gluing or drawing pictures of interest around the path and making an interesting "finish" box at the end (for

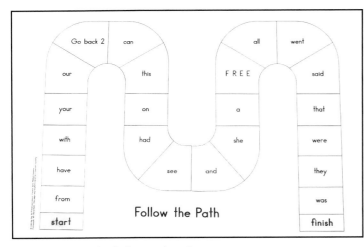

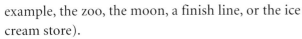

FIGURE 26 Follow the Path game board

FIGURE 27 Concentration game cards

example, the zoo, the moon, a finish line, or the ice cream store).

Playing the Game To play the game, each player shakes the die, lets it fall, and moves the corresponding number of spaces. If they are drawing cards, they draw the next card in the pile, read it aloud, and move to the next corresponding space. The player might also have to perform some action (such as saying the next letter of the alphabet, reading a word and saying the beginning or ending sound, looking at a picture and clapping syllables, and so on). The player who gets to the end of the path first wins the game.

Directions for Concentration

The goal of the Concentration card game is to make matches between cards that display letters, pictures, or words. The letters, pictures, and words will vary according to the purpose of the application activity (for example, matching beginning sounds or ending sounds, letters and sounds, beginning consonant clusters and pictures, and so on). The objective is to gather the most pairs by the end of the game.

Making the Game The Concentration game is provided in the lessons. However, if you wish to customize the game using the Custom Card Maker on the *Lesson Resources CD*, you can prepare a collection of cards with letters, pictures, or words that will be paired using the Deck Card Template. You may want to draw a simple picture or place a sticker on the reverse side of the cards to create a uniform deck. If you make the back of each set of cards different, keeping cards in different decks and selecting differ-

ent decks becomes easier. The total number of cards should be anywhere from twelve to twenty-four.

Playing the Game To play the game, place the cards face down on the table in orderly rows. Each player has a turn. The player turns two cards over to show the letter, picture, word, or word part. If the cards go together, the player takes the pair and takes another turn. If they don't match, the player turns the cards back over and the next player has a turn. The player who has the most pairs at the end of the game is the winner.

This game requires players not only to make matches among sounds and letters but to remember the position of potential matches.

You can teach the games in the word work section of many of the lessons. (Game directions are also on the *Lesson Resources CD*.) There will not be much time to play these games, but with only three players, they go quickly. Once children have learned the routines for the games, they can take them back to the classroom to play and they can also take home a copy to play with family members.

Letter Minibooks

Letter Minibooks are short books focused on a particular letter and its relation to a sound. They can be printed from the *Lesson Resources CD*. Letter Minibooks may also focus on letter clusters and their relation to sounds. Instructional benefits of Letter Minibooks are:

❑ Children develop familiarity with a letter and how it looks.

- ❑ Children can practice efficient directional movements for making a letter.

- ❑ Children learn letter names.

- ❑ Children have the opportunity to say a series of words that begin with the sound that is related to the letter. They see the letter and say the sound several times in sequence.

- ❑ Children build knowledge of a series of key examples of concrete objects that begin with the letter and can serve as examples of the letter/sound relationship.

Some routines for using the Letter Minibooks are the following:

1. Introduce the Letter Minibook by saying: "This is a book that is all about the letter [name of letter]. [Name of letter] makes the sound, [make the sound.]

2. "Let's make the letter right on top of the [name of letter] on the front."

3. Show children how to trace over the letter using the Verbal Path and *Prompting Guide 1*.

4. Have children trace the letter, using the Verbal Path, and then say the name of the letter.

5. Show children how to "read" each page of the Letter Minibook by saying the names of the letter and the objects.

6. After children know the routines for reading Letter Minibooks, they can read several of them quickly.

You will find suggested Letter Minibooks in the lessons. Based on your knowledge of the letters and sounds the children know and need to know, you may vary your selection of minibooks to use.

Magnetic Letters: Tools for Learning to Read and Write Words

Magnetic letters have many benefits for young readers (see Ways to Sort and Match Letters and 25 Ways to Use Magnetic Letters on the *Lesson Resources CD*). These multicolored letters are concrete. Children can manipulate them easily. They can feel them with their hands and notice their distinctive features. Some ways of working with magnetic letters are:

1. Have children make their names.

2. Have two or three sets. Children match letters: *a, a, a; t, t, t.*

3. Children match uppercase and lowercase letters: *Aa, Bb.*

4. Children put letters in the order of the alphabet. They match them letter by letter: *a-a, b-b, c-c.*

5. Children find all the vowels and separate them from the consonants.

6. Have children sort letters in a variety of ways: "Find the letters with long sticks and the letters with short sticks." "Find the letters with tunnels." "Find the letters with circles." "Find the letters with dots." "Find the letters with tails." "Find the letters with a slant." (see *Lesson Resources CD*)

7. Hand children letters in order to make a word. They make the word left to right, read it with a finger (left to right), and then check it letter by letter with a word card or a word you have written on a whiteboard.

8. Have children make a simple word (CVC or CVCe) with magnetic letters and then write the word on paper with marker—checking the word letter by letter when finished.

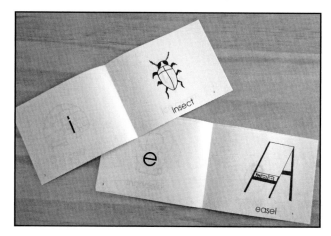

FIGURE 28 Letter Minibooks

FIGURE 29 Magnetic letters making a CVC word

9. Have children look at the array of letters (either all or a limited number), pick up a letter, and say its name (or sound).

10. Children lay out an array of letters. Play "Find a Letter." Say the name of a letter and have children find it quickly and pick it up and say its name. (Practice doing this quickly.)

11. Children have two circles drawn on paper, one with an *h* written in it and one with an *o*. Have children put letters in the *h* circle and say how they are like *h*. Do the same with the *o* circle. Vary the letters in the circles. This activity will help children attend to the visual features of letters.

12. Build a simple word (*cat* or *he*). Show the children how to change the first letter and make a new word (*sat* or *me*). Vary the words.

You will also want to refer to 25 Ways to Use Magnetic Letters at Home (see *Lesson Resources CD*).

My ABC Book

In the Orange and Green Systems, children may use their personal alphabet books, *My ABC Book,* to help them develop their knowledge of the whole alphabet, uppercase and lowercase letters, features of letters, and letter/sound relationships. You can print this book from the *Lesson Resources CD.* You can also take the CD version to a copy center to have it enlarged to 18 by 24 inches or 24 by 36 inches and mount it on tag board to make a Lap Book. This book has the upper and lowercase letter on each page, along with a key word and picture. The pages for vowels

have both short and long sounds. *My ABC Book* is built systematically across several lessons. Some ways to use it are:

❑ Read it from beginning to end, letters and words under key pictures.

❑ Each time a letter is colored or glued in on the Alphabet Linking Chart, the children can do the same in *My ABC Book.*

❑ Read only the letters.

❑ Read only the words under the key pictures.

❑ Search for a particular page and letter.

❑ Write a new word on the appropriate page.

❑ Draw more pictures that begin with the letter on a page.

My Poetry Book

In all three systems of LLI, children will enjoy working with *My Poetry Book.* In LLI, there are three different poetry books, one for each system, Orange, Green, and Blue. You can print this simple book from the *Lesson Resources CD* and staple or bind it on one side. It will contain all of the poems used in lessons for the system. Poems are introduced gradually as indicated in lessons so you will want to keep the book with all of the materials for a particular group. Hand them out to children when you want them to reread poems or read a new poem.

FIGURE 30 *My ABC Book*

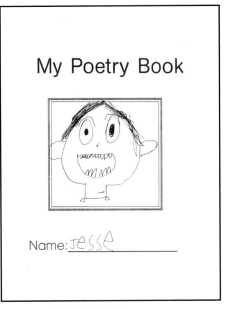

FIGURE 31 *My Poetry Book*

Usually, the poem is introduced with a larger chart size version that children can read in a shared way. You can take the *Lesson Resources CD* version to a copy center to have it enlarged to 18 by 24 inches or 24 by 36 inches and mount it on tag board to make a Lap Book or you can just print the poem by hand. Most poems are short. Then, children can take their own books and turn to the right page to read the poem. At the end of the series of LLI lessons, children will like taking home the book to read and keep. Some ways to use *My Poetry Book* are:

❏ Revisit and reread poems that are favorites.

❏ Take it back to the classroom to read and bring it back the next day.

❏ Draw pictures to go with the poems.

❏ Highlight words or word parts.

❏ Notice rhyming words and highlight them.

❏ Notice word endings and highlight them.

My Vowel Book

My Vowel Book is a simple 8.5-by-11-inch book that can be printed from the *Lesson Resources CD*. On each page, you have the upper and lowercase vowel and one picture that can be either the short or long sound of the vowel. You can print books for children that feature only the short or the long sound. In this case, children would complete the book for each and take it home. Or, you can print pages back to back so that the left page has the short sound and the right page has the long sound (or have the pages follow each

other consecutively. The vowel book is an optional tool that is introduced and included in the Green System lessons. Some ways to use the vowel books:

❏ Children can color in or glue in more pictures to represent the sounds.

❏ Children can write words that have the vowel in first position.

❏ Children can write words that have the vowel in other positions in the word. They highlight the vowel in yellow.

❏ Children can use the book to write words that are connected by the vowel sound, for example *about, around; say, day, way; an, and, sand.*

❏ Children can read their vowel books by saying the letter, the names of the pictures, and the words they have written.

My Writing Book

Each child will have a colorful blank writing book, called *My Writing Book*. Children can draw a picture of themselves in the box on the cover. You will have the children write independently, or dictate the writing having children start a new page on the right each time and adding illustrations. Use the left side for children to practice letters or for sound or letter box work (see page 69). Sometimes you will also have the children do some word writing in the Phonics/Word Work part of the lesson. The writing book is also used for children to glue and illustrate cut up sentences. All writing in the writing book is in conventional spelling to support reading.

FIGURE 32 *My Vowel Book*

FIGURE 33 *My Writing Book*

Name Chart

The name chart is a useful tool for helping children learn about letters, sounds, and words. It is a list of names, usually in alphabetical order by the first letter. Some teachers write the first letter of each name in red and rest of the name in black. The print should be clear, and names should not be jammed together. Use the name chart as a resource in interactive and independent writing.

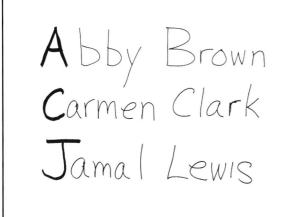

FIGURE 34 Name Chart

Name Puzzle

Name puzzles will help children begin to learn about letters, using their own names. By putting together their names, children learn how to look at letters and notice their distinguishing features and orientation. They learn that words are made up of letters and that the order of letters is always the same. Begin by telling children that they are going to put together their name puzzles.

1. Have children cut up a set of letter cards and use the letters to form their names. Letter cards can be printed from the *Lesson Resources CD*. They can store the letters in an envelope glued into their folders. Their folders should have their names already printed on them.

2. Arrange children in a circle so they can place their folders open flat on the floor in front of

them, where you will be able to observe their work.

3. Suggested language: "I'm going to show you how to put together your name puzzle. Take out the letters that are in the envelope glued in your folder. Open your folder and lay it flat in front of you. Be sure you can see your name. Use the letter pieces to make your name. Put down the first letter first; then put down the next letter. Be sure the letters match exactly."

4. Emphasize that each letter has to look the same as the letters written on the folder.

5. Using a chopstick or other small pointer, point to each letter, demonstrating how to check letter by letter and saying the letters as you go.

6. Show how to mix up the letters so they can form the name again.

7. Be sure all the children have formed their names at least once.

FIGURE 35 Name Folder and Puzzle

Oral Games: Developing Phonological Awareness

To help the children learn how to listen for and identify words in sentences, syllables in words, the first part (onset) and the last part (rime of a one-syllable word, e.g., c-at), and the individual phonemes in a word (c-a-t), you may want to play an oral game for a minute or two. You may want to use the Category Cards in the *Lesson Resources CD* so you can show the pictures or you can simply say the words.

BLENDING

You can have the children blend sounds, word parts, or syllables. For example, you say *c-a-t* and they say *cat*. Children also learn how to blend the onset with the rime, e.g., *c-at, d-og* or syllables, e.g., *ba-na-na, banana*.

SEGMENTING

You can have the children segment sounds in words. For example, you say *cat* or show the picture of a cat and they say *c-a-t*. Children also learn how to segment *dog* to *d-og* and *cat* to *c-at*.

MANIPULATING PHONEMES

You can have children add sounds to the beginning or end of words or change a sound in a word, e.g., *and-band, an-ant, look, took*.

All of these oral games can be played for less than a minute, as time allows, to build the children's sensitivity to sound units.

Sentence Strips

Sentence strips are made of about 1-by-12-inch manila oak tag. They can be cut into strips from larger sheets. A sentence or several sentences can be written on the strips. Then you cut them word by word, mix them up, and have the children put them together and reread them. Occasionally, you may want to cut parts of a word to call their attention to them. They can glue the words in *My Writing Book* and illustrate them. Or, they can take the parts in an envelope to the classroom or home to put together and glue on paper for practice.

Shared Reading

In shared reading, you point under each word on a large print text as you read it or as the children read with you. When the children have strong voice-print match, you can put the pointer at the beginning of each line. Alternatively, for further practice (in Getting Started only), children can point to the text in their small books and read in unison. In lessons, however, it is preferable for children to learn to read at their own rate and not rely on the support of the other children.

Sound and Letter Boxes (Elkonin Boxes): Helping Children Hear Sounds and Record Letters

D. B. Elkonin, a Russian psychologist, developed a tool for helping children think about the sounds and letters in the words. The technique has also been used by Marie Clay and by other researchers and educators. It is a powerful tool in the lessons. You can use the structure of Elkonin or sound boxes to help children listen for and identify each sound in a word. Draw the same number of boxes as sounds. For example, make three boxes for *like* (see figure below). Then ask the children to listen for each sound and write the letter in the box, e.g., *What sound do you hear first? Next? Last?* Add the other letters yourself in the correct boxes to make the words look right. Have the child practice writing the word in *My Writing Book* or have him write it immediately in the sentence. Later, you may decide to use letter boxes, which contain the same number of boxes as letters (see figure below), but do not make this decision until the children are independent in identifying sounds and letters in sequence. You have the children run their finger under the boxes and write each letter they would see in the word. (For more information, see *When Readers Struggle: Teaching that Works,* several chapters.)

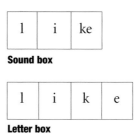

Sound box

Letter box

Table Charts

For shared reading of poetry and other texts, as well as the Phonics/Word Work part of the LLI lesson, you will sometimes need to make a chart to work on and/or refer to over several days. You will find it useful to keep these charts handy in a very compact way. The charts do not need to be as large as you would use for an entire class. You will be working closely with three children or a small group at a table. Use the 11-by-13-inch size of the LLI Lap Books as your guide. The print should be large enough for all children in the group to see across a table. Here are several alternatives:

❑ Make the charts on chart paper that you can fold once and keep in the folder for that group of children. You can use clothespins to hang charts from the top of an easel or keep them in a folder.

❑ Make the charts on stiff tagboard (about the size of a Lap Book). Keep the charts joined by two rings at the top for a group of children. You can keep it in the folder for that group of children. If you have a tabletop easel, you can prop this chart up against the easel or you can hang it temporarily from a chart rack or another easel.

❑ Purchase a large, unlined sketch pad (with stiff paper about 11 by 13 inches). Have one pad for each group, or use tabs to identify the section for each group. Make your charts right on the pages. You can draw columns and then write words and glue pictures and word cards in the correct columns. You can use tabs to identify phonograms or consonant clusters quickly.

Resist the temptation to "pre-prepare" these charts unless it is recommended in the lesson; for example, you would have poems already printed or handwritten, but phonics or word charts are far more powerful if the children participate in their construction and have a feeling of ownership. When you no longer need a chart, you have an opportunity to send it home with one of the children (taking turns). When a child explains the chart to someone at home, he is teaching himself a lesson!

Verbal Path for Letter Formation

The Verbal Path is designed to help children use words to get the hand going the right way to form letters. You can print the Verbal Path directions from the *Lesson Resources CD* or refer to it in *Prompting Guide 1*. The goal is for the motor routines to become automatic and unconscious without the support of the words. For letters formed in similar ways, you can have children practice a group of letters that are formed similarly before going to another group.

Ways to Sort and Match Letters

When children sort letters, they learn how to attend to their distinctive features. You can have them sort by uppercase and lowercase, by color, and by feature (tall, tails, circles). You can have them find all the letters that are the same as a letter. You might have them engage by looking only, or you may have them sort and name the letter each time. A minute or two of letter sorting will help the children process print more fluently and will support word analysis.

You will find letter sorting activities in the lessons. If you find you have extra time, you may want to do some extra sorting. Figure 38 on page 73 is a list of ways to have the children sort. You will also be able to print this sheet for reference (see *Lesson Resources CD*).

FIGURE 36 Table Chart

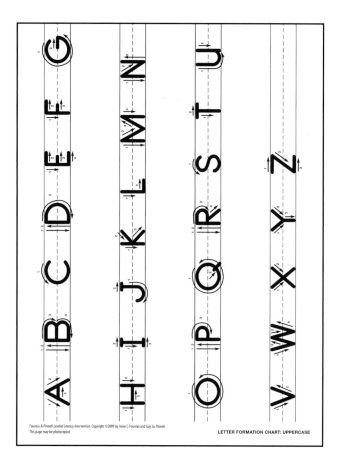

LETTER FORMATION CHART: UPPERCASE

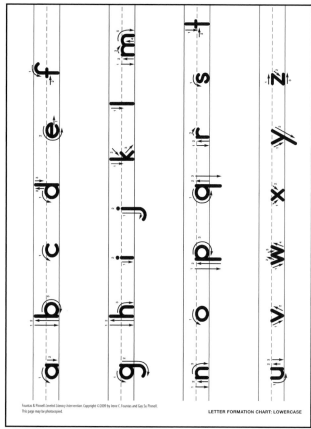

LETTER FORMATION CHART: LOWERCASE

Verbal Path for the Formation of Letters

Sometimes it helps children to say aloud the directions for "making" a letter. This "verbal path" helps them to understand the directional movement that is essential. In addition, it gives the teacher and child a language to talk through the letter and its features. Here, we suggest language for creating a verbal path to the distinctive features of letters.

Lowercase Letter Formation

a — pull back, around, up, and down
b — pull down, up, around
c — pull back and around
d — pull back, around, up, and down
e — pull across, back, and around
f — pull back, down, and cross
g — pull back, around, up, down, and under
h — pull down, up, over, and down
i — pull down, dot
j — pull down, curve around, dot
k — pull down, pull in, pull out
l — pull down
m — pull down, up, over, down and up, over and down

n — pull down, up, over, and down
o — pull back and around
p — pull down, up, and around
q — pull back, around, up, and down
r — pull down, up, and over
s — pull back, in, around, and back around
t — pull down and cross
u — pull down, around, up and down
v — slant down, up
w — slant down, up, down, up
x — slant down, slant down
y — slant in, slant and down
z — across, slant down, across

Uppercase Letter Formation

A — slant down, slant down, across
B — pull down, up, around and in, back and around
C — pull back and around
D — pull down, up, around
E — pull down, across, across, and across
F — pull down, across, across
G — pull back, around, across
H — pull down, pull down, across
I — pull down, across, across
J — pull down, curve around, across
K — pull down, slant in, slant out
L — pull down, across
M — pull down, slant down, slant down, pull down

N — pull down, slant down, pull up
O — pull back and around
P — pull down, up, and around
Q — pull back and around and cross
R — pull down, up, around, in, and slant down
S — pull back, in, around, down, and back around
T — pull down, across
U — pull down, around, up, and down
V — slant down, slant up
W — slant down up, down up
X — slant down, slant down
Y — slant in, slant, and down
Z — across, slant down, across

VERBAL PATH FOR THE FORMATION OF LETTERS: LOWERCASE

VERBAL PATH FOR THE FORMATION OF LETTERS: LOWERCASE

FIGURE 37 Verbal Path

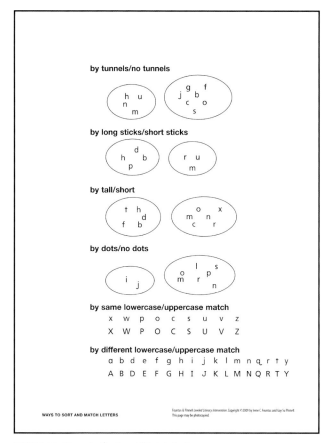

FIGURE 38 Ways to Sort and Match Letters

Word Bags: Collecting High-Frequency Word Cards

The purpose of the word card collection, called the "word bag" in LLI, is to help children gain control of a core of high-frequency words. You will find the word cards for each lesson in categories on the *Lesson Resources CD*. They need to learn how to recognize these words quickly and easily. These words are enormously beneficial to the beginning reader, who can use them to:

❑ understand the concept of a word as letters with white space on either side.

❑ understand the concept of a word in language.

❑ monitor voice-print match.

❑ monitor accuracy.

❑ self-correct.

❑ notice letter-sound relationships or word parts.

❑ notice connections between words to solve new words.

❑ begin to write words correctly.

Once children can recognize the words in every detail, they will be able to use them to help solve new words, for example, *the-then, is-in, an-and, an-man*. The word bag itself can be a simple one-quart, sealable, clear plastic bag in which to keep your materials.

FIGURE 39 Word Bag

To add a word to the word bag:

1. Foreshadow the addition by having the children locate the word in the new book that they are reading (or rereading the next day). See Words in Text below.

2. Show children the word (on chart paper, with magnetic letters, on the whiteboard, or on a card) and read it while running your finger under it, left to right.

3. Have children read the word, saying it and running a finger under it left to right.

4. Have them either read it several times, make it with magnetic letters, or write it on the whiteboard.

5. Add it to the word bag collection.

Some ways of working with the word bag collection are:

1. Have children turn over cards one at a time and read them. They place them in two piles: (1) words they know; and (2) words they are learning. They then choose one word card from "words they are learning" and read it, make it with magnetic letters, and write it. (They can highlight the beginning letter or another part of the word they write to help them remember it.)

2. Children lay out their word cards face up in front of them. Play a game: "Find a word that starts with the letter *a*." (You can choose any word feature—a phonogram, letter cluster, vowel, ending). Children find the word, read it, and put it away.

3. Children lay out their word cards face down in front of them. They turn over a word card and read it, leaving it face up. If they do not know a word, they turn the card over again. They continue until (with help) all word cards are face up.

4. Two children lay out their word cards face up in front of them. One child reads through the words from a stack. When the leader reads the word, the other two find their word cards and put them in a pile. They continue until all the word cards are in piles and then put them away.

5. Children choose a word, make it left to right with magnetic letters, read to check it by running a finger under it, and then check it letter by letter with the word card (pointing—*c-c, a-a, n-n*). Then they write the word, read to check it by running a finger under it, and then check it letter by letter with the word card.

6. Children choose a word card and look at it carefully. Then, without looking at the word, they attempt to make it with magnetic letters or to write it. Then, they check with the model and correct it, if needed.

7. Children take their group of word cards and lay them out face up. They find two words that are connected in some way. Then, they show the words to the rest of the group and they try to guess how the words are connected (same first letter, same number of letters, same ending, etc.).

FIGURE 40 Word Cards

Word Ladders

Word Ladders is a technique for helping children learn how to manipulate letters and word parts to construct new words. You start with a word, then, change, add, or remove one or more letters to make a new word, for example, *can, many, any, and* or *hand, handy, handle.* You can show children the word to start with using magnetic letters. You can then have children identify the new words you make by adding or removing letters. You may want the children to suggest the letter changes, and you can make the changes and show them the new word. You will want children to say each new word and understand its meaning.

Words in Text

It is beneficial for children to use their eyes to locate specific words in a text. The real challenge to the beginning reader is not to memorize a word in isolation but to read it within continuous text while keeping the meaning in mind. Locating words will help to develop this ability because it will familiarize children with the visual searching needed to recognize the word by its features. Children can locate *known* or *unknown* words. Locating known words helps them to recognize the word rapidly and without a great deal of effort while reading. Locating unknown words helps them think about and predict the beginning letter and remember other visual details about a word. Some routines for locating a word are:

1. Suggested language when the children know some beginning sounds: "Say *but*." (Children respond.) "What letter would you expect to see at the beginning of *but?*" (Children respond.) "Find it, run your finger under it, and say it."

2. Suggested language when children are recognizing high-frequency words: "You know the word *the*. Think how it looks." (Show a model on the whiteboard if you think they need it.) "Find *the* on this page and put your finger under it." (Children respond.) "Turn the page and find *the*. Put your finger under it." (Notice how quickly children can locate the word.)

FIGURE 41 Locating a word

Writing

DICTATED WRITING

In dictated writing, you read aloud a sentence and children write it in their writing books with your support. You help the children write it in conventional form as it becomes a text for rereading. As needed, model word construction using a whiteboard or prompt for letter formation using the Verbal Path. Use white correction tape as needed. The value of dictated writing is that children learn how to go from oral to written language. They experience word solving within a meaningful sentence.

INDEPENDENT WRITING

In independent writing, children write their own texts with your support. The value of independent writing is that children develop control of early writing strategies. They learn to represent ideas in different ways and to self-monitor their writing. All writing is in conventional form. Use white correction tape (or mailing labels) to assist children to cover mismatches quickly and make the text readable. You do not want cross-outs and you do not want children to spend time erasing.

INTERACTIVE WRITING

In interactive writing, a message is composed by the group. It is written on a chart that everyone can see with the teacher doing some of the writing and the children using the marker to write selected words or word parts. The value of interactive writing is that it duplicates every aspect of the writing process in a highly supported way. You can also use white correction tape to cover and correct errors, as the goal is conventional writing that will be reread. Be sure to use black marker on a white or cream background.

WRITING WORDS FLUENTLY

You will want children to learn to write some words quickly. When you want them to learn a word, have them write it fast several times in their writing books until they can write it without stopping.

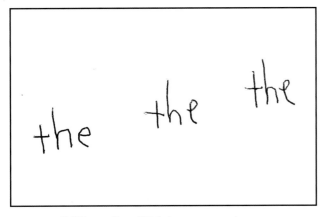

FIGURE 42 Child's practice of high-frequency word

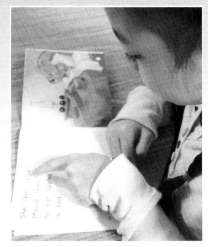

section 4

Assessment and Record-Keeping in the Leveled Literacy Intervention System

▶ Ongoing Assessment and Record-Keeping Forms

Assessment is the act of getting information about the learners you will teach. When you assessed the children for the start of the intervention, you collected important information about the child's reading level, comprehension, fluency, and processing strategies. This information is critical for beginning instruction at an appropriate level and with appropriate emphases. Collect information daily to inform your teaching.

▶ Record-Keeping Forms

Keep your record keeping simple, efficient, and informative. We have provided a few forms for daily record keeping and for keeping a record of each child's lessons. These forms can be printed out from the *Lesson Resources CD*.

Lesson Record Form

In Figure 43, you can see one page of a sample Lesson Record form showing two parts of a lesson and spaces to make notes for six children. A second version

---

Leveled Literacy Intervention Lesson Record: 3-Student Version   Odd-Numbered Lesson

Date: _____

Teacher: _____ Grade: _____ Lesson: _____

1 — REREADING BOOKS

2 — PHONICS/WORD WORK

Fountas & Pinnell *Leveled Literacy Intervention.* Copyright ©2009 by Irene C. Fountas and Gay Su Pinnell.
This page may be photocopied.

LESSON RECORD 3-STUDENT

FIGURE 43 Lesson Record Form

Intervention Record

Student Name: Stephen
Group: Grade One

Year: _____ Teacher: Ms. Samuels
System: Orange X Green (circled) Blue School: Parkman

Date	Week	M	T	W	Th	F	Lesson	Reading Record Book Title	Level	Acc. %	Comp.	SC	Fluency	#SGI
9/6	1		G-1	G-2	G-3	G-4	4							3
9/13	2	G-5	G-6	G-7	G-8	G-9								4
9/20	3	G-10	G-11	G-12	TA	G-13	10							4
9/27	4	G-14	G-15	CA	G-16/G-17	G-18	16	Jesse	A	100%	6	—	—	4
10/4	5	G-19	G-20	G-21	G-22	G-23	22	Orson's Tummy	B	97%	6	1:2	—	4
10/11	6	G-24	G-25	G-26	G-27	G-28	28	Our Garden	B	96%	6	1:3	—	4
10/18	7	G-29	G-30	G-31	G-32	G-33								3
10/25	8	G-34	G-35	G-36	G-37	G-38	34	Looking for Tazo	C	98%	6	1:3	2	3
11/1	9	G-39	G-40	G-41	G-42	G-43	40	Clouds	C	96%	5	1:3	2	4
11/8	10	G-44	G-45	G-46	G-47	G-48	46	Time for Lunch	D	95%	7	1:4	3	3
11/15	11	G-49	G-50	G-51	TA	G-52	52	Three Bears	E	95%	6	1:3	3	4

NOTES:
steady progress
consistent self-monitoring

KEY:

Acc. % = Accuracy
Comp. = Comprehension Total Score
SC = Self-Correction
#SGI = Small Group Instruction
(in addition to LLI)

TA = Teacher Absent
CA = Child Absent
TN = Teacher Not Available
CN = Child Not Available
SH = School Holiday

PROGRAM RECORD

FIGURE 44 Intervention Record

Leveled Literacy Intervention Student Achievement Log: 3-Student Version

School Year: _____ Teacher: Mrs. Phillips Assessment Used: F and P Benchmark 1
School: Windsor District/State: _____

GROUP ENTRY DATA

Student	Grade	Entry Date	Level	Accuracy %	Comp.	SC	Fluency	Notes
Sammantha	1	9/10	A	67%	6	1:10	n/a	no 1:1
Ronny	1	9/10	A	83%	5	1:10	n/a	no 1:1
Ethan	1	9/10	A	87%	6	1:8	n/a	inventing

GROUP EXIT DATA

Student	Grade	Exit Date	Level	Accuracy %	Comp.	SC	Fluency	Notes
Sammantha	1	12/23	G	95%	6	1:3	3	strong self-mon.
Ronny	1	12/23	G	97%	7	1:3	3	strong self mon
Ethan	1	12/23	G	98%	6	1:2	3	expressive strong 1:1

STUDENT ACTIVITY LOG: 3-STUDENT VERSION

FIGURE 45 Student Achievement Log

with spaces to make notes for three children is also available. Your notes should consist of significant details about what the child shows evidence of learning how to do or of needing to learn how to do. You can then use your notes to plan what you need to emphasize when you teach the next lesson. To see a complete, filled-in Lesson Record, see Figure 48 on page 81.

Intervention Record

This form is critical for monitoring the amount of Leveled Literacy Intervention (number or lessons per week) and the amount of small group instruction in the classroom each week. Accurate record keeping with the form will help you determine the effect of the supplementary instruction (LLI) on student achievement. You will find an explanation of the codes at the bottom of each form. You may want to keep this form in the Student Folders. (See Figure 44.)

Student Achievement Log

This optional form can be used to document children's performance as they enter or exit the LLI program. Use the categories of information that apply to your assessments and add any others in the final two columns. (See Figure 45.)

Communication Sheet—Individual

This optional form can be used to communicate with the classroom teacher regarding an individual's weekly progress. You may want the classroom teacher to share the same kind of information. You can simply write notes in each area. (See Figure 46.)

Communication Sheet—Group

This is an additional optional form that can be used to communicate with the classroom teacher about a group's weekly progress. Write notes in each area that you feel will be helpful. (See Figure 47.)

Leveled Literacy Intervention Communication Sheet: Individual

Date: _3/18_   Student: _James_   Classroom Teacher: _Mrs. Powell_

LLI Level: _G_   System: __Orange X Green __Blue   Reading Teacher: _Mrs. H._

Strengths:
fluent and phrased
uses multiple sources of information
self-corrects consistently

Working toward proficiency with the following strategic actions:
taking words apart using onset/rime, syllables
consistently checking with visual information

Recent writing vocabulary:
every   would
doesn't   could

Other comments:
working hard to become independent
writing more controlled and in proportion

Leveled Literacy Intervention Communication Sheet: Individual

FIGURE 46 Communication Sheet—Individual

Leveled Literacy Intervention Communication Sheet: Group

Group Level: _H_   Students: _Maria, Sam, Mark_

Strengths:

working at this level for almost two weeks
processing is smooth, except occasionally
Maria lacks syntax to keep flow

Working toward proficiency with the following strategic actions:

self monitoring consistently
using word parts — eg Do you see a
part you know?

Other comments:

several readings will be supportive
to Maria
If possible, pair with child she can read to?

FIGURE 47 Communication Sheet—Group

▶ Daily Lesson Observations on a Lesson Record

You have a Lesson Record (see *Lesson Resources CD*) on which to record your specific observations of the reading and writing behaviors of the children in each lesson. There are two versions of the record: one to be used with groups of three children and another to be used for groups of up to six children. Write notes about significant behaviors that are evidence of each readers' use of strategic actions we describe (see *When Readers Struggle: Teaching that Works,* Chapters 10, 14, 15, 16) and that are referenced in the *Fountas and Pinnell Prompting Guide 1*. You will also find the Guide for Observing and Noting Reading Behaviors useful (see *When Readers Struggle: Teaching that Works,* Chapter 4: Reading Behavior: What Does It Tell Us?). You will also want to write notes about significant writing behaviors that indicate children's ability to construct words and sentences (see Chapter 13 of *When Readers Struggle: Teaching that Works, Prompting Guide 1,* and Figure 48).

Letter/Word Record

You may want to use this optional form to keep track of each child's specific letter learning as well as the specific high-frequency words the group almost knows or controls consistently. When the children are learning letters, you may want to note for each child whether he knows the name of the letter, its sound, or how to form it. The lines in each box can be used to show the child's knowledge of the letter name (N), sound (S), or formation (F).

When you introduce a new word to the group, write it under the correct letter. You may want to check it off when the children can read it easily and place an x when they can write it easily.

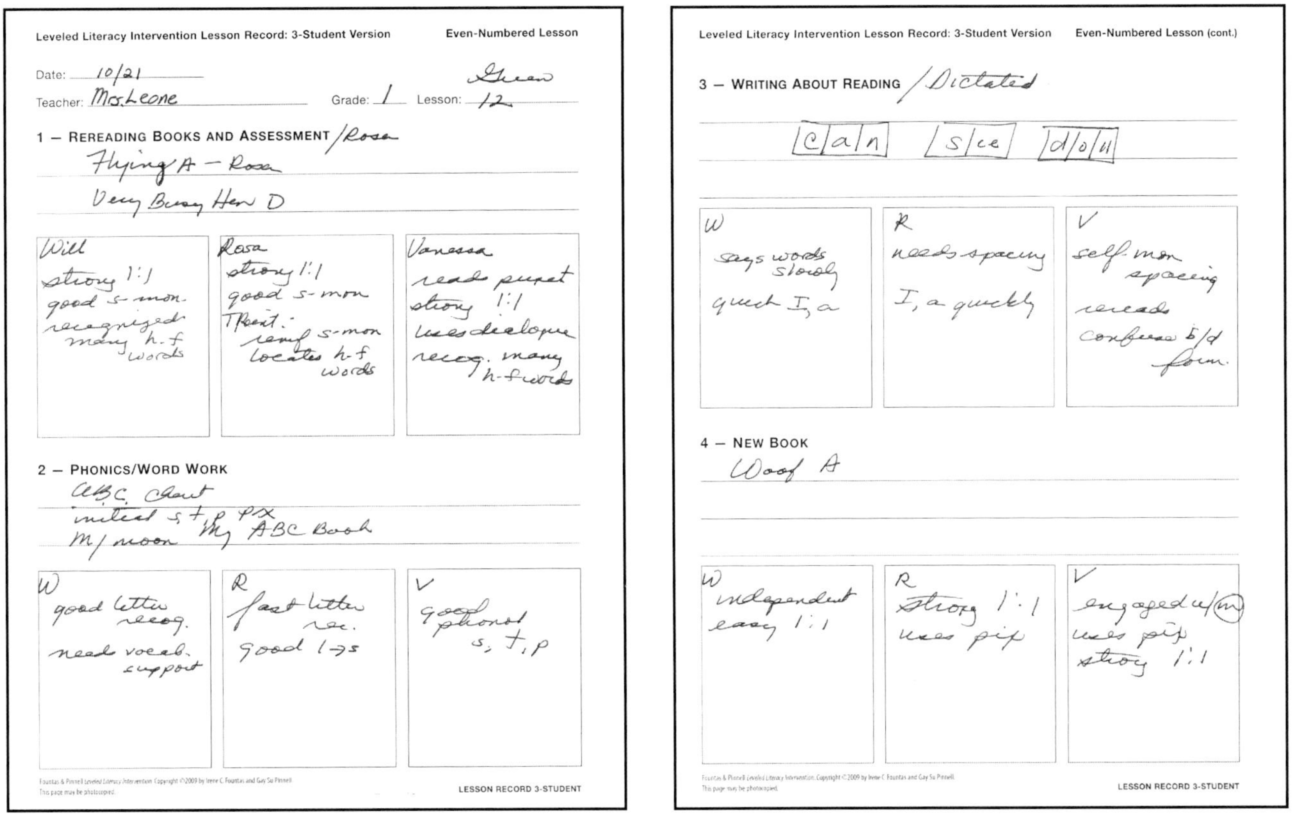
Leveled Literacy Intervention Lesson Record: 3-Student Version — Even-Numbered Lesson

Date: 10/21 — Green
Teacher: Mrs. Leone — Grade: 1 — Lesson: 12

1 — Rereading Books and Assessment / Rosa
Flying A – Rosa
Very Busy Hen D

Will	Rosa	Vanessa
strong 1:1 good s-mon. recognized many h.f words	strong 1:1 good s-mon. reread s-mon locates h-f words	reads puppet strong 1:1 uses dialogue recog. many h-f words

2 — Phonics/Word Work
ABC Chart
initial s, t, p px
M/moon My ABC Book

W	R	V
good letter recog. need vocab. support	fast letter rec. good 1→s	good phonol s, t, p

Fountas & Pinnell Leveled Literacy Intervention Copyright © 2009 by Irene C. Fountas and Gay Su Pinnell
This page may be photocopied. — LESSON RECORD 3-STUDENT

Leveled Literacy Intervention Lesson Record: 3-Student Version — Even-Numbered Lesson (cont.)

3 — Writing About Reading / Dictated
c/a/n s/ee d/o/ll

W	R	V
says words slowly quick I, a	needs spacing I, a quickly	self-mon spacing rereads confuses b/d form.

4 — New Book
Woof A

W	R	V
independent easy 1:1	strong 1:1 uses pix	engaged w/(m) uses pix strong 1:1

Fountas & Pinnell Leveled Literacy Intervention Copyright © 2009 by Irene C. Fountas and Gay Su Pinnell
This page may be photocopied. — LESSON RECORD 3-STUDENT

FIGURE 48 Sample Lesson Record, pages 1 and 2

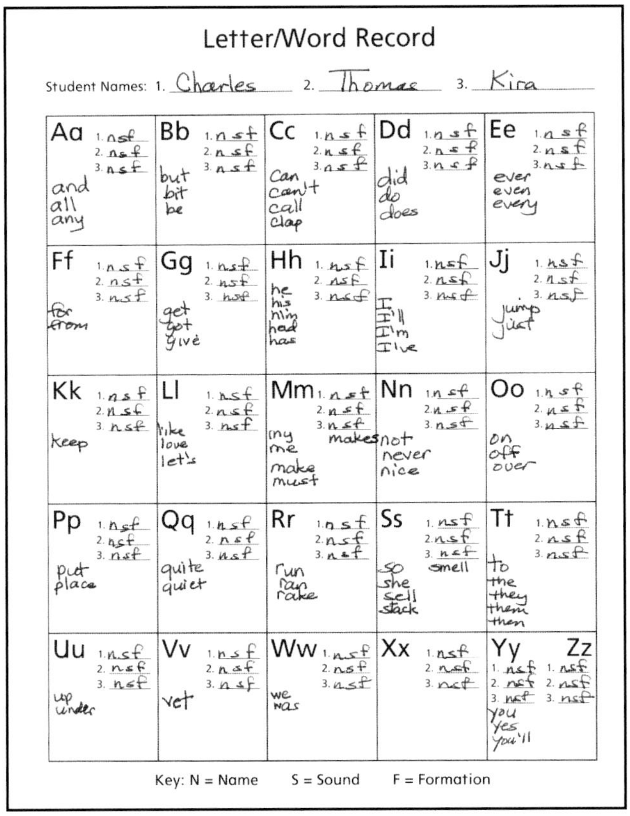
Letter/Word Record

Student Names: 1. Charles 2. Thomas 3. Kira

Aa 1. nsf 2. nsf 3. nsf — and, all, any	Bb 1. nsf 2. nsf 3. nsf — but, bit, be	Cc 1. nsf 2. nsf 3. nsf — can, can't, call, clap	Dd 1. nsf 2. nsf 3. nsf — did, do, does	Ee 1. nsf 2. nsf 3. nsf — ever, even, every
Ff 1. nsf 2. nsf 3. nsf — for, from	Gg 1. nsf 2. nsf 3. nsf — get, got, give	Hh 1. nsf 2. nsf 3. nsf — he, his, him, had, has	Ii 1. nsf 2. nsf 3. nsf — I, I'll, I'm, I've	Jj 1. nsf 2. nsf 3. nsf — jump, just
Kk 1. nsf 2. nsf 3. nsf — keep	Ll 1. nsf 2. nsf 3. nsf — like, love, let's	Mm 1. nsf 2. nsf 3. nsf — my, me, make, makes, must	Nn 1. nsf 2. nsf 3. nsf — not, never, nice	Oo 1. nsf 2. nsf 3. nsf — on, off, over
Pp 1. nsf 2. nsf 3. nsf — put, place	Qq 1. nsf 2. nsf 3. nsf — quite, quiet	Rr 1. nsf 2. nsf 3. nsf — run, ran, rake	Ss 1. nsf 2. nsf 3. nsf — so, she, sell, stack, smell	Tt 1. nsf 2. nsf 3. nsf — to, the, they, them, then
Uu 1. nsf 2. nsf 3. nsf — up, under	Vv 1. nsf 2. nsf 3. nsf — vet	Ww 1. nsf 2. nsf 3. nsf — we, was	Xx 1. nsf 2. nsf 3. nsf	Yy 1. nsf 2. nsf 3. nsf — you, yes, you'll; Zz 1. nsf 2. nsf 3. nsf

Key: N = Name S = Sound F = Formation

FIGURE 49 Letter/Word Record Form

Flip Record

An informal alternative form of record keeping is the Flip Record, which you can quickly make using index cards and a sheet of paper or stiff card stock. Holding a sheet of 8.5" x 11" paper or card stock lengthwise, tape 5" x 8" index cards to the paper so that the cards overlap down the sheet. If you use a sheet of paper, you can place the Flip Record on a clipboard for stability. Have one card for each child, and write each child's name at the bottom of a card so the names will be visible when the cards overlap. You can then flip up the cards to write anecdotal notes on each child's progress; words, letters, or patterns that are challenging to the child; or any other notes you wish to make on the child's reading and writing behaviors. As each card is filled, peel it off the sheet and place it in the child's Student Folder. (See Figure 50.)

Writing Samples in *My Writing Book*

My Writing Book also serves as a record of progress. Children generally do their writing on right-hand pages. The opposite page (left) in *My Writing Book* can

FIGURE 50 Record-Keeping Flip Chart

be used to work on letters and words. You can have children practice letter formation, writing a word quickly, or saying words using (Elkonin) sound or letter boxes. The book provides a record of the learning you are supporting in writing. The samples in the book show the child's progress over time in learning about letters, sounds, words, and the ability to compose and write sentences. Be sure to write the lesson number in the top corner.

Reading Records from Even-Numbered Lessons for Progress Monitoring

There is no substitute for the information you gain from taking systematic Reading Records of children's behavior as they process continuous text. During the Rereading Books and Assessment section of the even-numbered lessons, you take a Reading Record on one child using a Recording Form. This will mean that with a group of three children, you will take one Reading Record about once per week for each child (or once in a six-day cycle). Remember that for children reading the short books at levels A, B, and C, the record will take only the five minutes allotted (or less). For books that are longer, you can take the record on about 150 to 200 words, stopping at the end of a sentence. Reading Recording Forms on the CD will offer guidance, but you can also

shorten the record yourself if you count the words. [Since the record is taken on the second reading, you can continue with the comprehension conversation. Or, you can ask the child to continue reading to the end while you complete some of your analyses and then have the conversation.]

Your F & P calculator will help you to be time efficient. To serve as a reminder, you can place the child's name on a stick-on note on your lesson plan for the day (see specific part of lesson).

You can prepare for taking Reading Records by printing Recording Forms for the instructional texts at a particular level and keeping them in a hanging folder for those lessons. You will need only one copy of the book and your F & P calculator in addition to the forms you print from the *Lesson Resources CD*.

When you take a Reading Record, code the reading behavior using the standardized system for coding (see Coding and Scoring Errors at a Glance, page 86, and the *Professional Development and Tutorial DVD*), have a brief comprehension conversation, and make a teaching point. Score and analyze the record (see Scoring and Analyzing a Reading Record, pages 85–87, and the *Professional Development and Tutorial DVD*) to get important information on how the reader is using sources of information, initiating strategic actions, and comprehending the book.

Following the reading, look quickly at the evidence to provide insights about the way the child processed the text. Select one teaching point—something you can teach for, prompt for, or reinforce to improve the child's reading (see *When Readers Struggle: Teaching that Works*, Chapter 14: Processing Texts: Teaching for Problem-Solving and *Prompting Guide 1*).

Reading Graph and Reports

It will be helpful to keep a graph of progress for each reader. Every week (or two weeks), take a Reading Record of each child's second reading of the new book that was introduced in the odd-numbered lesson. Establish regular intervals for recording reading levels on the Reading Graph (*Lesson Resources CD* and interior of Student Folder). You can record the level by hand, using a circle with a dot in it for reading at the instructional level (90–94% for Levels A through K and 95–97% for Levels L through N). Use an open circle for reading at the independent level (98–100%). If the reading is below those levels, fill in the circle to make it black. If comprehension is unsatisfactory, make the circle black regardless of accuracy. This tool allows you to enter the information from the child's Reading Record each week to document the child's progress on a graph. You can share the information on the graph with the classroom teacher. Or you can enter the child's Reading Record information on your *Data Management CD* to generate a graph using the data you entered. (See Figure 51.)

Intervention Record

The Intervention Record is designed for your use in documenting the lessons each child received. Write the lesson number in the box and use the appropriate code to indicate the reason a child missed a scheduled lesson. In addition, you may want to ask the classroom teacher how many times the child had small group instruction in the classroom so you have a complete record of the amount of reading instruction the child received each week. A blank Intervention Record is available on the *Lesson Resources CD*.

Student Folder

You have a folder for each child. The color corresponds to the system you are using. On the inside of the folder is a reading graph for you to use weekly. On the outside of the folder, you can note program entry data and program exit data. This information is similar to the Student Achievement Log and the reading graph previously described. You can keep forms within the folder and pass it on with student records from grade to grade.

▶ Change Over Time in Children's Progress

Your Reading Records, writing books, and Lesson Records provide evidence of children's growth over time. For a detailed description of three LLI children and their progress in building effective processing systems across time, see *When Readers Struggle: Teaching that Works*, Chapter 5: Change Over Time: Processing Systems in the Making. Note how the children began at the same instructional

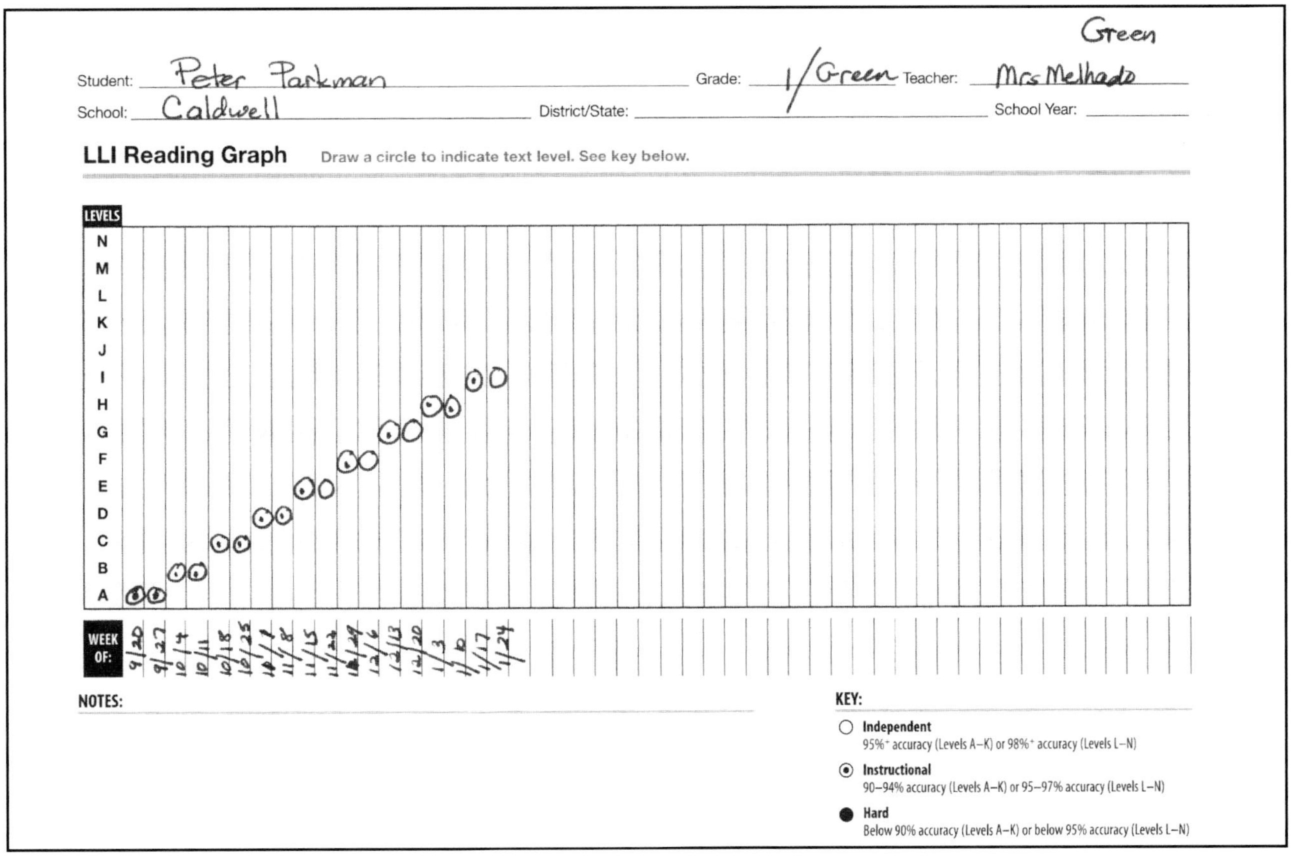

FIGURE 51 Reading Graph

level but built their processing systems differently from each other over time.

Using Communication Forms

On the *Lesson Resources CD* you will find two different types of forms, an Individual Communication sheet and a Group Communication sheet, that you can send to the classroom teacher every two weeks to keep him informed about the child's progress.

Using The Continuum of Literacy Learning to Monitor Progress and Guide Teaching

The section of *The Continuum of Literacy Learning* that is provided at the end of each level in the *Lesson Guide* lists specific behaviors and understandings that are required for children to read successfully at that level. These behaviors and understandings are accumulative across the levels. They include important competencies children need to think within, beyond, and about texts. In other words, the reader is taking on new demands as the texts grow more challenging. For example, a child reading on Level C and successfully meeting the demands of the text is also able to meet the demands of texts on Levels A and B. It is important to realize that the understandings include much more than simply reading the words accurately (see *Lesson Guide;* also see *The Continuum of Literacy Learning* at the end of each level). You will also find additional suggestions for word work. If your children have good control of the principles in the Phonics or Letter Word Work section of the lessons, you might want to substitute one of the options. Additionally, you may want to offer some of the suggestions to the classroom teacher.

The lessons are designed to help you accomplish the goals listed on the Continuum for the level. Basically, your goal is to help readers meet the demands of successive levels of text and, in the process, expand their systems of strategic actions. You will want to continually refer to the level Continuum at the end of each level in the *Lesson Guide* to monitor progress and guide teaching.

The following suggestions may contribute to effective teaching in your lessons:

- ❑ Read the new text carefully with the Continuum goals in mind.

- ❑ Think about what your children can do and then find behaviors and understandings that they control, partially control, or do not yet control.

- ❑ Read the introduction to the text and teaching points for the lesson, keeping in mind the processing needs of your children. Make any adjustments you think are necessary to meet the needs of your particular children.

- ❑ Look at the phonics and word work and at the suggestions for word work at that level on the Continuum. Make any adjustments you think are necessary to meet the needs of your particular children.

- ❑ As you near the end of a series of ten lessons, look at the Continuum to see what your children now control and what they need to know to successfully process texts easily at this level.

- ❑ As children grow more proficient and reading becomes easy at the level, look at the behaviors and understandings for the next higher level. You'll find many of the same strategies for which you've been teaching because the reading process is built by applying the same set of complex strategies to increasingly more difficult texts. You may find new understandings or more complex versions of the same understandings. Start to look toward this next level.

▶ Learning How to Take Reading Records to Monitor Progress and Guide Teaching

A Reading Record is a systematic tool used to code, score, and analyze a child's precise reading behaviors. You use a standardized system to gain an objective assessment of the child's reading without your teaching support. You learn what the child can do independently at the level.

In this guide, we will provide a brief overview of the systematized process for coding, scoring, and analyzing reading behaviors. The *Professional Development and Tutorial DVDs* tutorial will provide the in-depth information and as much practice, as you want.

Your professional guide, *When Readers Struggle: Teaching that Works* provides detailed descriptions of these areas as well with numerous examples. In these resources, you will learn what each type of behavior tells about the in-the-head systems the child is likely using or neglecting as he processes a text. This will help you determine the emphases for your teaching.

Coding Reading Behaviors on a Recording Form

In this section we briefly describe coding conventions. You can use the *Professional Development and Tutorial DVDs* and work at your own rate to learn how to code. You have many opportunities to practice. As the child reads, observe the precise behaviors and mark the typed text using the coding system shown in Figure 55. You can review the following charts to understand what the reader does (the observable behaviors) and how to code them.

Scoring the Reading Record

When you take a record of reading behavior, you get many different kinds of information. First, you will be able to determine the *accuracy*, that is, the percent of total words that were read correctly when a child reads a text. Accuracy is important and it is a key factor in effective processing. Accuracy depends on more than word recognition. It is also an indication of how well the child has used meaning and a sense of language structure to help in processing. If the accuracy level is between 90–94%, it is likely a good level for instruction. If it is higher (95–100%), it can also provide good opportunities for learning. (See Figure 52, a chart specific to the text that appears on each form.)

Accuracy Rate	Errors	7 or more	6	5	4	3	2	1	0
	%	Below 90%	90%	92%	93%	95%	97%	98%	100%

FIGURE 52 Accuracy Chart

Self-Correction

Determine the child's *self-correction ratio*. If a child makes an error and then corrects it, you have powerful evidence of what that reader is attending to and using. Think about how often the reader notices an error and corrects it or attempts to correct it. Notice what information the child used to correct the error. (See Figure 53.)

Self-Correction Ratio	$(E + SC) \div SC = 1:\_\_\_\_$

FIGURE 53 Self-Correction Chart

Comprehension Conversation

Have a brief comprehension conversation with the child to gain evidence of understanding. Begin with the general prompt to get the child talking about the book. If you want to use a systematic approach, check off each key understanding the child demonstrates. Probe for further information using the prompts as needed. The questions will help you determine the child's thinking with or beyond the text. You will have evidence of comprehending even while the child is reading. He might make errors that do not make sense and then correct them to make the reading meaningful. The tone of voice might reflect the child's understanding of meaning. If you use this evidence in combination with a brief conversation after reading, you are able to score the child's comprehension as unsatisfactory, limited, satisfactory, or excellent. For a text to be appropriate, the child's comprehension must be satisfactory or excellent.

Comprehension Scoring Key

0 Reflects **no** understanding of the text. Either does not respond or talks off the topic.

1 Reflects **very limited** understanding of the text. Mentions a few facts or ideas but does not express the important information or ideas.

2 Reflects **partial** understanding of the text. Includes important information and ideas but neglects other key understandings.

3 Reflects **excellent** understanding of the text. Includes almost all important information and main ideas.

FIGURE 54 Comprehension Rubric

Behavior	What Reader Does	How to Code	Example	How to Score	
Accurate Reading	Reads words correctly	Do not mark or place check (✓) above word	no mark or ✓✓✓ Get the ball		No error
Substitution	Gives an incorrect response	Write the substituted word above the word	can / could	Substitution, not corrected	1 error
Multiple Substitutions	Makes several attempts at a word	Write each substitution in sequence above the word	will|want was	Multiple substitutions, not corrected	1 error for each incorrect word in text
			will|want|sc was	Multiple substitutions, self-corrected (SC)	No error; 1 SC
			will was want was	Multiple misreadings of the same word, not corrected	1 error for each incorrect word in text
			Jay Jesse Jasey Jesse	Multiple misreadings of names and proper nouns	1 error first time missed; no errors after that
			did not didn't didn't did not	Misreading contractions (reads contraction as two words or two words as contraction)	1 error each time
Self-correction	Corrects a previous error	Write the error over the word, followed by SC	can|sc could		No error; 1 SC
Insertion	Adds a word that is not in the text	Write in the inserted word using a caret	only ∧		1 error per word inserted
Omission	Gives no response to a word	Place a dash (-) above the word	— and	Skipping a word	1 error per word
				Skipping a line	1 error per word
Repetition	Reads same word again	Write R after the word	✓R play		No error
Repeated Repetitions	Reads the same word more than once	Write R for first repetition, then write a number for additional repetitions	✓R2 each		No error
Rereading	Returns to the beginning of sentence or phrase to read again	Write an R with an arrow back to the place where rereading began	↓✓✓✓✓R		No error
	Rereads and self-corrects	Write an R with an arrow back to the place where rereading began and a SC at point of self-correction	↓✓✓✓ ants|sc ✓R bugs		No error; 1 SC
Appeal	Verbally asks for help	Write A above the word	each|A	Follow up with "You try it"	No error
"You Try It"	The child appeals, the teacher responds with "You try it"	Write Y after the word	each|A|Y	"You try it" followed by correct word	No error
				"You try it" followed by omission, incorrect word, or Told	1 error
Told	Child doesn't attempt a word even after "You try it"	Write T after the word or the Y	each|A|Y|T		1 error
Spelling Aloud	Child spells word by saying names of letters	Write the letters in all capital letters	N.E.T net	Spelling followed by correct word	No error. no SC
				Spelling followed by incorrect word	1 error
Sounding Out	The child makes the sounds associated with the letters in the word	Write the letters in lower case with hyphens between them	p-a-st-✓ past	"Sounding out" followed by correct word	No error; no SC
			p-a-st past	"Sounding out" followed by incorrect word or no word	1 error
			a-|sc bugs	Sounding the first letter incorrectly and then saying the word correctly	No error; 1 SC

Coding system developed by Marie Clay as part of the running record system in *An Observation Survey of Early Literacy Achievement, Revised Second Edition*, 2006, Heinemann.

FIGURE 55 Coding and Scoring Errors At-A-Glance

Fluency (Level C and higher)

Think about how the reading sounded. Consider the phrasing, expression, pausing, stress, and smoothness in processing the text. Make quick notes and/or circle the fluency rubric

Figure 56 provides a summary of the steps for scoring the Reading Record.

Scoring the Reading Record

The following is an explanation of the steps to take to score the Reading Record for fluency.

1. **Accuracy:** Circle number of errors on the graph (or use the calculator).

2. **Self-Correction Rate:** Calculate SC ratio and record. Starting at Level L, just record the number of self-corrections.

3. **Fluency:** Circle fluency rating (Level C and above)
   - 0 = no phrasing or expression
   - 1 = minimal phrasing or expression
   - 2 = some phrasing or expression
   - 3 = mostly phrased and expressive reading

4. **Comprehension:**
   - Assign points in each category (*Within, Beyond*), making a decision for each based on: 0 points = no understanding; 1 point = little understanding; 2 points = satisfactory understanding; 3 points = excellent understanding
   - Assign 1 extra point if appropriate.
   - Circle total comprehension score on the graph: Levels A–C: 0–4 = Unsatisfactory; 5 = Satisfactory; 6–7 = Excellent

In *The Continuum of Literacy Learning*, we describe thinking within, beyond, and about the text. In taking a Reading Record for Levels A to K, you are focusing assessment on the beginning reader's ability to think within and beyond a text. In your teaching during lessons, however, you can also support students' increasing ability to think analytically and critically. As texts become more complex at Levels E, F, and G, you can consider your students' ability to think about texts when you choose to award an extra point for "additional understanding."

▶ Analyzing Use of Sources of Information and Self-Correction Behaviors

The following explains how to analyze the coded form. You can also learn how to analyze the child's reading on the *Professional Development and Tutorial DVDs*.

Sources of Information Used and Neglected

For each error, write MSV in the error column (whether self-corrected or not). For each self-correction, write MSV (all three letters) in the SC column. It is important to think about what led the reader to make the error and what the reader might have neglected. Circle one, two, or three letters for each error or self-correction. Analyze each up to the point of the

Fluency Score	0 1 2 3	Fluency Scoring Key
		0 Reads primarily word-by-word with occasional but infrequent or inappropriate phrasing; no smooth or expressive interpretation, irregular pausing, and no attention to author's meaning or punctuation; no stress or inappropriate stress, and slow rate.
		1 Reads primarily in two-word phrases with some three- and four-word groups and some word-by-word reading; almost no smooth, expressive interpretation or pausing guided by author's meaning and punctuation; almost no stress or inappropriate stress, with slow rate most of the time.
		2 Reads primarily in three- or four-word phrase groups; some smooth, expressive interpretation and pausing guided by author's meaning and punctuation; mostly appropriate stress and rate with some slowdowns.
		3 Reads primarily in larger, meaningful phrases or word groups; mostly smooth, expressive interpretation and pausing guided by author's meaning and punctuation; appropriate stress and rate with only a few slowdowns.

FIGURE 56 Fluency Rubric

error or self-correction, not beyond. Think about the following as they apply to each error and self-correction:

- ❏ **Meaning.** Readers often make substitutions that indicate they are thinking about the meaning of the text. For example, a reader might say *ballet* for *dance.* Ask yourself the question: Did the meaning of the text influence the error? (Circle M in the column, Sources of Information.)

- ❏ **Structure.** A powerful source of information for a reader is the structure or syntax of language. From our knowledge of oral language, we have implicit knowledge of the way words are put together to form phrases and sentences. It "sounds right" to us. Readers often substitute nouns for nouns or verbs for verbs, indicating an awareness of the structure of language. For example, a reader might say, *"We like going"* for *"We like to ride."* Ask yourself the questions: Does the error fit an acceptable English language structure? Did structure influence the error? If it is the first word of the sentence, circle S if the word could start a sentence. (Circle S in the column for error.)

- ❏ **Visual Information.** Readers use the visual features of print—the letters and words—to read. They connect these features to phonetic information that exists in their heads. For example, looking at the picture, a reader might say *park* for *play.* Ask yourself: Did the visual information from the print influence any part of the error (letter, part, word)? (Circle V in the column for error.)

Readers often use multiple sources of information as they process texts. For example, a reader might substitute *steps* for *stairs*, indicating attention to all three—meaning, language structure, and visual information. Here, you would circle or check M, S, and V in the error column.

Self-Correction Behavior

Code the self-corrections that the reader makes. Here, you are hypothesizing *the additional information that the reader might have used to correct the error.* The self-correction, of course, indicates use of all three sources of information—meaning, language structure, and visual information—because it is the accurate word. But you are searching here for what the reader might

have used as *additional* information to correct the error.

If the reader made the error *ballet* for *dance*, for example, and then self-corrected, the error is analyzed as M and the self-correction column would be coded S and V, because the reader might have thought about the way the language sounded and might have noticed the *d*. If the reader said *park* for *play* and then self-corrected, code the SC column as M and S, because the English language structure and the meaning of the text likely influenced the correction.

There is not a linear relationship between self-correction ratio and progress in reading. As children progress, observable self-correction decreases and may become nonexistent. We would not desire a 1:1 or 1:2 SC ratio in highly accurate reading. Just listen to a reader who is making quite a few errors and self-correcting almost every one of them; the reading will not sound good even though the accuracy would be almost 100%. We assume that proficient readers are self-regulating both their oral and silent reading; but we will not be able to observe it. That is why we switch from reporting ratio to simply reporting the number of self-corrections when assessing reading at levels L through Z. If we find very high accuracy and also many self-corrections, we would notice it and work with the reader to get smoother processing.

These analyses will help you look qualitatively at the reader's use of these different sources of information. Think about what the reader is neglecting. You can help the reader attend to the information sources needed as you listen to him read orally or select teaching points after the reading. If readers in a group are neglecting to think about what might make sense, you can prompt them to do so. If they are not noticing the first letter or other part of a word that would be helpful, you can draw it to their attention. (See *Prompting Guide 1.*)

Analyzing Strategic Actions

Now that you have completed your analysis, look at the errors you have marked on the text in the second column (left part of the form where the text is typed). Think about the reader as a problem solver. Six areas will be helpful in your thinking.

- ❏ **Early Reading Behaviors.** These are behaviors indicating attention to print features. You want to look for evidence that the reader knows how print "works," for example matching one spoken word to one written word. If the reader does not show evidence of having these behaviors under control, you can do some explicit demonstrations.

❑ **Searching for and Using Information.** Effective readers *actively* search for the information they need to read with accuracy, fluency, and understanding. They make attempts that, even if not right, show you they are trying out what they know. You can teach readers many ways to search.

❑ **Solving Words.** You want readers to have and use many ways to solve or analyze words. As they learn more, they will recognize many words automatically, but they also need to be able to use phonics and word analysis strategies so that they can learn many more. You can teach the reader many different ways to solve words.

❑ **Self-Monitoring.** Rather than reading along and ignoring errors, you want the reader to *notice* when something doesn't fit. Effective readers are constantly monitoring their own reading accuracy. If the reader does not show signs of self-monitoring, you can draw attention to mismatches and show him how to fix them.

❑ **Self-Correcting.** Self-correction is a sign that the reader is self-monitoring and working actively to make everything fit—meaning, visual information, and the way the reading sounds. You can prompt for self-correction.

❑ **Maintaining Fluency.** Effective readers put all sources of information together so that their reading sounds fluent and expressive. You can think about how the reading sounded. If the reader is not fluent and the text is easy enough, you can demonstrate fluent reading and show the reader how to put words together so that it sounds good.

▶ ## Administering the Reading Record Using the Recording Form

We have provided a Recording Form for each new book read in the odd-numbered lessons. During the first part of each even-numbered lesson (Rereading Books and Assessment), listen to one child read, code the reading behavior on the Recording Form, have a brief comprehension conversation, and make a teaching point that you think will be most helpful to the reader. The other children will be reading books softly (or, at later levels, silently). If you think that the two children who are reading softly are influencing the reader with whom you are doing the assessment, have them start with yesterday's new book. For the Classic Tales, code the child reading the story in the first part of the book, and then reread the play in the last part of the book with all the children. Starting at about Level H-I, the children read an excerpt of approximately 250 words from the book for the Oral Reading section of the Reading Record.

While you are coding the child's reading behavior on the Recording Form, it is important for you to observe what the child can do without your support. Do not help or interfere in any way, verbally or nonverbally, except to say, "You try it," when the child appeals for help or give a Told when the child has tried something and/or will not move on. Say "You try it" if the child has not tried something and then wait no more than three seconds before you give a Told because the child needs to keep the reading going.

As you think about each reader, you may find it useful to use Figure 57, Guide for Observing and Noting Reading Behaviors, which is also provided on the *Lesson Resources CD*. Look at each category and think about the behavioral evidence you see in the Recording Form. Make notes that help you think about the child's strengths and needs and how the information can inform your teaching. Then think about *Prompting Guide 1* and how you can use it to teach for, prompt for, and reinforce effective processing strategies.

You may choose to use the rubric to score the child's comprehension as shown in Figure 58 during the conversation after the reading of the book. Or you may just have a conversation without the formal use of the rubric.

You will want to take a Reading Record on one child during the Rereading Books and Assessment section of the even-numbered lessons. The following are steps to administer the record. You will want to score

Name: _____ Date: _____

Guide for Observing and Noting Reading Behaviors	Notes

1. Early Reading Behaviors
Does the reader:
- Move left to right across a line of print?
- Return to the left for a new line?
- Match word by word while reading a line or more of print?
- Recognize a few easy high frequency words?

2. Searching for and Using Information
Meaning
Does the reader:
- Make meaningful attempts at unknown words?
- Use the meaning of the story or text to predict unknown words?
- Reread to gather more information to solve a word?
- Reread and use the meaning of the sentence?
- Reread to search for more details—information, characters, plot?
- Reread to gather information to clarify confusions?
- Use headings and titles to think about the meaning of a section of text?
- Use information in the pictures to help in understanding a text?
- Use knowledge of the genre (and its characteristics) to help in understanding a text?
- Use knowledge of the genre (and its characteristics) to help in finding information?
- Use readers' tools to help in finding information (glossary, index)?

Structure
Does the reader:
- Use knowledge of oral language to solve unknown words?
- Reread to see if a word "sounds right" in a sentence?
- Reread to correct using language structure?

Visual Information
Does the reader:
- Use the visual information to solve words?
- Use the sound of the first letter(s) to attempt or solve a word?
- Use some, most, or all of the visual information to solve words?
- Use sound analysis to solve a word?
- Make attempts that are visually similar?
- Use knowledge of a high frequency word to problem solve?
- Search for more visual information within a word to solve it?
- Use analogy to solve unknown words?
- Use syllables to solve words?
- Use prefixes and suffixes to take apart and recognize words?
- Use inflectional endings to problem solve words?
- Recognize most words quickly and easily?
- Reread and use the sound of the first letter to solve a word?
- Problem solve unknown words quickly and efficiently?
- Work actively to solve words?
- Use two or three sources of information together in attempts at words?
- Use all sources of information flexibly to solve words?
- Use all sources of information in an orchestrated way?

3. Solving Words
Does the reader:
- Recognize a core of high frequency words quickly?
- Recognize most words quickly and easily?
- Use a variety of flexible ways to take words apart?
- Use the meaning of the sentences to solve words?
- Use the structure of the sentence to solve words?

Guide for Observing and Noting Reading Behaviors *(cont.)*	Notes

- Use some of the visual information to solve words?
- Use known word parts to solve words?
- Use sound analysis (sounding out)?
- Use analogy to solve words?
- Make attempts that are visually similar?
- Use the sound of the first letter to solve words?
- Work actively to solve words?
- Use known words or parts to solve unknown words?
- Use syllables to problem solve?
- Use prefixes and suffixes to take words apart?
- Use inflectional endings to take words apart?
- Use sentence context to derive the meaning of words?
- Use base words and root words to derive the meaning of words?
- Make connections among words to understand their meaning?

4. Self-Monitoring
Does the reader:
- Hesitate at an unknown word?
- Stop at an unknown word?
- Stop at an unknown word and appeal for help?
- Stop after an error?
- Notice mismatches?
- Notice when an attempt does not look right?
- Notice when an attempt does not sound right?
- Notice when an attempt does not make sense?
- Reread to confirm reading?
- Use knowledge of some high frequency words to check on reading?
- Check one source of information with another?
- Check an attempt that makes sense with language?
- Check an attempt that makes sense with the letters (visual information)?
- Use language structure to check on reading?
- Request help after making several attempts?

5. Self-Correcting
Does the reader:
- Reread and try again until accurate?
- Stop after an error and make another attempt?
- Stop after an error and make multiple attempts until accurate?
- Reread to self-correct?
- Work actively to solve mismatches?
- Self-correct errors some of the time?
- Self-correct errors most of the time?

6. Maintaining Fluency
Does the reader:
- Read without pointing?
- Read word groups (phrases)?
- Put words together?
- Read smoothly?
- Read the punctuation?
- Make the voice go down at periods?
- Make the voice go up at question marks?
- Pause briefly at commas, dashes, and hyphens?
- Read dialogue with intonation or expression?
- Stress the appropriate words to convey accurate meaning?
- Read at a good rate—not too fast and not too slow?

7. Other

FIGURE 57 Guide for Observing and Noting Reading Behaviors

▶d analyze it as described in the previous section.

Steps in Administering the Reading Record in the Even-Numbered Lessons

1. Record identifying information on the Recording Form.

2. Use yesterday's new book (from odd-numbered lesson). Read the title to the child and ask him to begin reading orally. For books longer than 250–300 words, have children read an excerpt orally. It is not necessary for the child to read the whole book.

3. Press **RW** and enter the number of running words (RW) in the text on the Fountas and Pinnell Calculator/Stopwatch, if you are using this device.

4. Press **Start Time** on the calculator as the child begins oral reading. Press **End Time** when the reading is complete.

5. **Code** the reading behavior on the Recording Form. Mark a typed text (see *Lesson Resources CD*), making a check for each word read accurately and using the coding conventions to record errors, self-corrections, and other behaviors. Make notes about how the reading sounded (Level C and above).

6. Press **#Errors** and enter the number of errors on the calculator.

7. Press **#SC** and enter the number of self-corrections on the calculator.

8. Press **Time** to get **Elapsed Minutes or Seconds**.

9. Press **WPM** to see **Words per Minute**.

10. Press **Accur.%** for **Percentage of Accuracy**.

11. Press **SC** to get the **Self-Correction Ratio**.

12. Have a comprehension conversation with the child about the text. Make notes about the child's understanding. Alternatively, check off items the child talks about. Use prompts, as needed, to stimulate discussion. Score each area and decide on the additional point immediately after the conversation for a more systematized assessment.

13. Select one or two teaching points to help the reader learn how to process more effectively.

Figure 58 is a complete Reading Record on a child's reading of a Level E book, *A Walk with Meli.* Notice the accurate reading as well as the places where the child did some problem solving. The child read at an instructional level with satisfactory comprehension

FIGURE 58 Reading Record on Level E Instructional Book, *A Walk with Meli*

A Walk with Meli · Green System Lesson 59 · Level E · Nonfiction

Student: Matthew   Grade: 1   Date: _____

Teacher: _____   School: _____

Recording Form

Part One: Oral Reading

Place the book in front of the student and read the title.

Sources of Information Used

Page	Text (*A Walk with Meli* Level E, RW 200)	E	SC	E M	E S	E V	SC M	SC S	SC V
2	Here is Meli. / Meli is Ron's dog.								
3	"It's/It is time to go	1		M S V					
	for a walk," said/says Ron.	1		M S V					
	Ron gets Meli's red leash.								
	"Let's go, Meli," says Ron.								
5	Meli loves to go								
	on/to a walk.	1		M S V			M S V		
	She puts								
	her little black nose	1		—					
	on everything she sees.								
	Subtotal	3	1	3	3	2	0	0	1

Part One: Oral Reading *continued*

Page	Text	E	SC	E M	E S	E V	SC M	SC S	SC V
11	She/Meli jumps up and down.	1		M S V					
	She barks and barks.								
	"You can't get that squirrel!"								
	says/Ron Ron/says R	2		M S V M S V			M S V M S V		
	"Let's go, Meli."								
12	Meli and Ron go								
	to the dog park.								
	Ron takes off Meli's leash.								
	She loves to run/see sc			M S V M S V					
	her dog friends								
	at the park.								
	She sniffs and she sniffs them,	1		—					
	and they sniff								
	and sniff her.								
	Subtotal	2	3	4	4	0	0	0	3

Part One: Oral Reading *continued*

Page	Text	E	SC	E M	E S	E V	SC M	SC S	SC V
6	She sniffs and she sniffs								
	and she sniffs.								
7	Meli can smell so many/much sc	1		M S V M S V					
	with her little black nose! R								
	She knows that								
	another dog walked								
	on the grass.								
	She can smell him/it.	1		M S V					
8	Meli stops under a tree.								
	She sniffs.								
	Then she looks up.								
	What is in the/that tree?	1		M S V					
10	It's a squirrel!								
	Subtotal	2	1	3	3	2	0	1	0

Part One: Oral Reading *continued*

Page	Text	E	SC	E M	E S	E V	SC M	SC S	SC V
13	Meli runs								
	with her friends/friend.	1		M S V					
	She loves to run and run.								
14	Meli runs around and								
	around for a long time.								
15	Then Ron puts on Meli's								
	leash again, and/and sc and Meli	1		M S V M S V					
	and Ron go back home.	1		—					
16	That was								
	a very good walk. R								
	Meli and Ron had fun.								
	Now it's/it is time	1		M S V					
	for a good nap!								
	Subtotal	3	1	3	3	3	0	1	0
	Total	10	6	13	13	7	0	2	4

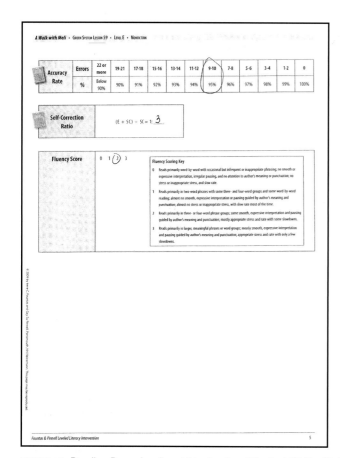

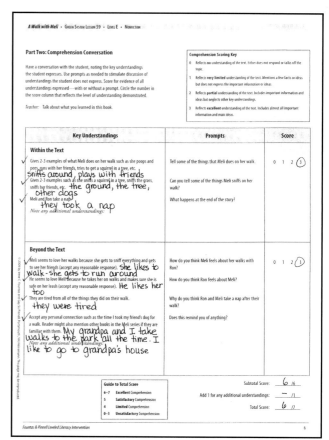

FIGURE 58 Reading Record on Level E Instructional Book, *A Walk with Meli, continued*

and fluency. Also notice that the teacher has made notes and checked key understandings.

Professional Development for LLI

▶ Professional Development Options for LLI Teachers

❏ *Program (System) Guide*—This guide offers guidance and suggestions for implementing the intervention, explains each of the LLI components and many of the forms you will be using throughout LLI, provides Word Analysis Charts for the small books, and contains a bibliography of professional books for your reference.

❏ *Professional Development and Tutorial DVDs*—You can use the *Professional Development and Tutorial DVDs* to support your work individually or with a study group of professionals. There are two disks for each system (Orange, Green, and Blue). The first provides an overview of the system and presents model lessons. The second DVD contains a tutorial on coding, scoring, and analyzing Reading Records and information on how to use the information to inform your teaching.

❏ *When Readers Struggle: Teaching that Works*—This professional book is a comprehensive tool for learning about a variety of difficulties readers have and how your teaching can move them forward.

❏ **LLI Website**—On the LLI Website, www.FountasAnd-PinnellLeveledLiteracy-Intervention.com, you will find frequently-asked questions and other information to use in implementing lessons.

❏ **Reflection Guide with a Videotaped Lesson**—You can use the Reflection Guide, Figure 57, to think about your own videotaped lesson, or you can tape your lesson and discuss it with colleagues. You might take turns bringing a videotaped lesson or part of a lesson for a group discussion. At the end of the viewing and discussion using the Reflection Guide, share the insights each of you gained that will influence your own teaching. This guide can be printed from the *Lesson Resources CD*.

❏ **Professional Development Calendar**—We provide monthly suggestions for your continued growth as an LLI teacher. Work with your LLI colleagues in your school or district to set up meeting times once per month for approximately one and a half to two hours. You may also have an array of suggested professional readings in the Professional Development section of each lesson that can be used for discussion. Bring your *Program (System) Guide* and *Lesson Guide* to each session. Your monthly LLI Calendar starts on page 95. This calendar assumes beginning lessons in September, so if you begin in mid-year, you can adjust the calendar accordingly.

Leveled Literacy Intervention Reflection Guide

EVEN NUMBERED LESSON: LESSON #: _____

Rereading • How did I teach for, prompt for, or reinforce effective use of reading strategies (fluency and phrasing, searching for and using information, solving words, self-monitoring, or self-correcting)?	
Phonics/Word Work • How clearly did I state the principle? • How clearly did I help the children understand how to apply the principle to other words? • What was the evidence of new learning?	
Writing • How did I engage children in composing sentences (interactive or independent writing)? • What were the characteristics of the sentences children composed (language complexity, vocabulary, word difficulty, accuracy, etc.)? • How did I help the children learn how to form letters efficiently? • How did I help the children learn how to use sound analysis or visual analysis? • How did I help children use writing conventions? • How did I draw children's attention to strategies for the construction of words? • What links did I make to the children's previous knowledge? • How did I use rereading to help children consider changes they needed to make? • What did children learn how to do as writers?	
New Book *Before Reading:* • How did I help the children expand their knowledge of language structures and vocabulary? • What print or text features did I help them notice? • How did I help the children understand how the book works and understand critical aspects of the text meaning? *During Reading* • How did I teach for, prompt for, or reinforce effective processing strategies? • What were the children able to do independently? *After Reading* • What was the evidence of the children's understanding of the text? • How did I support processing strategies through my teaching points? • What did the children learn how to do as readers?	

Leveled Literacy Intervention Reflection Guide

ODD NUMBERED LESSON: LESSON #: _____

Rereading • How did I teach for, prompt for, or reinforce effective use of reading strategies (fluency and phrasing, searching for and using information, solving words, self-monitoring, or self-correcting)?	
Phonics/Word Work • How clearly did I state the principle? • How clearly did I help the children understand how to apply the principle to other words? • What was the evidence of new learning?	
New Book *Before Reading:* • How did I help the children expand their knowledge of language structures and vocabulary? • What print or text features did I help them notice? • How did I help the children understand how the book works and understand critical aspects of the text meaning? *During Reading* • How did I teach for, prompt for, or reinforce effective processing strategies? • What were the children able to do independently? *After Reading* • What was the evidence of the children's understanding of the text? • How did I support processing strategies through my teaching points? • What did the children learn how to do as readers?	
Letter/Word Work • How did I organize my materials so that children could work on words independently? • How fluent were the children in recognizing letters/words or taking words apart? • What were the children noticing about words? • What did the children learn about how words work?	

FIGURE 57 Reflection Guide

AUGUST	SEPTEMBER	OCTOBER
Knowing the Readers	**Organizing and Making Transitions**	**Supporting Effective Reading**
You have collected important benchmark data on your children. Use the Reading Records from your assessment to talk with your colleagues about your groupings and the starting levels. Use the Guide for Observing and Noting Reading Behaviors to discuss the specific behaviors you observed in one group and the areas of *Prompting Guide 1* you will want to use as you start lessons. With a partner and the appropriate level book, role play how you will demonstrate the reading behaviors you have identified.	You have had a few weeks to get to know the children in your groupings and to help them get used to the predictability of the lesson. Select one of the lessons on your *Professional Development and Tutorial DVD* to watch. Observe the teacher's organization and the transition from one part of the lesson to the next. Discuss what you notice about her organization for teaching and how she was organized for smooth transitions and a quick-paced lesson.	Focus on the reading segment of your lesson. Think about how your introduction to the new text supports the children's effective processing. Prepare for your meeting by making careful notes of the problem-solving difficulties the children had as they read the new book during the last three lessons. Bring the book and share your observations with each other. Talk about what you might have done in the introduction to the text that would have prevented the processing difficulties.

NOVEMBER	DECEMBER	JANUARY
Using Ongoing Assessment to Inform Your Teaching	**Using the Continuum to Guide Teaching Decisions**	**Developing Phonics/Word Study Skills**
You have been taking a Reading Record on each child every six days. Bring the last three Reading Records for one child from one of your groups. Have enough copies for your colleagues. Use the Guide for Observing and Noting Reading Behaviors to discuss the three records. Talk about areas of strength and need indicated for each child. Also, talk about the change in the reader across the three records and what will be important to focus on next in your teaching.	At the end of each level is your guide to what children need to be able to do. Bring a set of Lesson Records, Reading Records, and writing books for one group of children. Focus on the level at which you are teaching the children now. Discuss what you feel the children control and what you will need to attend to so the children have good control of most of the competencies at the level.	Use your Lesson Guide. Divide the levels so that each pair of teachers in your group is assigned two or three levels to review. Look through the lessons in the level and on chart paper, make a list of all the kinds of phonics/word work the children engage in to expand competencies (e.g., sort letters, make high-frequency words). Look at the charts together and discuss the variety of opportunities. Then look at *Prompting Guide 1*. Discuss reading or writing areas you can refer to so that you can prompt for or reinforce what the children are learning about words.

continues

section 5

Professional Development

FEBRUARY	MARCH	APRIL
Observing Change in Writing	**Supporting Writing Development**	**Supporting Fluent, Phrased Reading**
Bring the writing book and Lesson Records for one of your children. With your colleagues, discuss the changes you see in the following areas using the writing page and the practice page next to it. Notice places where the child used correction tape. You can even look under the tape at the child's first attempt. Discuss: • letter formation • letter spacing • complexity of language structures • amount of writing • ability to hear sounds and record the letters that represent them • ability to notice how words look • the content or kinds of thinking the child is sharing about text Think about areas in *Prompting Guide 1* that will be useful in your teaching.	Bring the interactive writing pieces you created with one group of children. Take turns presenting your pieces to the group. Talk about your teaching decisions in each. • What do you notice about the sentences you and the children composed? • What writing did you do and why? • Where did you share the pen and what did you help the children learn at these selected points? • What do you think the children learned how to do as writers? • What might you have done differently? Look at the writing areas in *Prompting Guide 1*. What prompts did you find useful in supporting the writers as they constructed the text?	Bring one of each book at a level you are using with a group to your meeting. With a partner, look through the books for characteristics that provide opportunities to teach for fluent, phrased reading in each. Consider: • print layout (including phrase layout) • punctuation • use of dialogue • use of repetition • naturalness of language structures • use of bold letters or speech bubbles Share your insights with the group. As a group, talk about the implications for introducing the texts and supporting the reading of the texts with your children.

MAY	JUNE	
Expanding Language Across the Lesson	**Supporting Comprehension Across the Lesson**	
There are numerous opportunities to support children's use of language and expansion of their language across the lesson. With a partner in your group, look at each element of two consecutive lessons. Talk about: • the opportunities for children to use language in each element • ways to increase the amount of language children use • opportunities to model and expand the children's language	Bring two books you are using in LLI lessons. With a partner, look at the books and discuss how they work. Use the Analysis of New Book Characteristics in the corresponding lessons. Refer to the New Book segment of the lesson as well as the Writing segment on the following day. Ask yourself: • How can you support the children's attention to the meaning of the text in each element?	

continues

MAY	JUNE
Expanding Language Across the Lesson	**Supporting Comprehension Across the Lesson**
• opportunities for children to use book language • opportunities to expand the children's vocabulary Share your insights with the group. Talk about changes you want to make in your teaching of the lesson to provide stronger support for language development.	• What aspects of the texts may be tricky for your readers? • How do you want to strengthen their understanding through the use of these books? Share your insights with the group.

▶ Frequently Asked Questions Using LLI

Implementing the LLI System

How do I know whether to use Getting Started in the Orange and Green Systems?

If your assessment indicates that Level A is hard for the children and they know very little about print, then use Getting Started. You will find that Getting Started lessons provide a stretch and help the children learn how to work together in a group.

Why does the Orange System provide fourteen weeks of lessons?

At the kindergarten level, you will want to spend the first part of the year providing rich literacy opportunities. When you begin the intervention with the lowest achieving children, it should take no more than fourteen weeks to bring the children to Level C, which is grade level for kindergarten. If, in the rare case, you feel you need to spend more time with the lessons at Levels B or C, you can use lessons from the Green or Blue System to expand work at the level. Notice that in the Orange System children spend a

long period of time reading Level A texts so that early behaviors can be well established.

Can LLI be used before or after school?

LLI is ideally suited for before- or after-school programs. The goal would be to group children so that they are on appropriate levels. You may need to vary group size.

Can LLI be used for tutoring?

The lessons can be used for tutoring with excellent results, although you will miss some of the social interactions.

Does LLI replace Guided Reading?

LLI is intended to be *supplementary instruction.* That means that the power of the program is in the extra help children get in addition to good classroom teaching. Some classroom teachers have had successful results using LLI for a short time with their lowest achieving readers. These children also have guided reading with their peers at least three times per week.

Is LLI the same as Guided Reading?

No, LLI is a much more intensive framework of components designed to support the accelerated progress of low achieving children. It is highly systematic and sequential. The books are designed to build on one another. Although word work is provided in guided reading, LLI provides more intensive and longer work in phonics and word study. Most children do not need such an intensive approach.

Can a child continue in LLI if he/she has not made the progress that we'd like in the eighteen weeks?

Yes. If needed, a child could be regrouped with others and stay in LLI all year. Of course, you would want to do careful progress monitoring to be sure that the intervention is working. In some cases, you may want a thorough assessment of the child's learning needs by a psychologist.

Can I teach LLI lessons in the classroom?

The LLI lesson materials are portable enough that you can move from classroom to classroom to work with small groups. Work with the classroom teacher to find a small space that is far enough away from the guided reading table that the two groups will not interfere with each other. Be sure you have a table and an easel. This is a very efficient way to work because children will have very little transition time.

Do I have to complete all of the lessons within each level?

No, but be cautious. Look at the Continuum for the level to be sure the children control most of the behaviors. If your readers are finding the books very easy and in your judgment they understand the phonics and word work principles, you can skip to the next level. (Sometimes teachers spend a lesson doing a "read in" just to experience all the good books on the level. Or, they send the books back to the classroom for children to read. If you choose this option, be sure that the books are within independent range.)

Scheduling

How can I make the schedule work when there are so many conflicts?

A meeting of all the teachers at the grade level can be very helpful. Classroom teachers want children to

have extra help but also have to consider all the demands on their time. Review the schedule and go over the different groups you are trying to convene.

Does a four-day week (or an otherwise short week) count as a week of intervention?

Yes. You should be counting both days and weeks. Even a short week counts as a week.

Do all children need to finish the intervention at the same time?

No. If one child is clearly accelerating, you can assess him and move him out of the group (or into a higher group) at any time. If a child needs more time in the intervention, have him join a lower group. It is all right for him to reread, talk about, and write about some of the books in the collection. You can also "borrow" books and lessons from a parallel strand to provide new texts. Remember, there are no repetitions of books or lessons across the three systems.

Selection

Can a child who is labeled a special education child for readers participate in LLI?

It depends on what services the district provides under the label of "special education." If the educational specifications parallel the specific teaching opportunities provided in LLI, then it is an option.

Could I use LLI with all my children?

LLI was designed to supplement small group instruction that children receive in the classroom. Most children do not need such a structured approach, and teachers prefer more decision making in sequencing texts. Also, LLI does not provide enough lessons for daily group instruction across an entire year. However, you can decide to use the materials in any way you choose.

Can children who have been in Reading Recovery go into LLI?

Children should not be in both Reading Recovery and LLI at the same time. Reading Recovery children who reach grade level and exit should not need LLI. But for children who have made progress in Reading

Recovery but have not reached grade level and still need more support (a small number), LLI is an ideal option. If a child begins in LLI, she should enter Reading Recovery when a slot becomes available if she is the lowest achieving child in Grade 1.

How do you decide to group children who are at the same reading level but have different needs?

All children will have slightly different needs. But you are working to place together three children for whom a particular reading level is appropriate. If that is true, then you can begin reading the books on a level. You can fine tune your interactions with children during the lesson to account for their different needs. (For example, within a group reading at a level, one child may need more interactions around word solving and another around fluency). *Most of the time,* however, children have multiple needs and those will change from week to week. As with all teaching, observation is the key.

Attendance/Exiting the Intervention

What should I do when children are absent?

There will always be the problem of a child missing a lesson here and there. Meanwhile, others in the group will be moving on. You could introduce yesterday's new book while other children are rereading books in the rereading segment of the lesson. Often, the child can simply join in with the others on what they are doing. Or, you can send the missed book back to the classroom or home for the child to read and catch up. If attendance is spotty across the group, you can stop and have a "catch up" day to read and reread books they have missed and to review phonics principles. If a child has an extended absence, reassess him and make a decision as to the level he should be reading.

How do you handle evidence of recurring attendance issues?

In this case, the child may fall behind the group not because he can not make progress but simply because he is missing too many lessons. The circumstance may require you to take the same options

listed in another FAQ. (What happens if a child is lagging behind?) But, here, attendance is the real problem. Enlist the help of the classroom teacher or school administrator in investigating the problem. Talk with the family to be sure they know how important it is for the child to get to school. If there are health issues, work to understand them and try to work out a system for sending some materials home to the child.

What do I do if a child moves out of the school?

If possible, conduct a final assessment to get an ending level and record it on the Recording Form. Look at Reading Records and reflect on your observation of the children remaining in the group. Working with the classroom teacher, select another child reading at the same instructional level to enter the group from the classroom or from another group if this one is a better fit. The reader should be on the present level—not where the group originally started. It will not be necessary to "catch the child up" by reading all of the previous books. Just have this new group member begin where the others are. (If you think the child needs a "brush up" on high-frequency words, you can send some word cards back to the classroom and home for practice.)

Can a child leave LLI to enter Reading Recovery?

Yes, as soon as a slot in Reading Recovery is available, the neediest LLI child should be transferred to it and a new child entered into the LLI group. A child should not be in both LLI and RR at the same time.

Grouping

Do I have to limit group size to three?

We strongly recommend three children for best results. Where it is impossible to limit the groups to three, just try to keep the groups as small as possible. Occasionally, you will find that the children's levels do not work out for even group size. At various times, you may find yourself teaching groups of 2, 4, or even 5. It is very important for children to be working at an appropriate level.

Is it possible to have an LLI group with only two children?

Yes. There will always be variations because children's needs are so diverse. But, in general, you want the interaction that comes from having a group of three. Also, LLI provides more cost benefit if you try hard to keep the groups at three.

What if one child consistently lags behind the others in reading?

When you have children in a group, you can not expect them all to perform in exactly the same way. Assess the child carefully using a Reading Record to be sure the text level is within reach with instructional support. It is a good idea to seat the child closest to you (making sure the child can see charts). You can try to give a more individual support to this child to help the processing go a little faster as fluent reading is important. Also, someone might be able to have the child reread the books in the classroom or at home. If the level is really too hard, try regrouping to place the child with a group at a lower level.

Should I regroup children as I notice differences?

Group members need to get to know each other and learn how to behave as a group. But if a child is clearly not placed at the right level, then you will need to move him right away. If you are working with several groups and you notice a child or two needs a lower or higher level, adjust your groupings as best you can to meet the needs of the children. If there are small differences and no other grouping options, you may need to provide a bit more challenge or extra support to one of the group members.

What happens if one child in a group is accelerating more than the other two?

You can look for another group and move the child. It will not be necessary to have the child read all the books the children have read prior to entry. Just move the child into the group. If there is no group and the child still needs intervention, keep her in the LLI group and provide some extra writing or word work. Select other leveled books from the other collections to provide extra challenge. Most word work allows for children to go beyond the specific lesson.

What should I do if one child in the group is not moving along as quickly as the other two?

This problem will almost always exist when you are working with a group—even a small one. You have three choices: (1) Give the child some extra help when possible. You can enlist the classroom teacher or any school helper in doing some extra reading, word work, or writing with the child. Use the home option and have a conference with parents. (2) Slow the group down a bit by having a few "reading" or "writing" days to consolidate learning. (Be cautious with this option. It may not help and could slow the others down.) (3) Reassess the child and move him to another group.

Lesson Time

What if I have time left after I finish all lesson activities?

This is a good problem to have if you covered all of the elements thoroughly. You can use the time to work with high-frequency words, read *My Poetry Book,* read *My ABC Book,* or reread books that were introduced in previous lessons.

Can I take longer to get through the lengthy books at Levels such as M or N; for example, take three-day lessons and spread them out over four days?

Yes, but this should be rare. Remember that children should be reading at a faster pace by the time they reach these levels. They will also be reading silently. Use your own sense of what is appropriate but try not to "bog down." If you put in an extra day of reading, you can only briefly review the phonics principle and spend most of the time in extended reading, with discussion at the end.

What should I do if the teaching time is cut short and I do only half of a lesson?

You could start the same lesson again the next day for coherence. Or, you could do the second half and some extra reading of *My Poetry Book* or *My Writing Book.* Children can also work with high-frequency words or sort letters if needed.

What if my lessons are always too long and I find it hard to finish?

The thirty-minute time frame is important as we

found that children start to lose attention after that. As you and the children get used to the routines, you will find it easier to keep the pace. Teach children to be aware of time and help you manage it. For example, they should put word cards and other materials away quickly and make transitions smooth from one activity to another.

Organization will help. For example, keep the needed letter, picture, or word cards together in a plastic bag or small covered tub for a lesson. Keep all children's materials in one accordion file or hanging file and teach them to take them out and put them back quickly. Use a timer, as needed, to divide the sections into 10-minute intervals. Finally, check children's reading fluency to make sure they are not simply reading too slowly. If that is the case, concentrate on fluency (see *Prompting Guide 1*). You will notice that we often provide a second or third phonics activity. Be sure to do the first one and always teach the word cards. If time is a problem, eliminate the rest of the activities.

What happens if it takes more than thirty minutes to complete the lessons?

First, analyze—are you getting started on time? What is consuming time at the beginning? Try using a timer, set for each 10 minutes, to help you and the children keep up the pace. Where are you getting bogged down? Are the children reading too slowly? Is the discussion going in too many directions? Then tighten up the activities. It is important to get them all in. Remember that on the even-numbered lessons, the final "word work" is optional.

Levels

Why are there only ten lessons on a level?
In our experience, with the intensive support you provide in LLI lessons, children can move up the levels at the designated pace. If you think children need a few more days on a level, you can (where possible) "borrow" texts and lessons from across the three collections (Orange, Green, and Blue). Alternatively, you can select books from the level that you have in your school and create your own lessons using the framework. Be cautious about staying too long on a level.

Teach hard for the behaviors and understandings listed on the Continuum.

What if my group reaches the end of a level and I am not sure they are ready to move to the next level?

Look carefully at the Reading Records and then look at the first lesson on the next higher level. If you really think they need more time on the level, you can "borrow" from the same level in one of the other systems (Orange, Green, Blue). If you do not have the other systems, then find more books on the same level (from your guided reading books) and create your own lessons using the same lesson framework. You can review the phonics and word work from the level you are just finishing.

Is it all right to move to the next level without teaching all the lessons?

Yes, but be cautious. If children are finding the reading material and writing very easy, then you can skip the rest of the lessons at a level or even an entire level. Be sure to look at the Continuum for the level and think about evidence that children have strong control of most of the behaviors and understandings required for the level.

What do you do about children whose reading might be at one level, but their writing is well below that level?

Go with the reading level for instruction in LLI. Be sure to give emphasis and attention to writing in the even numbered lessons. Use the Classroom Connection option, which often involves more writing. Work closely with the classroom teacher to provide extra classroom writing opportunities.

Teaching Decisions

How much can I vary the lesson (depart from the specific instructions)?

We encourage you to adjust the lesson in any way justified by information from your ongoing assessment and observation of learners' strengths and needs. No lesson plan can be written to fit all children. Your decision-making across the lesson is critical. It would not make sense to consistently eliminate lesson components or to drastically slow down instruction, but you will find yourself tailoring lessons to meet children's needs.

If children are finding the new text too difficult, should I read it to them first?

No. If the text is so difficult that you need to read it to the children (or provide a very long introduction), then it is probably too hard. They need to experience independent processing of a new text that allows them to build their reading power. Move to an easier level.

When should children stop pointing?

At Level C they should drop the finger and let the eyes take over the process. Remind children to "read it with your eyes." (See *Prompting Guide 1*, Early Reading Behaviors.) If they can not do it, teach hard for it, or reassess the child. Some children may find this transition difficult and will need to practice on very easy texts.

When should children start to read silently?

At about Level H or I, the voice should start to drop to a very soft level. Children should be discovering that they can read more quickly when they read silently. By about Level I and J, the reading should be silent so the children can learn to read silently with competence. Of course, you will still be sampling oral reading from individual children, one at a time. Some children may find this transition difficult and will need to practice on very easy texts.

If children are finding the new text very easy, should I cut back on the information in the introduction?

You can cut back a little bit, but remember that the introduction is designed to start readers thinking. It may be that children can move a little faster through the level or that your placement is too easy.

What do you do about children who have low vocabulary (usually English language learners) when you get to books that have lots of concepts and new vocabulary?

You will need a richer introduction and perhaps a longer discussion after reading to be sure children are gaining the vocabulary they need. Also, they will be using these vocabulary words in the writing. After

rereading, you can visit a few words just to use them and talk about their meaning. Talk with the classroom teacher to be sure that children are being exposed to new vocabulary daily through interactive read aloud. Another way to help is to go to previous levels (for example, books that those children have not read) in any of the strands and give children some "extra" books to read that will be easy for them. They can do this in the classroom and will build vocabulary in the process. Finally, you could work into the lesson some word "collections," where you write words that are connected with each other in some way—names of pets, names of animals, words about weather, etc.

Can I carry the reading of the new book over more than one day?

Usually, carrying a book over two or more days will not be necessary. The selections are short enough for one day's reading. Be sure the children are reading fluently. But if you need to continue the reading the next day, you can make that decision. Check to be sure that children are not reading too slowly.

What do you do when children have gaps in the phonics/word analysis area? Do you keep giving them extra practice? Do you stay longer on a level to make up for the gaps? Do you go back and teach previous concepts that they don't have?

These are complex issues and will depend a great deal on teacher decision making. If a child can read the texts at a level (meeting the criteria for instructional level), then usually they have the phonics skills. But it would be a good idea to look at *The Continuum for Literacy Learning* and at the phonics and word study activities for that level and the previous level. It may be that you will need to spend a day or two just tidying up some phonics knowledge that will be essential as the children move into higher texts. Work closely with the classroom teacher to identify areas of support needed.

How do you help children take on high-frequency words, as there isn't enough practice time in the thirty-minute lesson?

You are showing children how to look closely at the words, connect them with other words, and learn them; so, their ability to take on new words should speed up. Children will be doing a great deal of reading and many new words will be acquired in this activity. Not all words have to be learned in isolation from word cards because the process of learning words is being established.

Some ways to get extra word learning in are: (1) Print out an extra copy of high-frequency words and show children how to cut them apart and take them home. Spend some lesson time "practicing" what they will do with their words at home. For example, they can lay them out and find connections. They can play Concentration. They can just turn them over and make piles of "easy words" and "words I'm still learning." (2) Have an extra "word bag" in the classroom and arrange with the teacher for the child to go over the words every day during independent work time. (3) Have parents come to a conference and show them a couple of easy games to play with their children at home (See the *Lesson Resources CD* for the rules for Lotto and Follow the Path).

How much flexibility do I have with regard to word work? Do I have to work with the suggested words?

The suggested words are there only for your convenience. You can select others that fit the principle you are teaching. If you feel a different principle is needed, make the decision to use the principle that fits your children's needs.

What should I do if the children are not learning words quickly enough?

Visit the section for Instructional Routines in this guide and reflect on whether you are being explicit enough in your teaching. Also, look at the chapter in *When Readers Struggle: Teaching that Works* on "Building a Repertoire of Words."

Should all the words in **My Writing Book** *be spelled conventionally?*

Yes, because children need to read their books at school and after they take them home. Use white correction tape to help children write conventional spellings and write some words in for them. Also, they will be using sound and letter boxes (see Instructional

Routines) to help them write some words. There may be an occasional difficult word on which the child has made an excellent attempt and you do not want to take the time to make the spelling conventional. You may decide to ignore a few temporary spellings.

If the lesson specifies interactive writing, could I use independent writing instead?

That is your decision. If you think children need a strong demonstration and to focus their attention on one text, then use interactive writing. If you think each child needs to actually do all of the writing rather than observing some of the time, use independent writing. Sometimes, you can write one sentence interactively for children to copy (or you to write quickly for them) and then they can go on to write another sentence independently.

How do I support English language learners?

On the last page of every LLI lesson, you will find suggestions for fine-tuning the lesson to support English language learners. You will also find a section in this guide. (Also see *When Readers Struggle,* Chapter 18.)

Assessment

Why do I need to take running records (Reading Records) when I have the benchmark entry information?

The literacy levels of children, especially younger ones, change very rapidly. You need up-to-date objective information to inform your decision-making and use of *Prompting Guide 1.* Your weekly Reading Records will provide important information for teaching individuals in the group. Also, this information will help you in planning introductions to the text, phonics, and writing.

What if I started on a level that is proving to be too difficult for the group?

As a general practice, begin at a level that you are confident will allow the children to read very successfully. You can stop where you are and move down to a less difficult level if you find you started at the wrong place. As children go up the levels, they may meet texts that they previously read and found hard. It will be a confidence booster to encounter them again and find them within reach.

How often should I take a Reading Record?

If you take a record the next day on the new book that was read in the odd-numbered lessons, then you will be taking a record every other day. Rotating around a group of three children, you will take one record on each every six days. Your daily observations and this procedure will provide enough specific information to guide your teaching.

Do I have to use the Recording Form to take Reading Records?

If you know how to take running records, you can use a blank form. (This may be more difficult at Levels K through N because there are so many words on a line and children read quickly.)

Do you recommend administering a Benchmark Assessment before moving to the next reading level?

No. That would be too much assessment. If you are observing and taking Reading Records once every six days on each child, then you will have a very good idea of how the child is performing at the present level. If they are reading at instructional level on the first reading and at solid instructional level or independent level on the second reading, then they are probably ready to go on to the next level. Look at the Continuum for the present level to be sure that you are seeing evidence of the needed behaviors and understandings for thinking within, beyond, and about the text.

Parents

How can I support the child if he/she is not doing his/her homework?

You have three ways to support the home option: (1) Make it special. Use the brightly colored Take-Home Bag. Spend some lesson time having children "practice" what they will do when they get home (taking out their book and other activities, doing them, putting them back in the bag, and putting the bag by the door so they won't forget it). Make it an event the first week when they bring back their bags and talk about what they did at home. (2) Enlist the classroom teacher in reminding children to take home their bags with books and activities and to do the work at home. (3) Have a parent conference and walk them through the kinds of activities the child will be bringing home to do. Help them realize how important it is for the child to do them and to receive praise.

How can I keep families involved?

Make good use of the Take-Home Books and Home Connection options. Help families understand how to use them by sending home the daily letters. Also, you can always invite family members to observe a lesson and talk with them afterwards.

Should I send the LLI books home with children?

LLI provides "take-home" versions of the books that are designed for children to read and keep in a basket at home. Home reading is important for low-achieving readers who may not have great access to books. Readers must have large amounts of practice. You have the option to purchase more "take-home" books at a very reasonable price so that children benefit from rereading. Or, you can send home the full color versions in the bag and have the children bring them back. The book is sent home for rereading after it has been read twice in lessons.

Should I tell parents the level I am working on?

You can explain the program to parents and other family members or caregivers as continuous progress. Show them the books their child was reading at the beginning of LLI and what he is reading now. Help them look at the books to understand progress. Explain that the level helps you to monitor progress and teach the child. Try to avoid the "level" being something that parents and caregivers focus on too much.

appendix

System Book Chart

Book/Lesson	1	2	3	4	5
Getting Started	Waking Up	Frog Food	The New Puppy	Friends	Sam and Papa
Book/Lesson	6	7	8	9	10
Getting Started	Too Much Stuff	Ant Can't	Eggs	Where Things Grow	The Very Busy Hen
Book/Lesson	11	12	13	14	15
Level A	Flying	Woof!	The Painter	Smells	Jesse
Book/Lesson	16	17	18	19	20
Level A	Monkey	Oh No!	Getting Dressed	Family Pictures	My Bath

Level B Begins

Book/Lesson	21	22	23	24	25
Level B	Orson's Tummy Ache	At the Park	Bubbles	The Farmers	Mom and Kayla
Book/Lesson	26	27	28	29	30
Level B	My Puppy	Our Garden	My New School	Boots and Shoes	Traffic

Level C Begins

Book/Lesson	31	32	33	34	35
Level C	A Day at the Park	Jump	Looking for Taco	Swim!	Meli on the Stairs
Book/Lesson	36	37	38	39	40
Level C	The Sky	Homes	The Picnic	Clouds	Look!

Level D Begins

Book/Lesson	41	42	43	44	45
Level D	The Three Pigs	Snap!	Up in a Tree	Apple Pie	Time for Lunch
Book/Lesson	46	47	48	49	50
Level D	A Rainy Day	The Good Dog	My Friend	What Am I?	Trucks

Level E Begins

Book/Lesson	51	52	53	54	55
Level E	The Three Bears	The Puppets	The Surprise	Play Ball!	Talent Show
Book/Lesson	56	57	58	59	60
Level E	Kate's Truck	Baby Pictures	A Visit to the City	A Walk with Meli	Pets

Shaded Box = Independent books at easier level.

System Book Chart

Level F Begins

Book/Lesson	61	62	63	64	65
Level F	The Three Little Pigs and a Big Bad Wolf	The Box	The Soccer Game	Books	Bunny and the Monster

Book/Lesson	66	67	68	69	70
Level F	The Pool	Pictures of Hugs	Farmer Dan's Ducks	The Big Storm	My Five Senses

Level G Begins

Book/Lesson	71	72	73	74	75
Level G	Goldie and the Three Bears	Helping Mom	Papa's Birthday	The Storm	Baby Bird

Book/Lesson	76	77	78	79	80
Level G	Lizzy	The Goat in the Garden	A Surprise for Mom	How Frogs Grow	Brave Taco

Level H Begins

Book/Lesson	81	82	83	84	85
Level H	The Skunk with No Stripes	The Tree House	The Gingerbread Man	Out for Lunch	Dinner for Maisy

Book/Lesson	86	87	88	89	90
Level H	Just Wait and See	In Winter	All About Animal Babies	The Gecko That Came to School	Grandma's Glasses

Level I Begins

Book/Lesson	91	92	93	94	95
Level I	Fun for Hugs	Home Sweet Home	Bear's Birthday	The Bossy Pig	Stone Soup

Book/Lesson	96	97	98	99	100
Level I	Best New Friends	The Missing Cat	The Lucky Penny	All About Honeybees	A Walk at Night

Level J Begins

Book/Lesson	101	102	103	104	105
Level J	Too Tall	Two Teams	All About Dolphins	The Cherries	The Lion and the Mouse

Book/Lesson	106	107	108	109	110
Level J	All About Boats	The Three Billy Goats	All About Chimps	Bad-Luck Day	A Trip to the Laundromutt

Shaded Box = Independent books at easier level.

▶ Text Analyses for Books in the Green Collection

On the first page of every lesson, you will see an analysis of the new book that covers the ten text factors we have found helpful in determining the challenges in a text. These factors are described in the chart below.

The text analysis will provide valuable information to guide your introduction and teaching of the new text. Additionally, in this section, we provide a detailed analysis of the word challenges of the new text. Next, you will find this analysis for each title. This information is helpful to us as teachers because it helps us to understand the kinds of word-solving challenges young readers are facing. You will not want to attend to all of these word features in teaching any one lesson. Instead, you will find some selected features in the text factor analysis. These features have been selected because they are key to the text *and* appropriate for the learning needs that children typically have when reading at these levels. We are always thinking about what the children need to know next.

Factors Related to Text Difficulty

Factor	Definition
Genre	The "genre" is the type of text and refers to a system by which fiction and nonfiction texts are classified. Each genre has characteristic features.
Text Structure	The "structure" is the way the text is organized and presented. It may be *narrative*, as in most fiction and biographical texts. Factual texts are organized categorically or topically and may have sections with headings. Writers of factual texts use several underlying structural patterns to provide information to readers: *enumeration, chronological sequence, compare/contrast, cause/effect,* and *problem/solution.* The presence of these structures, especially in combination can increase the challenge for readers.
Content	The "content" refers to the subject matter of the text—the concepts that are important to understand. In fiction, content may be related to the setting or to the kinds of problems characters have. In factual texts, content refers to the topic of focus. Content is considered in relation to the prior experience of readers.
Themes and Ideas	The "themes and ideas" are the big ideas that are communicated by the text. A text may have multiple themes or a main theme and several supporting themes or ideas.
Language and Literary Features	Written language is qualitatively different from spoken language. Fiction writers use dialogue, figurative language, and other kinds of literary structures. Factual writers use description and technical language. In hybrid texts you may find a wide range of literary language.
Sentence Complexity	Meaning is mapped out onto the syntax of language. Texts with simpler, more natural sentences are easier to process. Sentences with embedded and conjoined clauses make a text more difficult.
Vocabulary	"Vocabulary" refers to the meaning of the words and is part of our oral language. The more the words are accessible to readers in terms of meaning, the easier a text will be. The individual's *reading and writing vocabularies* refer to words that they understand and can also read or write.
Words	"Words" refer to recognizing and solving the printed words in the text. The challenge in a text partly depends on the number and the difficulty of the words that the reader must solve by recognizing them or decoding them. Having a great many of the same high-frequency words makes a text more accessible to readers.
Illustrations	The "illustrations" include drawings, paintings or photographs that accompany the text and add meaning and enjoyment. In factual texts, illustrations also include graphics that provide a great deal of information that readers must integrate with the text. Illustrations are an integral part of a high quality text. Increasingly, fiction texts are including a range of graphics.
Book and Print Features	The "book and print features" are the physical aspects of the text—what readers cope with in terms of length, size, and layout. Book and print features also include tools like the table of contents, glossary, pronunciation guides, indices, and sidebars.

Appendix

Lesson	1
Book Title	***WAKING UP***
Feature	**Examples from the Text**
Content words	rooster, wakes, cock-a-doodle-doo, cow, moo, pig, oink, horse, neigh, turkey, gobble, sheep, baa, duck, quack, chick, peep
High-frequency words	the*, up*, and*
Words with inflectional endings	wakes
Difficult word patterns	cow, moo, oink, horse, neigh, quack
Difficult multisyllable words	rooster, cock-a-doodle-doo, turkey, gobble
Words with vowel and *r*	horse, rooster, turkey
Vowel patterns *ow, ay, ey*	cow, turkey
CVC words **Regular pattern *(run)*** **Other *(how)***	1. pig 2. cow
Onomatopoetic words	cock-a-doodle-doo, moo, oink, neigh, gobble, baa, quack, peep
CVV words *(see)*	baa, moo
VCC words *(all)*	and
CVCC words *(fish)*	duck
CVVC words *(soap, foot)*	peep
CCVVC words *(cream)*	sheep
CVCe words **Regular pattern *(make)*** **Other *(have)***	1. wake(s) 2.
CCVCC words *(black)*	chick
CVCCe words *(table, taste)*	horse
Sentence length	2–5
Sentences per page	1 (1 page with 2)
Number of words	50

Lesson	2
Book Title	*FROG FOOD*
Feature	**Examples from the Text**

Content words	bugs, pancakes, popcorn, soup, bread, pizza, salad, cake
High-frequency words	I*, like*, on*
Pronouns	I
Prepositions	on
Compound words	popcorn
Plurals	bugs, pancakes
Difficult word patterns	pizza
Difficult multisyllable words	pancakes, popcorn, salad, pizza
Words with *a* as *schwa*	pizza
Words with vowel and *r*	popcorn
CVC words **Regular pattern** *(run)* **Other** *(how)*	1. bug(s) 2.
CVVC words *(soap, foot)*	soup
CCVVC words *(cream)*	bread
CVCe words **Regular pattern** *(make)* **Other** *(have)*	1. like, cake 2.
Sentence length	5 (one sentence has 3 words)
Sentences per page	1
Number of words	38

continues

Lesson	3
Book Title	*THE NEW PUPPY*
Feature	**Examples from the Text**

Labels/Names	Meli
Content words	dish, blanket, collar, bed, toy, brush, bone, puppy
High-frequency words	I, got*, a*, little*
Pronouns	I
Difficult word patterns	toy
Difficult multisyllable words	blanket, collar, puppy
Words ending in *y* Sounding like (1) *i* or (2) *e*	1. 2. puppy
Words with vowel and *r*	collar
CVC words Regular pattern *(run)* Other *(how)*	1. got, bed 2. toy
CVCC words *(fish)*	dish
CVCe words Regular pattern *(make)* Other *(have)*	1. bone 2.
CCVCC words *(black)*	brush
Sentence length	5
Sentences per page	1
Number of words	40

Lesson	4
Book Title	*FRIENDS*
Feature	**Examples from the Text**

Labels/Names	Orson, Taco
Content words	dog, collar, bone, ball, bark, woof, bowl, bed, friend
High-frequency words	is*, a, big*, little, has*
Difficult word patterns	friend
Difficult multisyllable words	collar
Words with vowel and *r*	collar, bark
Vowel patterns *ow, ay, ey*	bowl
CVC words **Regular pattern** *(run)* **Other** *(how)*	1. big, dog, has, bed 2.
Onomatopoetic words	woof
CVCC words *(fish)*	ball, bark, bowl
CVVC words *(soap, foot)*	woof
CVCe words **Regular pattern** *(make)* **Other** *(have)*	1. bone 2.
CCVVCC words *(friend)*	friend
Sentence length	5
Sentences per page	1
Number of words	80

Appendix

continues

Lesson	5
Book Title	*SAM AND PAPA*
Feature	**Examples from the Text**

Labels/Names	Papa
Content words	read, books, lunch, ball, draw, pictures, shopping, watch, TV, cookies
High-frequency words	I, like, to*, with*, my*, eat*, play*, go*, make*, love*, and, loves*, me*
Pronouns	I, my, me
Prepositions	with
Words with inflectional endings	shopping, loves, cookies
Plurals	books, pictures, cookies
Difficult word patterns	read, books, lunch, draw, watch, with, eat, play, love
Difficult multisyllable words	pictures, shopping, cookies
Words with *a* as *schwa*	Papa (final *a*)
Words ending in *y* **Sounding like (1) *I* or (2) *e***	1. my 2.
Words with vowel and *r*	pictures
Vowel patterns *ow, ay, ey*	play
VVC words *(out)*	eat
VCC words *(all)*	and
CVCC words *(fish)*	ball, with
CVVC words *(soap, foot)*	read, book(s), cook(ies)
CVCe words **Regular pattern *(make)*** **Other *(have)***	1. like, make 2. love
CCVC words *(then)*	draw, shop(ping), play
Sentence length	8 (4 and 5 on last page)
Sentences per page	1 (2 on last page)
Number of words	65

Lesson	6
Book Title	*TOO MUCH STUFF*
Feature	**Examples from the Text**

Labels/Names	Bear
Content words	truck, closet, bike, train, plane, hat, book, ball
High-frequency words	got, his*, he*, put*, it*, in*, the, too*, oh*, no*
Pronouns	he, his, it
Prepositions	in
Difficult word patterns	oh, put, too
Difficult multisyllable words	closet
CVC words **Regular pattern** *(run)* **Other** *(how)*	1. hat, got, his 2. put
CVV words *(see)*	too
CVCC words *(fish)*	ball
CVVC words *(soap, foot)*	Bear, book
CCVVC words *(cream)*	train
CVCe words **Regular pattern** *(make)* **Other** *(have)*	1. bike 2.
CCVCC words *(black)*	truck
CCVCe words *(white)*	plane
Sentence length	4–7 (one sentence with 2 words)
Sentences per page	2 (one page with 1 sentence)
Number of words	75

Lesson	7
Book Title	***ANT CAN'T***
Feature	**Examples from the Text**
Labels/Names	Ant
Content words	met, bird, fly, bee, buzz, frog, hop, cow, moo, fish, swim, pig, oink, dog, bark, spider, crawl, wall
High-frequency words	a, can*, you*, said*, the, no, I, can't*, up, yes*
Pronouns	you, I
Prepositions	up
Contractions	can't
Difficult word patterns	oink, crawl
Difficult multisyllable words	spider
Words ending in *y* **Sounding like (1) *I* or (2) *e***	1. fly 2.
Words with vowel and *r*	bird, bark, spider
Vowel patterns *ow, ay, ey*	cow
CVC words **Regular pattern** *(run)* **Other** *(how)*	1. met, can, hop, pig, dog, yes 2. cow
Onomatopoetic words	buzz, moo, oink
CVV words *(see)*	you, bee, moo
VCC words *(all)*	ant, fly
CVCC words *(fish)*	bird, buzz, fish, bark, wall
CVVC words *(soap, foot)*	said
CCVC words *(then)*	frog, swim
CCVCC words *(black)*	crawl
Sentence length	4–6
Sentences per page	3
Number of words	131

Lesson	8
Book Title	***EGGS***
Feature	**Examples from the Text**
Labels/Names	Mother Hen, Mother Snake, Mother Fish, Mother Turtle, Mother Spider, Mother Penguin, Mother Duck
Content words	hen, laid, eggs, crack, baby, chicks, snakes, pop, fish, turtles, spiders, penguins, ducks, quack
High-frequency words	some*, came*, out*
Prepositions	out
Plurals	eggs, chicks, snakes, turtles, spiders, penguins, ducks
Difficult word patterns	penguins, quack
Difficult multisyllable words	turtles, spiders, penguins
Words ending in *y* Sounding like (1) *i* or (2) *e*	1. 2. baby
Words with vowel and *r*	mother, turtle, spider
CVC words Regular pattern *(run)* Other *(how)*	1. hen, pop 2.
Onomatopoetic words	crack, pop, quack
VVC words *(out)*	out
VCC words *(all)*	egg(s)
CVCC words *(fish)*	fish, duck(s)
CVVC words *(soap, foot)*	laid
CVCe words Regular pattern *(make)* Other *(have)*	1. came 2. some
CCVCC words *(black)*	crack, chick(s)
CCVCe words *(white)*	snake
Sentence length	4–5
Sentences per page	1 (with one-word sentences for effect)
Number of words	87

continues

Appendix

Lesson	9
Book Title	***WHERE THINGS GROW***
Feature	**Examples from the Text**
Content words	apples, grow, trees, pick, oranges, potatoes, ground, dig, carrots, grapes, vines, pumpkins, blueberries, bushes
High-frequency words	on, we*, can, the, too, I, in, up, big
Pronouns	I, we, they
Prepositions	on, in, up
Compound words	blueberries
Plurals	apples, trees, oranges, potatoes, carrots, grapes, vines, pumpkins, blueberries, bushes
Difficult word patterns	oranges, ground, blueberries
Difficult multisyllable words	apples, oranges, potatoes, carrots, pumpkins, blueberries, bushes
Words with vowel and *r*	carrots, blueberries
Vowel patterns *ow, ay, ey*	grow
CVC words **Regular pattern** *(run)* **Other** *(how)*	1. can, dig, big 2.
CVV words *(see)*	too
CVCC words *(fish)*	pick, bush(es)
CVCe words **Regular pattern** *(make)* **Other** *(have)*	1. vine(s) 2.
CCVC words *(then)*	grow
CCVCe words *(white)*	grape(s), where
CCVVCC words *(friend)*	ground
Sentence length	4–6
Sentences per page	2
Number of words	81

Lesson	10
Book Title	*THE VERY BUSY HEN*
Feature	**Examples from the Text**
Content words	dog, hen, busy, planting, wheat, cat, watering, mouse, cutting, horse, mixing, bread, cow, baking, yum
High-frequency words	come*, and, play, said, the, no, I, am*, very*, eat, they*, did*
Pronouns	I, they
Words with inflectional endings	planting, watering, cutting, mixing, baking
Difficult word patterns	mouse
Difficult multisyllable words	watering, planting, cutting, mixing, baking
Words ending in *y* **Sounding like (1)** *i* **or (2)** *e*	1. 2. very, busy
Words with vowel and *r*	very, watering, horse
Vowel patterns *ow, ay, ey*	play, cow, they
CVC words **Regular pattern** *(run)* **Other** *(how)*	1. hen, dog, cat, did, yum 2. cow
VVC words *(out)*	eat
VCC words *(all)*	and
CVCC words *(fish)*	very, busy
CVVC words *(soap, foot)*	said
CCVVC words *(cream)*	wheat, bread
CVCe words **Regular pattern** *(make)* **Other** *(have)*	1. 2. come
CCVC words *(then)*	play, they
CVCCe words *(table, taste)*	horse
Sentence Length	3–6 (with one repetitive 18-word sentence)
Sentences per page	1–4
Number of words	123

continues

Appendix

Lesson	11
Book Title	*FLYING*
Feature	**Examples from the Text**

Content words	train, duck, doll, horse, pig, bunny, car, party
High-frequency words	I, can, see*, a
Pronouns	I
Words with inflectional endings	flying
Difficult multisyllable words	bunny, party
Words ending in _y_ **Sounding like (1) _i_ or (2) _e_**	1. 2. bunny, party
Words with vowel and _r_	horse, car, party
CVC words **Regular pattern** *(run)* **Other** *(how)*	1. can, pig, car 2.
CVV words *(see)*	see
CVCC words *(fish)*	duck, doll
CCVVC words *(cream)*	train
CVCCe words *(table, taste)*	horse
Sentence length	5
Sentences per page	1
Number of words	40

Lesson	12
Book Title	*WOOF!*
Feature	**Examples from the Text**

Feature	Examples from the Text
Labels/Names	Taco
Content words	bird, woof, cat, truck, car, squirrel, bike, bug, dog
High-frequency words	sees*, a
Words with inflectional endings	sees
Difficult multisyllable words	squirrel
Words with vowel and *r*	bird, car, squirrel
CVC words **Regular pattern** *(run)* **Other** *(how)*	1. cat, bug, dog 2. car
Onomatopoetic words	woof
CVV words *(see)*	see(s)
CVCC words *(fish)*	bird
CVVC words *(soap, foot)*	sees, woof
CVCe words **Regular pattern** *(make)* **Other** *(have)*	1. bike 2.
CCVCC words *(black)*	truck
Sentence length	4
Sentences per page	1
Number of words	42

continues

Appendix

Lesson	13
Book Title	*THE PAINTER*
Feature	**Examples from the Text**
Content words	paint, chair, bike, house, flowers, tree, swing, friends, myself
High-frequency words	I, can, my
Pronouns	I, my, myself
Compound words	myself
Plurals	flowers, friends
Difficult word patterns	house, swing
Difficult multisyllable words	painter, flowers, myself
Words ending in *y* Sounding like (1) *i* or (2) *e*	1. my 2.
Words with vowel and *r*	chair, flowers
Vowel patterns *ow, ay, ey*	flowers
CVC words Regular pattern *(run)* Other *(how)*	1. can 2.
CVCC words *(fish)*	self (myself)
CCVVC words *(cream)*	chair
CVCe words Regular pattern *(make)* Other *(have)*	1. bike 2.
CCVCC words *(black)*	swing
CCVVCC words *(friend)*	friend(s)
Sentence length	4–5
Sentences per page	1
Number of words	39

Lesson	14
Book Title	*SMELLS*
Feature	**Examples from the Text**

Feature	Examples from the Text
Content words	smell, flowers, pizza, soap, cookies, popcorn, bread, soup, skunk
High-frequency words	I, can, the
Pronouns	I
Compound words	popcorn
Plurals	flowers, cookies
Difficult word patterns	pizza
Difficult multisyllable words	flowers, pizza, cookies, popcorn
Words with *a* as *schwa*	pizza
Words with vowel and *r*	flowers, popcorn
Vowel patterns *ow, ay, ey*	flowers
CVC words Regular pattern *(run)* Other *(how)*	1. can 2.
CCVVC words *(cream)*	bread
CCVCC words *(black)*	smell, skunk
Sentence length	5
Sentences per page	1
Number of words	40

continues

Lesson	15
Book Title	*JESSE*
Feature	Examples from the Text

Content words	purple, shirt, pants, socks, shoes, jacket, cap, glasses
High-frequency words	I, like, my, love
Pronouns	I, my
Plurals	socks, shoes, glasses
Difficult multisyllable words	purple, jacket, glasses
Words ending in *y* **Sounding like (1) *i* or (2) *e***	1. my 2.
Words with vowel and *r*	purple, shirt
CVC words **Regular pattern** *(run)* **Other** *(how)*	1. cap 2.
CVCC words *(fish)*	socks
CVCe words **Regular pattern** *(make)* **Other** *(have)*	1. like 2. love
CCVCC words *(black)*	shirt
Sentence length	5 (one sentence with 3 words)
Sentences per page	1
Number of words	38

Lesson	16
Book Title	*MONKEY*
Feature	**Examples from the Text**

Feature	Examples from the Text
Content words	monkey, jump, climb, ride, hug, sleep
High-frequency words	the, can, eat, sit*, walk*
Difficult word patterns	climb, walk
Difficult multisyllable words	monkey
Vowel patterns *ow, ay, ey*	monkey
CVC words **Regular pattern** *(run)* **Other** *(how)*	1. can, sit, hug 2.
VVC words *(out)*	eat
CVCC words *(fish)*	jump, walk
CCVVC words *(cream)*	sleep
CVCe words **Regular pattern** *(make)* **Other** *(have)*	1. ride 2.
CCVCC words *(black)*	climb
Sentence length	4
Sentences per page	1
Number of words	32

continues

Lesson	17
Book Title	*OH NO!*
Feature	**Examples from the Text**

Content words	mail, water, trash, paper, flowers, pillow, paint, dog
High-frequency words	look*, at*, the, oh, no
Prepositions	at
Plurals	flowers
Difficult word patterns	paint
Difficult multisyllable words	water, paper, flowers, pillow
Words with vowel and *r*	water, paper, flowers
Vowel patterns *ow, ay, ey*	flowers, pillow
CVC words **Regular pattern** *(run)* **Other** *(how)*	1. dog 2.
CVVC words *(soap, foot)*	look, mail
CCVCC words *(black)*	trash
Sentence length	4
Sentences per page	1
Number of words	46

Lesson	18
Book Title	*GETTING DRESSED*
Feature	**Examples from the Text**

Content words	socks, pants, shirt, shoes, sweater, hat, backpack
High-frequency words	look, at, my, me
Pronouns	my, me
Prepositions	at
Compound words	backpack
Plurals	socks, pants, shoes
Difficult word patterns	shoes, sweater
Difficult multisyllable words	sweater, backpack
Words ending in *y* Sounding like (1) *i* or (2) *e*	1. my 2.
Words with vowel and *r*	shirt, sweater
CVC words Regular pattern *(run)* Other *(how)*	1. hat 2.
CVCC words *(fish)*	sock(s), pant(s), back(pack)
CVVC words *(soap, foot)*	look
CCVCC words *(black)*	shirt
Sentence length	4 (one sentence with 3 words)
Sentences per page	1
Number of words	31

Appendix

continues

Lesson	19
Book Title	***FAMILY PICTURES***
Feature	**Examples from the Text**

Content words	mom, dad, brother, sister, grandma, cat, bear, family
High-frequency words	this*, is, my
Pronouns	my, this
Compound words	grandma
Plurals	pictures
Difficult multisyllable words	family, pictures, brother, sister, grandma
Words with *a* as *schwa*	grandma
Words ending in *y* **Sounding like (1) *i* or (2) *e***	1. my 2. family
Words with vowel and *r*	pictures, brother, sister
CVC words **Regular pattern** *(run)* **Other** *(how)*	1. mom, dad, cat 2.
CVVC words *(soap, foot)*	bear
CCVC words *(then)*	this
Sentence length	4
Sentences per page	1
Number of words	32

Lesson	20
Book Title	*MY BATH*
Feature	**Examples from the Text**
Content words	duck, boat, soap, fish, ball, frog, mom, bath
High-frequency words	this, is, my
Pronouns	my, this
Words ending in *y* **Sounding like (1)** *i* **or (2)** *e*	1. my 2.
CVC words Regular pattern *(run)* **Other** *(how)*	1. mom 2.
CVCC words *(fish)*	bath, duck, fish, ball
CVVC words *(soap, foot)*	soap
CCVC words *(then)*	this, frog
Sentence length	4
Sentences per page	1
Number of words	32

continues

Lesson	21
Book Title	*ORSON'S TUMMY ACHE*
Feature	**Examples from the Text**
Content words	dog, ate, food, grass, cookie, stick, bone, apple, bug, burp
High-frequency words	the, big, a, little
Difficult multisyllable words	cookie, apple
Words with vowel and *r*	burp
CVC words **Regular pattern** *(run)* **Other** *(how)*	1. big, dog, bug 2.
Onomatopoetic words	burp
CVCC words *(fish)*	burp
CVVC words *(soap, foot)*	food
CVCe words **Regular pattern** *(make)* **Other** *(have)*	1. bone 2.
CCVCC words *(black)*	grass, stick
Sentence length	7–8
Sentences per page	1
Number of words	51

Lesson	22
Book Title	*AT THE PARK*
Feature	**Examples from the Text**

Content words	swinging, park, jumping, walking, riding, climbing, sliding, running, eating
High-frequency words	I, am, at, the
Pronouns	I
Prepositions	at
Words with inflectional endings	swinging, jumping, walking, riding, climbing, sliding, running, eating
Difficult multisyllable words	swinging, jumping, walking, riding, climbing, sliding, running, eating
Words with vowel and *r*	park
CVC words **Regular pattern** *(run)* **Other** *(how)*	1. run (running) 2.
VVC words *(out)*	eat (eating)
CVCC words *(fish)*	park, jump (jumping), walk (walking)
CVCe words **Regular pattern** *(make)* **Other** *(have)*	1. ride (riding) 2.
CCVCC words *(black)*	swing (swinging), climb (climbing)
CCVCe words (*white*)	slide (sliding)
Sentence length	6
Sentences per page	1
Number of words	48

Appendix

continues

Lesson	23
Book Title	*BUBBLES*
Feature	**Examples from the Text**

Content words	bubbles, sky, pool, milk, tub, sea, fish, bowl, dog, bubble
High-frequency words	see, the, in, my, on, me
Pronouns	my, me
Prepositions	in, on
Plurals	bubbles
Difficult word patterns	sky, sea, bowl
Difficult multisyllable words	bubble
Words ending in *y* **Sounding like (1) *i* or (2) *e***	1. sky, my 2.
Vowel patterns *ow, ay, ey*	bowl
CVC words **Regular pattern** *(run)* **Other** *(how)*	1. tub, dog 2.
CVV words *(see)*	see, sea
CVCC words *(fish)*	milk, fish, bowl
CVVC words *(soap, foot)*	pool
Sentence length	5–7
Sentences per page	1
Number of words	48

Lesson	24
Book Title	*THE FARMERS*
Feature	**Examples from the Text**

Content words	cows, horses, pigs, goats, sheep, hens, farmers
High-frequency words	look, at, the
Prepositions	at
Plurals	cows, horses, pigs, goats, sheep, farmers
Difficult multisyllable words	horses, farmers
Words with vowel and *r*	horses, farmers
Vowel patterns *ow, ay, ey*	cows
CVC words **Regular pattern** *(run)* **Other** *(how)*	1. pig(s), hen(s) 2. cow(s)
CVVC words *(soap, foot)*	look, goat(s)
CCVVC words *(cream)*	sheep
CVCCe words *(table, taste)*	horse
Sentence length	4
Sentences per page	1
Number of words	28

continues

Appendix

Lesson	25
Book Title	*MOM AND KAYLA*
Feature	**Examples from the Text**

Labels/Names	Mom, Kayla
Content words	hat, jacket, pants, boots, dog, hose, truck
High-frequency words	has, a, too, big, little, looks*, like
Words with inflectional endings	looks
Plurals	pants, boots
Difficult multisyllable words	jacket
CVC words **Regular pattern** *(run)* **Other** *(how)*	1. mom, has, hat, big, dog 2.
CVV words *(see)*	too
VCC words *(all)*	and
CVCC words *(fish)*	pant(s)
CVVC words *(soap, foot)*	boot(s), look(s)
CVCe words **Regular pattern** *(make)* **Other** *(have)*	1. hose, like 2.
CCVCC words *(black)*	truck
Sentence length	3–5
Sentences per page	2
Number of words	69

Lesson	26
Book Title	***MY PUPPY***
Feature	**Examples from the Text**
Content words	puppy, hat, shoe, sock, bear, ball, mitten, blanket
High-frequency words	my, got, a, me
Pronouns	my, me
Difficult word patterns	shoe
Difficult multisyllable words	mitten, blanket
Words ending in *y* **Sounding like (1) *i* or (2) *e***	1. my 2. puppy
CVC words **Regular pattern** *(run)* **Other** *(how)*	1. got, hat 2.
CVCC words *(fish)*	sock, ball
CVVC words *(soap, foot)*	bear
Sentence length	4–5
Sentences per page	1
Number of words	39

Appendix

continues

Lesson	27
Book Title	*OUR GARDEN*
Feature	**Examples from the Text**
Content words	corn, garden, beans, flowers, strawberries, tomatoes, pumpkins, carrots, bunnies
High-frequency words	we, have*, some, in, our*
Pronouns	we, our
Prepositions	in
Compound words	strawberries
Plurals	beans, flowers, strawberries, tomatoes, pumpkins, carrots, bunnies
Difficult word patterns	strawberries, tomatoes, pumpkins, bunnies
Difficult multisyllable words	garden, flowers, strawberries, tomatoes, pumpkins, carrots, bunnies
Words with vowel and *r*	garden, corn, flowers, strawberries, carrots
Vowel patterns *ow, ay, ey*	flowers
VVC words *(out)*	our
CVCC words *(fish)*	corn
CVVC words *(soap, foot)*	bean(s)
CVCe words **Regular pattern *(make)*** **Other *(have)***	1. 2. have, some
Sentence Length	7
Sentences per page	1
Number of words	54

Lesson	28
Book Title	*MY NEW SCHOOL*
Feature	**Examples from the Text**
Content words	cap, jacket, backpack, lunchbox, school, teacher, book, friend
High-frequency words	I, have, a, new*
Pronouns	I
Words with inflectional endings	teacher
Compound words	backpack, lunchbox
Difficult word patterns	school, lunchbox, teacher
Difficult multisyllable words	jacket, backpack, lunchbox, teacher
Words ending in *y* **Sounding like (1) *i* or (2) *e***	1. my 2.
Words with vowel and *r*	teacher
CVC words **Regular pattern** *(run)* **Other** *(how)*	1. cap 2. new
CVCC words *(fish)*	back, pack (backpack)
CVVC words *(soap, foot)*	book
CVCe words **Regular pattern** *(make)* **Other** *(have)*	1. 2. have
CCVVCC words *(friend)*	friend
Sentence length	5
Sentences per page	1
Number of words	40

continues

Lesson	29
Book Title	***BOOTS AND SHOES***
Feature	**Examples from the Text**

Content words	boots, ride, shoes, dance, ski, kick, jump
High-frequency words	look, at, my, I, can, run*, walk, in, with
Pronouns	my, I
Prepositions	at, in, with
Plurals	boots, shoes
Difficult word patterns	shoes
Words ending in *y* **Sounding like (1)** *i* **or (2)** *e*	1. my 2.
CVC words **Regular pattern** *(run)* **Other** *(how)*	1. can, run 2.
VCC words *(all)*	and
CVCC words *(fish)*	walk, kick, with, jump
CVVC words *(soap, foot)*	boot(s), look
CVCe words **Regular pattern** *(make)* **Other** *(have)*	1. ride 2.
CVCCe words *(table, taste)*	dance
Sentence length	4–6
Sentences per page	2
Number of words	74

Lesson	30
Book Title	*TRAFFIC*
Feature	**Examples from the Text**

Feature	Examples from the Text
Content words	bike, motorcycle, van, bus, truck, car, traffic
High-frequency words	look, at, the
Prepositions	at
Compound words	motorcycle
Difficult word patterns	motorcycle
Difficult multisyllable words	motorcycle, traffic
Words with vowel and *r*	motorcycle, car
CVC words Regular pattern *(run)* Other *(how)*	1. van, bus 2. car
CVVC words *(soap, foot)*	look
CVCe words Regular pattern *(make)* Other *(have)*	1. bike 2.
CCVCC words *(black)*	truck
Sentence length	4
Sentences per page	1
Number of words	28

Appendix

continues

Lesson	31
Book Title	*A DAY AT THE PARK*
Feature	Examples from the Text

Labels/Names	Jesse, Sam, Papa
Content words	map, ball, hit, bugs, birds, cars, car, swings, swing, kites, climb, tree, bench, ice, cream
High-frequency words	likes*, to, look, at, the, but*, wants*, play, sit, in, with, on, see, run, like, and, too
Prepositions	at, in, with, on
Words with inflectional endings	likes, wants
Plurals	bugs, birds, cars, swings, kites
Words with *a* as *schwa*	Papa
Words with vowel and *r*	birds, cars, car
Vowel patterns *ow, ay, ey*	play
CVC words **Regular pattern** *(run)* **Other** *(how)*	1. Sam, map, hit, bug(s), sit, but, run 2. car
CVV words *(see)*	see, too
VCC words *(all)*	and
CVCC words *(fish)*	ball, bird(s), want(s), with
CVVC words *(soap, foot)*	look
CCVVC words *(cream)*	cream
CVCe words **Regular pattern** *(make)* **Other** *(have)*	1. like, kite(s) 2.
CCVCC words *(black)*	swing, climb
Sentence length	4–9
Sentences per page	2
Number of words	105

Lesson	32
Book Title	*JUMP*
Feature	**Examples from the Text**

Content words	frog, jump, rabbit, duck, fox, dog, pig, moose
High-frequency words	the, can, oh, no
Difficult word patterns	moose
Difficult multisyllable words	rabbit
CVC words **Regular pattern** *(run)* **Other** *(how)*	1. can, fox, dog, pig 2.
CVCC words *(fish)*	jump, duck
CCVC words *(then)*	frog
Sentence length	4 (one sentence with 2 words)
Sentences per page	1
Number of words	30

continues

Lesson	33
Book Title	***LOOKING FOR TACO***
Feature	**Examples from the Text**
Labels/Names	Jack, Taco, Orson, Mom's
Content words	yard, under, rose, bush, garage, car, bathroom, bathtub, bedroom, bed, room, desk, kitchen, table
High-frequency words	looked*, and, for*, come, here*, said, in, the, no, was*, not*, he, his, I, see, you, too
Pronouns	he, his, I, you
Prepositions	for, in, under
Words with inflectional endings	looked, Mom's
Compound words	bathroom, bathtub, bedroom
Difficult word patterns	bush, garage, table, said, was, you
Difficult multisyllable words	garage, bathroom, bathtub, bedroom, kitchen, table
Words with *a* as *schwa*	garage
Words with vowel and *r*	yard, under, garage, car, for
CVC words **Regular pattern** *(run)* **Other** *(how)*	1. bed, not, his, tub (bathtub), Mom('s) 2. car, for, was
CVV words *(see)*	see, you
VCC words *(all)*	and
CVCC words *(fish)*	Jack, yard, bush, bath (bathroom, bathtub), desk
CVVC words *(soap, foot)*	room, look(ed), said
CVCe words **Regular pattern** *(make)* **Other** *(have)*	1. rose, here 2. come
CVCCe words *(table, taste)*	table
Sentence length	1–8
Sentences per page	2–3
Number of words	94

Lesson	34
Book Title	***SWIM!***
Feature	**Examples from the Text**
Content words	ducks, swim, fish, dogs, frogs, turtles, bears, seals
High-frequency words	the, can, I
Pronouns	I
Plurals	ducks, dogs, frogs, turtles, bears
Difficult multisyllable words	turtles
Words with vowel and *r*	turtles, bears
CVC words **Regular pattern *(run)*** **Other *(how)***	1. can, dog(s) 2.
CVCC words *(fish)*	duck(s), fish
CVVC words *(soap, foot)*	bear(s), seal(s)
CCVC words *(then)*	swim, frog(s)
Sentence length	3–4
Sentences per page	1
Number of words	31

Appendix

continues

Lesson	35
Book Title	***MELI ON THE STAIRS***
Feature	**Examples from the Text**

Labels/Names	Meli
Content words	stairs, take, shoe, toy, dog, ball
High-frequency words	look, at, likes, to, play, on, the, she, run, up, down*, a, her*
Pronouns	she, her
Prepositions	on, at, to, up, down
Words with inflectional endings	likes
Plurals	stairs
Difficult word patterns	stairs, shoe
Words with vowel and *r*	her
Vowel patterns *ow, ay, ey*	play, down
CVC words **Regular pattern** *(run)* **Other** *(how)*	1. run, dog 2. toy, her
CVCC words *(fish)*	down, ball
CVVC words *(soap, foot)*	look
CCVVC words *(cream)*	stair(s)
CVCe words **Regular pattern** *(make)* **Other** *(have)*	1. like(s), take 2.
Sentence length	3–9 (one sentence with 13 words)
Sentences per page	1–3
Number of words	91

Lesson	36
Book Title	***THE SKY***
Feature	**Examples from the Text**

Content words	sky, sun, plane, birds, balloon, clouds, rain, rainbow
High-frequency words	look, up, at, the
Prepositions	at
Compound words	rainbow
Plurals	birds, clouds
Difficult multisyllable words	balloon, rainbow
Words ending in *y* **Sounding like (1)** *i* **or (2)** *e*	1. sky 2.
Words with vowel and *r*	birds
CVC words **Regular pattern** *(run)* **Other** *(how)*	1. sun 2.
CVCC words *(fish)*	bird(s)
CVVC words *(soap, foot)*	look, rain
CCVVC words *(cream)*	cloud(s)
CCVCe words *(white)*	plane
Sentence length	5
Sentences per page	1
Number of words	40

Appendix

continues

Lesson	37
Book Title	***HOMES***
Feature	**Examples from the Text**
Content words	tree, home, owl, log, fox, shell, crab, cave, bats, hive, bees, web, spider, hole, mouse, house, dog
High-frequency words	here, is, a, this, for, an, look, at, the
Pronouns	this
Prepositions	for
Plurals	bats, bees
Difficult word patterns	mouse, house
Difficult multisyllable words	spider
Words with vowel and *r*	for, spider
CVC words **Regular pattern** *(run)* **Other** *(how)*	1. for, log, fox, web, bat(s), dog 2.
CVV words *(see)*	bee(s)
VCC words *(all)*	owl
CVVC words *(soap, foot)*	look
CVCe words **Regular pattern** *(make)* **Other** *(have)*	1. home, here, hole, hive, cave 2.
CCVC words *(then)*	this, crab
CCVCC words *(black)*	shell
Sentence length	4–8
Sentences per page	1
Number of words	90

Lesson	38
Book Title	*THE PICNIC*
Feature	**Examples from the Text**

Content words	tree, blanket, basket, milk, bread, cheese, pie, picnic
High-frequency words	here, is, the
Difficult word patterns	bread, pie
Difficult multisyllable words	blanket, basket, picnic
CVV words *(see)*	pie
CVCC words *(fish)*	milk
CCVVC words *(cream)*	bread
CVCe words Regular pattern *(make)* Other *(have)*	1. here 2.
CCVVCe words *(cheese)*	cheese
Sentence length	4
Sentences per page	1
Number of words	32

continues

Lesson	39
Book Title	***CLOUDS***
Feature	**Examples from the Text**

Labels/Names	Kate, Tony
Content words	cloud, bird, cat, car, horse, house, rabbit, hat, bear
High-frequency words	look, at, the, said, it, looks, like, a, I, see, big, that*, one*, my
Pronouns	it, I, my
Prepositions	at
Words with inflectional endings	looks
Difficult word patterns	house
Words ending in *y* **Sounding like (1) *i* or (2) *e***	1. my 2.
Words with vowel and *r*	bird, car, horse
CVC words **Regular pattern** *(run)* **Other** *(how)*	1. cat, big, hat 2. car
CVV words *(see)*	see
CVCC words *(fish)*	bird
CVVC words *(soap, foot)*	said, bear
CCVVC words *(cream)*	cloud
CVCe words **Regular pattern** *(make)* **Other** *(have)*	1. like 2.
CCVC words *(then)*	that
CVCCe words *(table, taste)*	horse
Sentence length	3–9
Sentences per page	2
Number of words	92

Lesson	40
Book Title	*LOOK!*
Feature	**Examples from the Text**

Content words	feet, legs, tail, neck, eyes, nose, ears
High-frequency words	look, at, my, me
Pronouns	my, me
Prepositions	at
Plurals	legs, eyes, ears
Difficult word patterns	eyes
Words ending in *y* Sounding like (1) *i* or (2) *e*	1. my 2.
CVC words **Regular pattern** *(run)* **Other** *(how)*	1. leg(s) 2.
VVC words *(out)*	ear(s)
CVCC words *(fish)*	neck
CVVC words *(soap, foot)*	look, feet, tail
CVCe words **Regular pattern** *(make)* **Other** *(have)*	1. nose 2.
Sentence length	4 (one sentence with 3 words)
Sentences per page	1
Number of words	31

Appendix

continues

147

Lesson	41
Book Title	*THE THREE PIGS*
Feature	**Examples from the Text**

Content words	wolf, pig, blow, house, road, two, pigs, three
High-frequency words	let*, me, in, said, the, no, one, little, then*, I, will*, your*, down, and, he, did, ran*, but, not, get*, went*
Pronouns	me, I, your, he
Prepositions	in
Plurals	pigs
Difficult word patterns	house
Vowel patterns *ow, ay, ey*	blow, down
CVC words **Regular pattern** *(run)* **Other** *(how)*	1. let, pig, did, ran, not, get 2.
CVCC words *(fish)*	wolf, will, down, went
CVVC words *(soap, foot)*	said, your, road
CCVC words *(then)*	then, blow
Sentence length	3–10
Sentences per page	1–2
Number of words	113

Lesson	42
Book Title	*SNAP!*
Feature	**Examples from the Text**

Content words	turtle, grass, trees, flowers, water, duck, frog, fly, snap
High-frequency words	the, little, can, see, a
Plurals	trees, flowers
Difficult multisyllable words	turtle, flowers, water
Words ending in *y* **Sounding like (1) *i* or (2) *e***	1. fly 2.
Words with vowel and *r*	turtle, water
Vowel patterns *ow, ay, ey*	flower
CVC words **Regular pattern *(run)*** **Other *(how)***	1. can 2.
Onomatopoetic words	snap
CVV words *(see)*	see
CVCC words *(fish)*	duck
CCVC words *(then)*	snap, frog
CCVCC words *(black)*	grass
Sentence length	6
Sentences per page	1
Number of words	50

continues

Lesson	43
Book Title	*UP IN A TREE*
Feature	**Examples from the Text**
Labels/Names	Meg, Hugs, Gram
Content words	tree, toy, cat, food
High-frequency words	was, up, in, a, come, down, said, but, did, not, got, and, get, your, want*, the, he, can, of*, eat, to, will, I, go, up, she, went, sat*
Pronouns	your, he, I, she
Prepositions	in, of, to, up
Words with inflectional endings	Hugs
Difficult word patterns	toy, was, come, said, your, want
Vowel patterns *ow, ay, ey*	down
CVC words **Regular pattern** *(run)* **Other** *(how)*	1. Hug(s), Meg, cat, sat, but, did, not, got, get, can 2. was, toy
VVC words *(out)*	eat
VCC words *(all)*	and
CVCC words *(fish)*	down, want, will, went
CVVC words *(soap, foot)*	food, said, your
CVCe words **Regular pattern** *(make)* **Other** *(have)*	1. 2. come
CCVC words *(then)*	Gram
Sentence length	3–8
Sentences per page	1–3
Number of words	111

Lesson	44
Book Title	*APPLE PIE*
Feature	**Examples from the Text**

Content words	pick, apples, wash, peel, cut, mix, bake, pie, smell
High-frequency words	we, like, to, the, eat
Pronouns	we
Prepositions	to
Plurals	apples
Difficult multisyllable words	apple
CVC words **Regular pattern** *(run)* **Other** *(how)*	1. mix, cut 2.
CVV words *(see)*	pie
VVC words *(out)*	eat
CVCC words *(fish)*	pick, wash
CVVC words *(soap, foot)*	peel
CVCe words **Regular pattern** *(make)* **Other** *(have)*	1. like, bake 2.
CCVCC words *(black)*	smell
Sentence length	6
Sentences per page	1
Number of words	51

Lesson	45
Book Title	*TIME FOR LUNCH*
Feature	**Examples from the Text**

Labels/Names	Mother Bear, Baby Bear, Little Bear, Father Bear
Content words	time, lunch, berries, yum, nuts, fish, honey, bees
High-frequency words	it's*, for, said, likes, I, will, get, some, got, like, too, oh, no, ran, and, but, do*, not
Pronouns	I
Prepositions	for
Words with inflectional endings	likes
Contractions	it's
Plurals	berries, nuts, bees
Difficult multisyllable words	berries, honey
Words ending in *y* **Sounding like (1) *i* or (2) *e***	1. 2. Baby
Words with vowel and *r*	Mother, Father, for
Vowel patterns *ow, ay, ey*	honey
CVC words **Regular pattern** *(run)* **Other** *(how)*	1. yum, nut(s), get, got, ran, but, not 2. for
CVV words *(see)*	bee(s)
VCC words *(all)*	and
CVCC words *(fish)*	fish, will
CVVC words *(soap, foot)*	said, Bear
CVCe words **Regular pattern** *(make)* **Other** *(have)*	1. time, like 2. some
Sentence length	3–7
Sentences per page	2–3
Number of words	122

Lesson	46
Book Title	***A RAINY DAY***
Feature	**Examples from the Text**
Content words	paint, rainy, bake, hide, dance, sing, read, write
High-frequency words	we, like, to, on, a, day*, love
Pronouns	we
Prepositions	on
Words with inflectional endings	rainy
Difficult word patterns	rainy
Words ending in *y* **Sounding like (1) *i* or (2) *e***	1. 2. rainy
Vowel patterns *ow, ay, ey*	day
CVCC words *(fish)*	sing
CVVC words *(soap, foot)*	read
CVCe words **Regular pattern *(make)*** **Other *(have)***	1. like, bake, hide 2. love
CCVCe words *(white)*	write
CVCCe words *(table, taste)*	dance
CVVCC words *(paint)*	paint
Sentence length	5–8
Sentences per page	1
Number of words	61

continues

Appendix

Lesson	47
Book Title	*THE GOOD DOG*
Feature	**Examples from the Text**

Labels/Names	Orson, Jack
Content words	dog, time, roll, rolled, beg, paws, paper, ball, nap, boy
High-frequency words	said, sit, was, a, good*, he, sat, oh, no, it's, for, walk, went, with, come, very, ran, to, over*, and, up, liked*, be, put, his, get, the, wanted*, got, then
Pronouns	he, his
Prepositions	with, to, over, up, for
Words with inflectional endings	rolled, liked, wanted
Contractions	it's
Plurals	paws
Difficult word patterns	paws, boy
Difficult multisyllable words	paper
Words ending in *y* **Sounding like (1) *i* or (2) *e***	1. 2. very
Words with vowel and *r*	for, over, paper
CVC words **Regular pattern** *(run)* **Other** *(how)*	1. sit, dog, sat, ran, beg, his, get, got, nap 2. was, for, put, paw(s)
VCC words *(all)*	and
CVCC words *(fish)*	walk, went, with, roll, want(ed), ball
CVVC words *(soap, foot)*	said, good
CVCe words **Regular pattern** *(make)* **Other** *(have)*	1. time, like(d) 2. come
CCVC words *(then)*	then
Sentence length	4–10 (one page with 2)
Sentences per page	2–3
Number of words	125

Lesson	48
Book Title	**MY FRIEND**
Feature	**Examples from the Text**

Content words	friend, pizza, read, books, ride, bikes, jump, rope, bake, cookies, ball, puzzles
High-frequency words	my, likes, to, eat, with, me, play, do, like
Pronouns	my, me
Prepositions	with
Words with inflectional endings	likes
Plurals	books, bikes
Difficult word patterns	cookies
Difficult multisyllable words	pizza, cookies
Words with *a* as *schwa*	pizza
Words ending in *y* Sounding like (1) *i* or (2) *e*	1. my 2.
Vowel patterns *ow, ay, ey*	play
VVC words *(out)*	eat
CVCC words *(fish)*	jump, ball
CVVC words *(soap, foot)*	read, book(s)
CVCe words Regular pattern *(make)* Other *(have)*	1. like, ride, bike(s), rope, bake 2.
Sentence length	8 (one page with 4)
Sentences per page	1 (one page with 2)
Number of words	64

Appendix

continues

Lesson	49
Book Title	*WHAT AM I?*
Feature	**Examples from the Text**
Content words	tree, swing, grass, hide, dirt, home, under, ground, sea, swim, fast, cave, sleep, sand, woods, eating, green, leaves, monkey, snake, ant, shark, bat, crab, deer
High-frequency words	I, am, in, a, from, to, what*, the, can, my, is, here, all*, day, came, out, of, an
Pronouns	I, my
Prepositions	in, under, out, of
Words with inflectional endings	eating
Plurals	leaves
Difficult word patterns	ground, leaves
Difficult multisyllable words	under, monkey
Words ending in *y* **Sounding like (1) *i* or (2) *e***	1. my 2. monkey
Words with vowel and *r*	dirt, under, shark
Vowel patterns *ow, ay, ey*	day, monkey
CVC words **Regular pattern** *(run)* **Other** *(how)*	1. can, bat 2. day
CVV words *(see)*	sea
VVC words *(out)*	out
VCC words *(all)*	all, ant
CVCC words *(fish)*	dirt, fast, sand
CVVC words *(soap, foot)*	deer
CCVVC words *(cream)*	sleep, green
CVCe words **Regular pattern** *(make)* **Other** *(have)*	1. hide, home, cave, here, came 2.
CCVC words *(then)*	what, from, swim, crab
CCVCC words *(black)*	swing, grass, shark
CCVCe words *(white)*	snake

CCVVCC words *(friend)*	ground
Sentence length	3–6
Sentences per page	3
Number of words	111

continues

Lesson	50
Book Title	***TRUCKS***
Feature	**Examples from the Text**
Content words	truck, logs, cars, trash, hay, trees, sand, ice, cream, house
High-frequency words	look, at, this, has, on, it, in, a
Pronouns	this, it
Prepositions	at, on, in
Plurals	logs, cars, trees
Difficult word patterns	ice, house
Words with vowel and *r*	cars
Vowel patterns *ow, ay, ey*	hay
CVC words Regular pattern *(run)* Other *(how)*	1. has, log(s) 2. car(s)
CVCC words *(fish)*	sand
CVVC words *(soap, foot)*	look
CCVVC words *(cream)*	cream
CCVC words *(then)*	this
CCVCC words *(black)*	truck, trash
Sentence length	4–6
Sentences per page	2
Number of words	75

Lesson	51
Book Title	***THE THREE BEARS***
Feature	**Examples from the Text**
Labels/Names	Mama Bear, Papa Bear, Baby Bear
Content words	girl, walk, house, woods, home, three, bowls, chairs, beds, bears
High-frequency words	one, day, a, little, went, for, she, saw*, in, the, no, was, I, like, this, said, came, oh, he, his, sat, up, then, ran, all, way*
Pronouns	she, I, he, his, this
Prepositions	for, in, up
Words with inflectional endings	woods
Plurals	bowls, chairs, beds, bears
Difficult word patterns	walk, house, woods, three, bowls, oh, one, little, saw, said
Difficult multisyllable words	Baby, little
Words with *a* as *schwa*	Papa
Words ending in *y* Sounding like (1) *i* or (2) *e*	1. 2. Baby
Words with vowel and *r*	girl, for
Vowel patterns *ow, ay, ey*	bowls, way, day
CVC words Regular pattern *(run)* Other *(how)*	1. bed(s), sat, ran, his 2. way, day, for, saw, was
VCC words *(all)*	all
CVCC words *(fish)*	girl, walk, bowl(s), went
CVVC words *(soap, foot)*	wood(s), Bear, said
CCVVC words *(cream)*	chair(s)
CVCe words Regular pattern *(make)* Other *(have)*	1. home, like, came 2.
CCVC words *(then)*	this, then
Sentence length	3–9
Sentences per page	1–3
Number of words	116

Appendix

continues

Lesson	52
Book Title	*THE PUPPETS*
Feature	**Examples from the Text**

Content words	rabbit, hop, frog, dog, cat, bird, fly, duck, fish, swim, puppet, show
High-frequency words	look, at, me, I'm*, a, little, I, can, and, too, run, us*, our
Pronouns	me, I'm, I, us, our
Prepositions	at
Contractions	I'm
Words ending in *y* **Sounding like (1)** *i* **or (2)** *e*	1. fly 2.
Words with vowel and *r*	bird
CVC words **Regular pattern** *(run)* **Other** *(how)*	1. can, hop, dog, run, cat 2.
VCC words *(all)*	and
CVCC words *(fish)*	bird, duck, fish
CVVC words *(soap, foot)*	look
CCVC words *(then)*	frog, swim
Sentence length	3–7
Sentences per page	3 (one page with 1)
Number of words	91

Lesson	53
Book Title	***THE SURPRISE***
Feature	**Examples from the Text**
Labels/Names	Fox, Bear, Rabbit, Deer, Squirrel, Bird, Raccoon
Content words	dear, house, surprise, met, hello, happy, birthday
High-frequency words	come, to, my, I, have, a, for, you, went, see, on, the, way, he, where*, are*, going*, asked*, I'm, said, has, me, can, too, and, they, we, will, with, us, all, so*, in
Pronouns	my, I, you, he, me, we, they, us
Prepositions	to, for, on, in
Words with inflectional endings	going, asked
Compound words	birthday
Contractions	I'm
Difficult word patterns	house, Squirrel
Difficult multisyllable words	surprise, Rabbit, happy
Words ending in *y* **Sounding like (1)** *i* **or (2)** *e*	1. my 2. happy
Words with vowel and *r*	surprise, for, are, birthday
Vowel patterns *ow, ay, ey*	way, they, birthday
CVC words **Regular pattern** *(run)* **Other** *(how)*	1. Fox, met, has, can 2. way
CVV words *(see)*	you, see, too
VCC words *(all)*	ask(ed), and, all
CVCC words *(fish)*	went, with, will
CVVC words *(soap, foot)*	dear, Bear, Deer, said
CVCe words **Regular pattern** *(make)* **Other** *(have)*	1. 2. come, have
CCVC words *(then)*	they
CCVCe words *(white)*	where
Sentence length	4–13 (one sentence with 17)
Sentences per page	2–4 (two pages with 1)
Number of words	225

Appendix

continues

Lesson	54
Book Title	***PLAY BALL!***
Feature	**Examples from the Text**
Content words	ball, round, kick, bounce, game, school, home
High-frequency words	here, is, a, big, the, you, can, this, play, with, it, too, not, run, at
Pronouns	it, you
Prepositions	with, at
Difficult word patterns	round, bounce, school
Vowel patterns *ow, ay, ey*	play
CVC words **Regular pattern** *(run)* **Other** *(how)*	1. big, can, not, run 2.
CVV words *(see)*	you, too
CVCC words *(fish)*	ball, kick, with
CVCe words **Regular pattern** *(make)* **Other** *(have)*	1. here, game, home 2.
CCVC words *(then)*	play, this
Sentence length	4–10
Sentences per page	1–2
Number of words	80

Lesson	55
Book Title	***TALENT SHOW***
Feature	**Examples from the Text**
Labels/Names	Horse, Sheep, Goat, Dog, Rabbit, Pig
Content words	talent, show, I'll, sing, sang, song, dance, drum, read, book, jump, rope, jumped, time, you'll, began, danced
High-frequency words	went, to, see, I'm, going, have, a, said, you, can, be, in, my, good, your, then, for, did, will, yes, play, this, played*, I, what, do, it's, the, he, with, it, was, very
Pronouns	my, your, then, I, he, it, this, you
Prepositions	to, in, for, with
Words with inflectional endings	going, played, jumped, danced
Contractions	I'm, I'll, it's, you'll
Difficult multisyllable words	talent
Words ending in *y* Sounding like (1) *i* or (2) *e*	1. my 2. very
Words with vowel and *r*	horse, for, very
Vowel patterns *ow, ay, ey*	show, play
CVC words Regular pattern *(run)* Other *(how)*	1. can, did, dog, yes, pig 2. for, was
CVV words *(see)*	see, you
CVCC words *(fish)*	went, sing, sang, song, will, jump, with
CVVC words *(soap, foot)*	said, your, goat, read, book
CCVVC words *(cream)*	sheep
CVCe words Regular pattern *(make)* Other *(have)*	1. rope, time 2. have
CCVC words *(then)*	show, then, play, this, drum, what
CVCCe words *(table, taste)*	horse, dance
Sentence length	3–9
Sentences per page	1–4
Number of words	227

Appendix

continues

163

Lesson	56
Book Title	***KATE'S TRUCK***
Feature	**Examples from the Text**

Labels/Names	Kate
Content words	truck, ride, bear, dolls, books, dinosaur, dog, ruff
High-frequency words	got, her, the, I, can, in, my, she, said, want, put, oh, no
Pronouns	her, I, my, she
Prepositions	in
Plurals	dolls, books
Difficult word patterns	dinosaur
Difficult multisyllable words	dinosaur
Words ending in *y* **Sounding like (1) *i* or (2) *e***	1. my 2.
Words with vowel and *r*	her
CVC words **Regular pattern** *(run)* **Other** *(how)*	1. got, can, dog 2. her, put
Onomatopoetic words	ruff
CVCC words *(fish)*	want, doll(s), ruff
CVVC words *(soap, foot)*	said, bear, book(s)
CVCe words **Regular pattern** *(make)* **Other** *(have)*	1. ride 2.
CCVCC words *(black)*	truck
Sentence length	4–8
Sentences per page	2
Number of words	92

Lesson	57
Book Title	**BABY PICTURES**
Feature	**Examples from the Text**
Labels/Names	Froggy, Duck, Otter, Turtle, Mommy
Content words	house, pictures, baby, picture, cute, otter, friends, mom, book, frogs, fish, tadpole, frog
High-frequency words	went, to, play, was, looking*, at, some, this, is, my, said, I, a, very, yes, you, were*, and, can, we, see, your, here, am, all, had*, wanted, know*, what, his, looked, like, so, he, ask*, asked, saw, lots*, they, little, that, me, it, now*
Pronouns	this, my, I, you, we, your, his, he, they, that, me, it
Prepositions	to, at
Words with inflectional endings	looking, wanted, looked, asked
Plurals	pictures, friends, lots, frogs
Difficult word patterns	pictures, house, asked
Difficult multisyllable words	baby, pictures, mommy, little, tadpole
Words ending in *y* **Sounding like (1)** *i* **or (2)** *e*	1. my 2. Froggy, baby, Mommy, very
Words with vowel and *r*	pictures, very, were, otter, turtle
Vowel patterns *ow, ay, ey*	play, they, now
CVC words **Regular pattern** *(run)* **Other** *(how)*	1. yes, can, had, his, mom, lot(s) 2. was, saw, now
CVV words *(see)*	you, see
VCC words *(all)*	all, ask, and
CVCC words *(fish)*	went, duck, want(ed), fish
CVVC words *(soap, foot)*	look(ing), said, your, book
CVCe words **Regular pattern** *(make)* **Other** *(have)*	1. here, like, cute 2. were, some
CCVC words *(then)*	play, this, know, what, frog, they, that
Sentence length	5–10
Sentences per page	1–3 (one page with 4)
Number of words	203

Appendix

continues

Lesson	58
Book Title	*A VISIT TO THE CITY*
Feature	**Examples from the Text**

Content words	dad, truck, mom, car, van, brother, taxis, bicycles, police, bus, sister, city
High-frequency words	look, said, my, at, the, big, I, little
Pronouns	my, I
Prepositions	to, at
Plurals	taxis, bicycles
Difficult word patterns	taxis, bicycles, police
Difficult multisyllable words	brother, taxis, bicycles, police, sister
Words ending in *y* **Sounding like (1)** *i* **or (2)** *e*	1. my 2. city
Words with vowel and *r*	car, brother, sister
CVC words **Regular pattern** *(run)* **Other** *(how)*	1. dad, big, mom, van, bus 2. car
CVVC words *(soap, foot)*	look, said
CCVCC words *(black)*	truck
Sentence length	4–9
Sentences per page	1–2
Number of words	64

Lesson	59
Book Title	***A WALK WITH MELI***
Feature	**Examples from the Text**
Labels/Names	Meli, Ron
Content words	dog, time, red, leash, black, nose, everything, sniffs, smell, much, another, grass, under, tree, squirrel, jumps, barks, park, takes, friends, friend, around, long, again, home, fun, nap
High-frequency words	here, is, it, to, go, for, a, walk, says*, gets*, let's*, loves, she, puts*, her, little, on, sees, and, can, so, with, knows*, that, walked*, the, stops*, then, looks, up, what, in, it's, down, you, can't, get, off*, see, at, them*, they, runs, run, back*, was, very, good, had, now
Pronouns	she, her, it, you, them, they
Prepositions	for, on, under, up, in, down, to, off, with
Words with inflectional endings	says, gets, loves, puts, sees, knows, looks, runs, sniffs, stops, jumps, barks, takes, runs
Compound words	everything
Contractions	let's, it's, can't
Plurals	friends
Difficult word patterns	leash, squirrel, friends
Difficult multisyllable words	everything, squirrel, under, around, again
Words with *a* as *schwa*	around, again
Words ending in *y* **Sounding like (1) *i* or (2) *e***	1. 2. very
Words with vowel and *r*	for, her, under, squirrel, barks, park
Vowel patterns *ow, ay, ey*	say(s), down, they
CVC words **Regular pattern *(run)*** **Other *(how)***	1. dog, get, red, let('s), her, can('t), run, had, fun, nap 2. for, put(s), was, now
CVV words *(see)*	see, you
VCC words *(all)*	and, off
CVCC words *(fish)*	walk, with, jump(s), down, bark(s), park, long, back
CVVC words *(soap, foot)*	looks, good

Appendix

continues

CVCe words **Regular pattern** *(make)* **Other** *(have)*	1. here, time, nose, take(s), home 2. love(s)
CCVC words *(then)*	stop(s), then, what, that, them, they, that
CCVCC words *(black)*	black, sniff(s), grass
Sentence length	2–11 (1 has 14 words)
Sentences per page	1–4
Number of words	200

Lesson	60
Book Title	***PETS***
Feature	**Examples from the Text**

Content words	pet, cat, dog, mouse, bird, fish, rabbit, pets
High-frequency words	this, is, my, it, a, I, like, our, we, love
Pronouns	this, my, it, I, our, we
Plurals	pets
Difficult word patterns	mouse
Difficult multisyllable words	rabbit
Words ending in *y* **Sounding like (1)** *i* **or (2)** *e*	1. my 2.
Words with vowel and *r*	bird, our
CVC words **Regular pattern** *(run)* **Other** *(how)*	1. pet, cat, dog 2.
VVC words *(out)*	our
CVCC words *(fish)*	bird, fish
CVCe words **Regular pattern** *(make)* **Other** *(have)*	1. like 2. love
CCVC words *(then)*	this
Sentence length	4–5
Sentences per page	3 (one page with 1)
Number of words	88

continues

Lesson	61
Book Title	***THREE LITTLE PIGS AND A BIG BAD WOLF***
Feature	**Examples from the Text**
Content words	once, three, pigs, needed, homes, first, pig, house, straw, fine, second, sticks, third, bricks, bad, wolf, let, I'll, huff, puff, blow, sister's, next, brother's, tried, huffed, puffed, plan, hello, splash, lived, happily, ever
High-frequency words	there*, were, little, they, new, the, made*, his, out, of, what, a, he, said, her, she, one, day, big, came, to, me, in, no, then, your, down, and, did, ran, away*, went, their, but, could*, not, so, up, with, had, too, after*
Pronouns	they, his, he, her, she, me, your
Prepositions	out, of, to, in, up, with
Words with inflectional endings	needed, tried, huffed, puffed, lived, happily
Contractions	I'll
Plurals	pigs, homes, sticks, bricks
Difficult word patterns	once, first, house, third, tried, huffed, puffed, splash
Difficult multisyllable words	second, sister's, brother's, hello, happily, after
Words with *a* as *schwa*	away
Words ending in *y* Sounding like (1) *i* or (2) *e*	1. 2. happily
Words with vowel and *r*	first, her, third, ever, after
Vowel patterns *ow, ay, ey*	they, day, blow, down, away, play
CVC words Regular pattern *(run)* Other *(how)*	1. pig, big, bad, let, did, ran, but, not, had, his 2. new, her, day
Onomatopoetic words	huff, puff, splash
CVV words *(see)*	too
VVC words *(out)*	out
VCC words *(all)*	and
CVCC words *(fish)*	wolf, huff, puff, down, next, went, with
CVVC words *(soap, foot)*	need(ed), said, your

CVCe words **Regular pattern** *(make)* **Other** *(have)*	1. were, home(s), made, fine, came 2. live(d)
CCVC words *(then)*	they, what, then, blow, plan, play
CCVCC words *(black)*	stick, third, brick
CCVCe words *(white)*	there
Sentence length	3–15
Sentences per page	1–4
Number of words	267

continues

Lesson	62
Book Title	*A BOX*
Feature	**Examples from the Text**
Content words	box, wheels, car, plates, cups, table, sail, boat, door, windows, house, puppets, stage, top, rocket, signs, store, doghouse
High-frequency words	we, got, a, big, put, on, the, now, is, and, made, for, then, new, too, this
Pronouns	we
Prepositions	on, for
Compound words	doghouse
Plurals	wheels, plates, cups, windows, puppets, signs
Difficult word patterns	wheels, house, signs
Difficult multisyllable words	table, windows, puppets, rocket, doghouse
Words with vowel and *r*	car, for, store
Vowel patterns *ow, ay, ey*	now, windows
CVC words **Regular pattern** *(run)* *Other (how)*	1. box, got, big, cup(s), top 2. put, now, car, for, new
CVV words *(see)*	too
VCC words *(all)*	and
CVVC words *(soap, foot)*	sail, boat, door
CCVVC words *(cream)*	wheel(s)
CVCe words **Regular pattern** *(make)* *Other (have)*	1. made 2.
CCVC words *(then)*	then, this
CCVCe words *(white)*	plate(s), stage, store
CVCCe words *(table, taste)*	table
Sentence length	4–9
Sentences per page	2–4
Number of words	118

Lesson	63
Book Title	***THE SOCCER GAME***
Feature	**Examples from the Text**

Labels/Names	Sam, Jesse, Papa
Content words	soccer, fast, jump, kick, ball, net, bugs, more, boys, past, kicked, stopped, didn't, help, each, other, looking, ant, hill, ants, red, black, six, legs, yelled, coming, roll, foot, save, gave, hard, smiled, team
High-frequency words	let's, play, said, was, good, at, he, liked, to, run, could, and, the, into*, I, want, too, you, do, but, see, if, can, me, it, go, in, then, have, back, had, get, come, on, an, were, they, looked, up, going, over, put, his, out, went, yes, we, did, no, just*, wanted, your, a, make
Pronouns	he, I, you, me, they, his, we, your
Prepositions	at, to, into, in, on, up, over
Words with inflectional endings	liked, kicked, stopped, looking, yelled, looked, coming, wanted, smiled, going
Compound words	into
Contractions	let's, didn't
Plurals	bugs, boys, ants, legs
Difficult word patterns	boys, each, other, coming, smiled
Difficult multisyllable words	soccer, Jesse, didn't, coming, other, over
Words with *a* as *schwa*	Papa
Words with vowel and *r*	soccer, more, other, hard, were, over
Vowel patterns *ow, ay, ey*	play, they
CVC words **Regular pattern** *(run)* **Other** *(how)*	1. let('s), Sam, run, net, bug(s), red, six, leg(s), but, can, had, get, his, yes, did 2. boy(s), put, was
CVV words *(see)*	too, you, see
VVC words *(out)*	out
VCC words *(all)*	ant, and
CVCC words *(fish)*	fast, jump, kick, ball, past, help, hill, yell(ed), roll, hard, want, back, went, just
CVVC words *(soap, foot)*	look(ed), team, said, good, your

continues

Appendix

CVCe words **Regular pattern** *(make)*	1. like(d), more, save, gave, make
Other *(have)*	2. come, have, were
CCVC words *(then)*	stop(ped), play, then, they
CCVCC words *(black)*	black
CCVCe words *(white)*	smile(d)
Sentence length	3–12
Sentences per page	1–5
Number of words	278

Lesson	64
Book Title	***BOOKS***
Feature	**Examples from the Text**

Labels/Names	Mom, Dad
Content words	cars, asked, book, snakes, bears, try, birds, bikes, trains, planes, read, books
High-frequency words	do, you, like, asked, yes, I, said, here, is, a, good, will, this, oh, and, love, to
Pronouns	I, you
Prepositions	to
Words with inflectional endings	asked
Plurals	books, cars, snakes, bears, birds, bikes, trains, planes,
Words ending in *y* **Sounding like (1) *i* or (2) *e***	1. try 2.
Words with vowel and *r*	cars, birds
CVC words **Regular pattern** *(run)* **Other** *(how)*	1. Mom, Dad, yes 2. car(s)
CVV words *(see)*	you
VCC words *(all)*	ask(ed), will, and
CVCC words *(fish)*	bird(s)
CVVC words *(soap, foot)*	said, good, book, bear(s), read
CCVVC words *(cream)*	train(s)
CVCe words **Regular pattern** *(make)* **Other** *(have)*	1. here, like, bike(s) 2. love
CCVC words *(then)*	this
CCVCe words *(white)*	snake(s), plane(s)
Sentence length	4–7, one page with 15
Sentences per page	1–2
Number of words	145

Appendix

continues

Lesson	65
Book Title	***BUNNY AND THE MONSTER***
Feature	**Examples from the Text**

Labels/Names	Rabbits, Grandma, Dad, Bunny, Sunny, Jack
Content words	ride, hop, far, hopped, under, fence, stomp, hole, pink, monster, behind, bush, black, white, tall, grass, long, lots, hair, car, home, pictures, three, lines
High-frequency words	one, day, the, went, for, a, stop*, said, you, can, go, little, but, do, not, and, they, who*, is, there, it's, run, into, she, saw, in, he, with, of, back, to, at, made, of, it, looked, like, this, no, did, we, see, some, look, same*, was, all
Pronouns	you, they, who, it, she, he, they, this, we
Prepositions	for, under, into, behind, in, with, to, at, of
Words with inflectional endings	hopped, looked
Compound words	Grandma, into
Contractions	it's
Plurals	rabbits, lots, pictures, lines
Difficult word patterns	pictures
Difficult multisyllable words	Bunny, Rabbits, monster, Grandma, Sunny, under, behind, pictures
Words ending in *y* Sounding like (1) *i* or (2) *e*	1. 2. Bunny, Sunny
Words with vowel and *r*	monster, for, far, under, car, pictures
Vowel patterns *ow, ay, ey*	day, they
CVC words Regular pattern *(run)* Other *(how)*	1. Dad, can, hop, but, not, run, did 2. day, for, far, saw, car, was
Onomatopoetic words	stomp
CVV words *(see)*	you, see
VCC words *(all)*	and, all
CVCC words *(fish)*	went, pink, bush, tall, long, with, back
CVVC words *(soap, foot)*	said, hair, look

CVCe words **Regular pattern *(make)*** **Other *(have)***	1. ride, hole, home, made, like, line(s), same 2. some
CCVC words *(then)*	stop, they, this
CCVCC words *(black)*	stomp, black, grass
CCVCe words *(white)*	there, white
CVCCe words *(table, taste)*	fence
Sentence length	3–9
Sentences per page	1–3
Number of words	161

continues

Lesson	66
Book Title	**THE POOL**
Feature	**Examples from the Text**

Labels/Names	Mouse, Frog, Dog, Pig, Goat, Cow
Content words	hot, jumped, pool, cool, jump, yelled
High-frequency words	was, so, she, into, the, too, he, saw, in, is, it, said, yes, then, and, I, am, can, with, you, looked, at, looks, will, no, this, little, are, big, but, ran, to, stop, out, they, did
Pronouns	she, he, it, I, you, this, they
Prepositions	into, in, with, at, to, out
Words with inflectional endings	jumped, looked, looks
Compound words	into
Words with vowel and *r*	are
Vowel patterns *ow, ay, ey*	cow, they
CVC words **Regular pattern** *(run)* **Other** *(how)*	1. hot, yes, dog, pig, can, big, but, ran, did 2. was, saw, cow
CVV words *(see)*	too, you
VVC words *(out)*	out
VCC words *(all)*	and
CVCC words *(fish)*	jump, with, will, yell(ed)
CVVC words *(soap, foot)*	pool, cool, said, goat, look(ed)
CCVC words *(then)*	frog, then, this, stop
Sentence length	3–9
Sentences per page	1–4
Number of words	141

Lesson	67
Book Title	**PICTURES OF HUGS**
Feature	**Examples from the Text**

Labels/Names	Meg, Hugs, Gram
Content words	pet, week, school, take, picture, share, crayons, paper, doesn't, more, cat, camera, show, use, toy, mouse, leaned, click, took, moved, that's, shoe, again, tail, chased, around, room, hard, every, time, these, maybe, use, once, puzzle, printed, side, didn't, help, held, sleeping
High-frequency words	it, was, at, had, to, a, of, she, got, her, and, some, this, look, like, said, but, could, not, make, good, work*, do, you, want, my, I, can, how*, yes, playing*, with, over, his, is, all, the, he, are, them, all, put, by*, do, me, asked, for, where, then, saw, him, up, when*
Pronouns	it, she, her, this, you, my, I, that, his, he, these, them, me, him
Prepositions	of, at, to, with, over, around, by, for, up
Words with inflectional endings	playing, leaned, moved, chased, printed, asked, sleeping
Compound words	around, maybe
Contractions	doesn't, that's, didn't, it's
Plurals	pictures, crayons
Difficult word patterns	school, could, mouse, leaned, shoe, again, around, once, asked
Difficult multisyllable words	picture(s), crayons, paper, doesn't, camera, again, every, puzzle, printed, sleeping
Words with *a* as *schwa*	camera, again, around
Words ending in *y* **Sounding like (1) *i* or (2) *e***	1. my, by 2. every
Words with vowel and *r*	pictures, her, paper, more, camera, over, hard, every, are, work, for
Vowel patterns *ow, ay, ey*	crayons, show, how, playing, maybe
CVC words **Regular pattern *(run)*** **Other *(how)***	1. pet, had, got, but, not, cat, can, yes, his, for, him 2. was, how, toy, put, saw
Onomatopoetic words	click
CVV words *(see)*	you
VCC words *(all)*	and, all, ask(ed)
CVCC words *(fish)*	want, hard, work, help, held

Appendix

continues

CVVC words *(soap, foot)*	week, look, said, good, lean(ed), took, tail, room
CCVVC words *(cream)*	sleep(ing)
CVCe words **Regular pattern** *(make)*	1. take, like, make, time, side
Other *(have)*	2. some, more, move(d)
CCVC words *(then)*	this, show, play(ing), that, them, then, when
CCVCC words *(black)*	click, print(ed)
CCVCe words *(white)*	share, chase(d)
Sentence length	3–12
Sentences per page	2–4
Number of words	230

Lesson	68
Book Title	***FARMER DAN'S DUCKS***
Feature	**Examples from the Text**

Labels/Names	Farmer Dan
Content words	two, ducks, cows, seen, hens, horses, pigs, sheep, grass
High-frequency words	looked, for, his, he, and, but, did, not, see, them, saw, the, have, you, my, said, no, yes, look, in
Pronouns	his, he, you
Prepositions	in, for
Words with inflectional endings	looked
Plurals	ducks, cows, hens, horses, pigs
Difficult multisyllable words	farmer, horses
Words ending in *y* **Sounding like (1) *i* or (2) *e***	1. my 2.
Words with vowel and *r*	farmer, for, horses
Vowel patterns *ow, ay, ey*	cows
CVC words **Regular pattern** *(run)* **Other** *(how)*	1. but, did, not, his, hen(s), pig(s), yes 2. for, saw, cow(s)
CVV words *(see)*	see, you
CVCC words *(fish)*	duck(s)
CVVC words *(soap, foot)*	look(ed), seen, said
CCVVC words *(cream)*	sheep
CVCe words **Regular pattern** *(make)* **Other** *(have)*	1. 2. have
CCVC words *(then)*	them
CCVCC words *(black)*	grass
CVCCe words *(table, taste)*	horse(s)
Sentence length	4–8
Sentences per page	2–3, one page with 1
Number of words	126

Appendix

continues

Lesson	69
Book Title	*THE BIG STORM*
Feature	**Examples from the Text**

Labels/Names	Orson
Content words	storm, coming, storms, table, getting, close, sky, dark, hid, behind, chair, started, rain, fat, raindrops, hit, window, under, sofa, rained, harder, squeezed, plant, fit, ball, light, lit, door, BAM, loud, hurt, ears, crawled, rug, CRASH, BOOM, basket, lights, house, best, place
High-frequency words	a, was, did, not, like, he, ran, the, got, very, it, to, big, went, but, of, up, that, at, all, in, back, of, out, then
Pronouns	he, it, that
Prepositions	under, behind, to, of, at, in, out, of
Words with inflectional endings	coming, getting, started, rained, harder, squeezed, crawled
Compound words	raindrops
Plurals	storms, raindrops, ears, lights
Difficult word patterns	coming, table, close, dark, window, squeezed, light, door, loud, hurt, Orson's, ears, crawled, house, place, was, very, out
Difficult multisyllable words	coming, table, getting, behind, raindrops, window, sofa, very
Words with *a* as *schwa*	sofa
Words ending in *y* **Sounding like (1) *i* or (2) *e***	1. sky 2. very
Words with vowel and *r*	storm, Orson, under, dark, started, harder, hurt
Vowel patterns *ow, ay, ey*	window
CVC words **Regular pattern *(run)*** **Other *(how)***	1. ran, get(ting), hid, fat, hit, fit, lit, BAM, rug, did, not, got, big, but 2. was
Onomatopoetic words	BAM, CRASH, BOOM
VVC words *(out)*	ear(s), out
VCC words *(all)*	all
CVCC words *(fish)*	dark, hard(er), ball, hurt, best, went, back
CVVC words *(soap, foot)*	rain, door, loud, BOOM

CCVVC words *(cream)*	chair
CVCe words **Regular pattern** *(make)* **Other** *(have)*	1. like 2. come (coming)
CCVC words *(then)*	drop (raindrops), that, then
CCVCC words *(black)*	storm, start(ed), plant, crawl(ed), CRASH
CCVCe words *(white)*	close, place
CVCCe words *(table, taste)*	table
Sentence length	3–10
Sentences per page	1–4
Number of words	123

continues

Appendix

183

Lesson	70
Book Title	*MY FIVE SENSES*
Feature	**Examples from the Text**
Content words	two, eyes, flowers, park, pretty, ears, hear, bird, sings, song, nose, smell, food, smells, mouth, taste, ice, cream, tastes, sweet, hands, touch, dog, feels, soft, five, senses
High-frequency words	I, have, use*, my, to, see, in, the, look, a, good, can, all, at
Pronouns	my, I
Prepositions	in, at
Words with inflectional endings	sings, smells, feels
Plurals	senses, eyes, flowers, ears, hands
Difficult word patterns	flowers, mouth, taste, touch
Difficult multisyllable words	senses, flowers
Words ending in *y* **Sounding like (1) *i* or (2) *e***	1. my 2. pretty
Words with vowel and *r*	flowers, park, ears, hear, bird
Vowel patterns *ow, ay, ey*	flowers
CVC words **Regular pattern** *(run)* **Other** *(how)*	1. dog, can 2. use
CVV words *(see)*	see
VCC words *(all)*	all
CVCC words *(fish)*	park, bird, sing(s), song, hand(s), soft
CVVC words *(soap, foot)*	look, hear, food, feel(s)
CCVVC words *(cream)*	cream, sweet
CVCe words **Regular pattern** *(make)* **Other** *(have)*	1. five, nose 2. have
CCVCC words *(black)*	smell
CVCCe words *(table, taste)*	sense(s), taste
Sentence length	4–7
Sentences per page	2
Number of words	127

Lesson	71
Book Title	***GOLDIE AND THE THREE BEARS***
Feature	**Examples from the Text**

Labels/Names	Goldie, Baby Bear, Mama Bear, Papa Bear
Content words	woods, house, door, open, hello, called, answered, wonder, lives, think, inside, hungry, bowls, soup, table, tried, hot, cold, right, ate, gone, cold, chairs, fireplace, high, low, broke, sleepy, wanted, nap, beds, bed, soft, hard, lay, down, fell, asleep, bears, home, hungry, walk, cried, broken, broke, someone, sleeping, girl, she's, fast, woke, heard, jumped, eek, gave, hug, kiss, never, again
High-frequency words	one, day, went, for, a, walk, in, the, soon*, she, came, to, little, was, but, no, I, who, here, said, I'll*, go, and, did, from, her, saw, three*, of, on, them, all, this, is, too, just, so, it, by, sat, he, got, his, my, who, don't*, know, that, it's, up, when, ran, out, way, as*, could, mother*, big, back
Pronouns	she, I, who, her, them, this, it, he, his, my, that
Prepositions	for, in, to, from, of, on, out
Words with inflectional endings	called, answered, lives, tried, sleepy, wanted, cried, broken, sleeping, jumped
Compound words	inside, fireplace, someone
Contractions	I'll, don't, it's, she's
Plurals	bowls, chairs, beds, bears, characters
Difficult word patterns	house, answered, wonder, three, right, heard, jumped, could, again
Difficult multisyllable words	open, hello, answered, wonder, hungry, table, sleepy, wanted, asleep, baby, fireplace, someone, sleeping, again, characters, narrator
Words with *a* as *schwa*	asleep, again
Words ending in *y* Sounding like (1) *i* or (2) *e*	1. my, by 2. hungry, sleepy, baby
Words with vowel and *r*	for, answered, wonder, her, hard, girl, mother, never
Vowel patterns *ow, ay, ey*	day, bowls, lay, down, know, way, play
CVC words Regular pattern *(run)* Other *(how)*	1. but, did, hot, sat, nap, bed, got, his, ran, big, hug 2. for, day, was, her, saw, low, lay, way
Onomatopoetic words	eek
CVV words *(see)*	too

continues

VVC words *(out)*	out
VCC words *(all)*	and, all,
CVCC words *(fish)*	walk, call(ed), bowl, cold, just, high, want(ed), soft, hard, down, fell, went, girl, fast, jump(ed), kiss, back
CVVC words *(soap, foot)*	soon, door, said, soup, bear
CCVVC words *(cream)*	tried, chair, sleep(y), cried
CVCe words **Regular pattern** *(make)* **Other** *(have)*	1. came, here, home, woke, gave 2. live(s), gone
CCVC words *(then)*	them, this, then, know, that, when, play
CCVCC words *(black)*	think
CCVCe words *(white)*	broke
CVCCe words *(table, taste)*	table
Sentence length	3–14
Sentences per page	2–6
Number of words	365

Lesson	72
Book Title	***HELPING MOM***
Feature	**Examples from the Text**

Labels/Names	Mom
Content words	flowers, garden, help, plant, fun, pushed, pulled, hard, these, pots, next, dig, holes, job, much, dirt, hot, keep, working, water, hose, turned, hold, watered, lot
High-frequency words	got, for, a, she, said, you, can, me, I, do, have, to, don't, know, how, but, come, on, it, will, be, so, and, was, work, let's, put, here, are, too, big, had, some, not, then, we, in, the, that, is, over, there, just, like, this, of
Pronouns	she, you, me, I, we
Prepositions	for, in, over, of
Words with inflectional endings	pushed, pulled, working, turned, watered
Contractions	let's, don't
Plurals	flowers, pots, holes
Difficult word patterns	flowers, pushed, pulled, water, know, there
Difficult multisyllable words	flowers, garden, watered
Words with vowel and *r*	for, are, over, flowers, garden, hard, work, dirt, water, turned
Vowel patterns *ow, ay, ey*	flowers, know, how
CVC words **Regular pattern** *(run)* **Other** *(how)*	1. Mom, fun, let('s), pot(s), dig, job, hot, lot, got, can, but, put, big, had, not 2. for, how, was
CVV words *(see)*	you, too
VCC words *(all)*	and
CVCC words *(fish)*	help, push(ed), pull(ed), hard, work, next, much, dirt, turn(ed), hold, will, just
CVVC words *(soap, foot)*	keep, said
CVCe words **Regular pattern** *(make)* **Other** *(have)*	1. hole(s), hose, here, like 2. have, come, some
CCVC words *(then)*	know, then, that, this
CCVCC words *(black)*	plant
CCVCe words *(white)*	these, there
Sentence length	1–10
Sentences per page	1–5
Number of words	165

continues

Appendix

Lesson	73
Book Title	***PAPA'S BIRTHDAY***
Feature	**Examples from the Text**

Labels/Names	Sam, Jesse, Papa, rocket ship, race car
Content words	Papa's, birthday, Sam, Jesse, Papa, present, shh, quiet, hear, outside, rocket, ship, blast, space, loved, rockets, costs, much, I'd, race, car, cars, cost, lot, dimes, penny, quarter, money, computer, basketball, it's, old, doesn't, loves, read, book, even, card, beautiful, paper, paint, crayons, drew, painted, red
High-frequency words	it, was, and, wanted, to, give*, a, let's, him, he, will, love, said, what, can, we, asked, have, be, or*, us, so, went, get, all, off, into, too, like, loved, how, does*, I, two*, had, don't, very, of, my, you, do, know, make, yes, for, his, got, big, on, just
Pronouns	it, him, he, what, we, us, I, my, you
Prepositions	outside, to, into, of, for, on
Words with inflectional endings	Papa's, wanted, asked, loved, costs, does, loves, painted
Compound words	birthday, outside, basketball, into
Contractions	let's, I'd, it's, doesn't, don't
Plurals	rockets, cars, dimes, crayons
Difficult word patterns	want(ed), quiet, hear, does, quarter, money, love, have, even, drew, said, what, how, two, very, much, know
Difficult multisyllable words	birthday, wanted, present, quiet, outside, rocket, quarter, money, computer, basketball, beautiful, paper, crayons, painted, very
Words with *a* as *schwa*	Papa (final *a*)
Words ending in *y* **Sounding like (1) *i* or (2) *e***	1. my 2. penny
Words with vowel and *r*	birthday, car, quarter, computer, card, paper, or, for
Vowel patterns *ow, ay, ey*	know, how, birthday, money
CVC words **Regular pattern *(run)*** **Other *(how)***	1. Sam, let('s), lot, red, him, can, get, had, yes, got, big 2. day (birthday), car, for, was, how
Onomatopoetic words	shh
CVV words *(see)*	too, you
VVC words *(out)*	out (outside)

VCC words *(all)*	ask(ed), off, old, and, all
CVCC words *(fish)*	want(ed), cost, much, ball (basketball), card, will, went, just
CVVC words *(soap, foot)*	hear, read, book, said
CVCe words **Regular pattern** *(make)* **Other** *(have)*	1. side (outside), race, dime(s), like, make 2. give, love, have
CCVC words *(then)*	ship, know, drew, what
CCVCC words *(black)*	blast
CCVCe words *(white)*	space
Sentence length	1–12
Sentences per page	1–8
Number of words	249

Appendix

continues

Lesson	74
Book Title	*THE STORM*
Feature	**Examples from the Text**

Labels/Names	Bunny, Hoppy
Content words	storm, coming, bam, paws, ears, hid, under, blanket, scared, chair, bed, thunder, hopped, peeked, himself, eyes, wide, open, boom, hurt, feel, better, fast, any, more
High-frequency words	a, was, put, her, over, she, under*, little, I, want, said, him, to, give, me, a, big, then, will, not, be, in, his, got, out, of, and, went, get, but, the, back, at, he, all, by, were, looked, it, is, just, can't, you, can, make, ran, very
Pronouns	her, she, I, him, me, his, he, himself, it, you
Prepositions	over, under, to, in, out, of, at, by
Words with inflectional endings	coming, scared
Compound words	himself
Contractions	can't
Plurals	paws, ears, eyes
Difficult word patterns	hopped, peeked, eyes, looked, boom, can't, feel
Difficult multisyllable words	coming, bunny, under, blanket, thunder, himself, open, better
Words ending in *y* **Sounding like (1) *i* or (2) *e***	1. by 2. Bunny, Hoppy, very, any
Words with vowel and *r*	storm, her, over, under, thunder, were, hurt, better, very, more
CVC words **Regular pattern** *(run)* **Other** *(how)*	1. bam, hid, him, big, hug, not, his, got, bed, get, but, hop (hopped), hid, can, ran 2. put, her, was, paw(s)
Onomatopoetic words	bam, boom
CVV words *(see)*	you
VVC words *(out)*	out
VCC words *(all)*	and, all
CVCC words *(fish)*	want, will, went, back, just, hurt, fast
CVVC words *(soap, foot)*	said, peek(ed), boom, feel, look(ed)
CCVVC words *(cream)*	chair

Word Analysis Charts, *continued*

CVCe words **Regular pattern** *(make)* **Other** *(have)*	1. wide, make, more 2. give, were
CCVC words *(then)*	then
CCVCC words *(black)*	storm
CCVCe words *(white)*	scare(d)
Sentence length	3–11
Sentences per page	1–4
Number of words	154

continues

Lesson	75
Book Title	***BABY BIRD***
Feature	**Examples from the Text**

Content words	once, baby, bird, small, beak, legs, wings, warm, happy, something, happened, began, grow, getting, stronger, longer, bigger, grew, much, more, room, lot(s), space, ouch, long, peck, strong, sharp, pecked, crack, egg, free, hop, flap, bug
High-frequency words	there, was, a, the, had, she, very, but, and, then, to, oh, my, said, is, are, too, look, at, me, I, am, if, will, run, out, of, here, this, just, know, big, for, what, can, do, with, get, me, did, not, stop, got, now, have, mother
Pronouns	she, my, me, I, this
Prepositions	to, at, of, for, with
Words with inflectional endings	happened, getting, stronger, longer, bigger, pecked
Compound words	something
Plurals	legs, wings
Difficult word patterns	once, ouch, know, strong
Difficult multisyllable words	happy, something, happened, getting, stronger, longer, bigger
Words ending in *y* **Sounding like (1)** *i* **or (2)** *e*	1. my 2. baby, very, happy
Words with vowel and *r*	bird, warm, stronger, longer, bigger, more, are, for, sharp, mother
Vowel patterns *ow, ay, ey*	grow, know, now
CVC words **Regular pattern** *(run)* **Other** *(how)*	1. had, leg(s), but, run, lot, for, big, can, get, did, not, got, hop, bug 2. was, now
Onomatopoetic words	crack
CVV words *(see)*	too
VVC words *(out)*	out
VCC words *(all)*	and, egg
CVCC words *(fish)*	bird, wing(s), warm, much, will, just, long, peck
CVVC words *(soap, foot)*	beak, said, look, room
CVCe words **Regular pattern** *(make)* **Other** *(have)*	1. more, here 2. have

CCVC words *(then)*	then, grow, grew, this, know, what, stop, flap
CCVCC words *(black)*	small, sharp, crack
CCVCe words *(white)*	there, space
Sentence length	3–12
Sentences per page	5–7 (1 on last page)
Number of words	251

continues

Lesson	76
Book Title	*LIZZY*
Feature	**Examples from the Text**

Labels/Names	Lizzy, Ben, Anna, Mom
Content words	pet, lizard, cage, must, hiding, couch, rug, chair, plant, table, plan, strawberry, hi
High-frequency words	was, not, in, her, where, is, asked, she, be, said, good, at, let's, look, on, the, I, don't, see, did, go, under, have, a, come, with, me, may*, have, yes, here, big, put, and
Pronouns	her, she, I, me, in
Prepositions	at, on, under, with, in
Words with inflectional endings	asked, hiding
Contractions	let's, don't
Difficult word patterns	couch, asked
Difficult multisyllable words	lizard, table, strawberry
Words with *a* as *schwa*	lizard
Words ending in *y* **Sounding like (1) *i* or (2) *e***	1. 2. Lizzy, strawberry
Words with vowel and *r*	lizard, under
Vowel patterns *ow, ay, ey*	may
CVC words **Regular pattern** *(run)* **Other** *(how)*	1. pet, not, let('s), did, rug, Mom 2. was, put
CVV words *(see)*	see
VCC words *(all)*	ask(ed), and
CVCC words *(fish)*	must, with
CVVC words *(soap, foot)*	said, good, look
CCVVC words *(cream)*	chair
CVCe words **Regular pattern** *(make)* **Other** *(have)*	1. cage 2. have, come
CCVC words *(then)*	plan
CCVCC words *(black)*	plant

CCVCe words *(white)*	where
CVCCe words *(table, taste)*	table
CVVCC words *(paint)*	couch
Sentence length	4–9
Sentences per page	1–4
Number of words	155

continues

Appendix

Lesson	77
Book Title	***THE GOAT IN THE GARDEN***
Feature	**Examples from the Text**

Labels/Names	Goat, Dog, Duck, Cow, Ant
Content words	long, ago, farmer, wife, planted, garden, ate, plants, barked, kicked, farmer's, quacked, mooed, sad, soon, would, nothing, help, ant, tiny, watch, climbed, bit, ouch, cried, again, thank, saved, stay, keep
High-frequency words	a, and, his, one, day, went, into, the, stop, said, but, let's, get, he, will, make, go, away, so, at, out, of, she, where, is, too, were, they, have, eat, I, can, little, how, you, us, are, just, up, then, back, ran, our, like, it, here
Pronouns	his, he, she, they, I, you, us, our, it
Prepositions	in, into, to, on, at, of, up, out
Words with inflectional endings	planted, kicked, quacked, mooed, climbed, cried, saved
Compound words	into, nothing
Contractions	let's
Plurals	plants
Difficult word patterns	quacked, mooed, would, watch, soon, ouch, again
Difficult multisyllable words	garden, farmer, planted, farmer's, nothing, again
Words with *a* as *schwa*	again
Words ending in *y* Sounding like (1) *I* or (2) *e*	1. 2. tiny
Words with vowel and *r*	garden, farmer, barked, were, are
Vowel patterns *ow, ay, ey*	day, away, cow, they, how, stay
CVC words Regular pattern *(run)* Other *(how)*	1. his, but, let('s), get, dog, sad, can, bit, ran 2. day, cow, how
CVV words *(see)*	too, you
VVC words *(out)*	eat, out, our
VCC words *(all)*	and, ant
CVCC words *(fish)*	long, went, will, bark(ed), kick, duck, help, just, back
CVVC words *(soap, foot)*	goat, said, soon, keep

CVCe words **Regular pattern** *(make)* **Other** *(have)*	1. wife, make, save(d), like, here 2. were, have
CCVC words *(then)*	stop, they, then, stay, play
CCVCC words *(black)*	plant(ed), climb(ed), thank
CCVCe words *(white)*	where
Sentence length	3–13
Sentences per page	1–4
Number of words	227

Appendix

continues

Lesson	78
Book Title	*A SURPRISE FOR MOM*
Feature	**Examples from the Text**

Labels/Names	Mom, Dad
Content words	market, surprise, tomatoes, carrots, potatoes, peppers, corn, home, pot, filled, water, spoon, time, mixed, soup, soon, hot
High-frequency words	and, I, went, to, the, we, wanted, make, a, for, got, some, like, eat, too, from, big, he, it, with, was, put, in, then, liked, she, loved
Pronouns	I, we, he, it, she
Prepositions	for, to, in, with
Words with inflectional endings	wanted, liked, loved, mixed, filled
Plurals	tomatoes, potatoes, carrots, peppers
Difficult word patterns	mixed
Difficult multisyllable words	surprise, tomatoes, potatoes, carrots, peppers, market, water
Words with vowel and *r*	surprise, market, for, peppers, corn, water
CVC words **Regular pattern** *(run)* **Other** *(how)*	1. mom, dad, pot, big, hot, mix(ed) 2. put, hot, got
CVV words *(see)*	too
VCC words *(all)*	and
CVCC words *(fish)*	went, corn, fill(ed), with, want(ed),
CVVC words *(soap, foot)*	soup, soon
CVCe words **Regular pattern** *(make)* **Other** *(have)*	1. like, make, time, home 2. love(d), some
CCVC words *(then)*	then, from
Sentence length	4–9
Sentences per page	1–3
Number of words	177

Lesson	79
Book Title	*HOW FROGS GROW*
Feature	**Examples from the Text**
Content words	frog, lays, eggs, water, many, tadpole, tadpoles, baby, frogs, fish, tails, legs, grow, short, long, yet, longer, shorter, grown, lay
High-frequency words	this, mother, in, the, are, little, there, come, out, of, do, to, not, look, like, they, have, and, get, up, very, no, now, it, can, is, a, from
Pronouns	this, they, it
Prepositions	in, of, up, to
Words with inflectional endings	lays, longer, shorter, larger
Plurals	frogs, eggs, tadpoles, tails, legs
Difficult word patterns	grown
Difficult multisyllable words	water, tadpoles, longer, shorter, larger
Words ending in *y* **Sounding like (1) *i* or (2) *e***	1. 2. many, baby, very
Words with vowel and *r*	mother, water, are, short, longer, shorter, very, larger
Vowel patterns *ow, ay, ey*	how, grow, lay, they, now, grown
CVC words **Regular pattern** *(run)* **Other** *(how)*	1. not, leg(s), yet, get, can 2. how, lay, now
VVC words *(out)*	out
VCC words *(all)*	egg, and
CVCC words *(fish)*	fish, long
CVVC words *(soap, foot)*	tail(s)
CVCe words **Regular pattern** *(make)* **Other** *(have)*	1. like 2. come, have
CCVC words *(then)*	frog, grow, this, grew, from
CCVCC words *(black)*	short, grown
CCVCe words *(white)*	there
CVCCe words *(table, taste)*	large(r)
Sentence length	4–9
Sentences per page	2–4
Number of words	116

continues

Appendix

Lesson	80
Book Title	***BRAVE TACO***
Feature	**Examples from the Text**
Labels/Names	Taco, Orson
Content words	red, thing, noise, vroom, barked, didn't, woof, more, hid, behind, chair, again, under, table, time, bed, until
High-frequency words	a, big, made, he, and, at, the, but, stop, ran, away, under, did, not, this, give, up, went
Pronouns	he
Prepositions	at, behind, under, this, up
Words with inflectional endings	barked
Contractions	didn't
Difficult word patterns	noise, again
Difficult multisyllable words	didn't, behind, again, under, until
Words with *a* as *schwa*	away, again
Words with vowel and *r*	barked, more, under
Vowel patterns *ow, ay, ey*	away
CVC words **Regular pattern *(run)*** **Other *(how)***	1. big, red, ran, hid, did, not, run, bed 2.
Onomatopoetic words	vroom, woof
VCC words *(all)*	and
CVCC words *(fish)*	bark(ed), went
CCVVC words *(cream)*	vroom, chair
CVCe words **Regular pattern *(make)*** **Other *(have)***	1. made, more, time 2. give
CCVC words *(then)*	stop, this
CCVCC words *(black)*	thing
CVCCe words *(table, taste)*	table
Sentence length	2–9
Sentences per page	1–3
Number of words	129

Lesson	81
Book Title	***THE SKUNK WITH NO STRIPES***
Feature	**Examples from the Text**

Labels/Names	Brother Skunk, Sister, Skunk, Little Skunk
Content words	baby, skunks, lived, soft, black, fur, long, bushy, tail, white, stripes, maybe, skunk, cat, purr, squirrel, tree, bear, short, stubby, followed, home, cried, spray, stinky, smell, raised, sprayed, roared, ran, wow, yucky, sure
High-frequency words	three, with, their, mother, look, at, me, said, I, have, a, two, down, my, back, little, looked, and, he, but, do, not, all, you, so, are, she, has, no, am, asked, can, run, up, that, go, away, or, will, with, like, his, then, on, oh, ran, for
Pronouns	their, me, I, my, he, you, she, his
Prepositions	with, at, up, on, for
Words with inflectional endings	lived, bushy, looked, asked, stubby, followed, cried, stinky, raised, sprayed, roared, yucky
Compound words	maybe
Plurals	skunks, stripes
Difficult word patterns	asked, squirrel, raised, sprayed, sure
Difficult multisyllable words	baby, brother, sister, maybe, bushy, stubby, followed, stinky
Words with *a* as *schwa*	away
Words ending in *y* **Sounding like (1) *i* or (2) *e***	1. my 2. baby, bushy, stubby, stinky, yucky
Words with vowel and *r*	mother, brother, fur, sister, are, purr, squirrel, short, or, for, sure
Vowel patterns *ow, ay, ey*	down, maybe, followed, away, spray
CVC words **Regular pattern *(run)*** **Other *(how)***	1. but, not, cat, has, run, can, his, ran, for 2. fur, wow
Onomatopoetic words	purr
CVV words *(see)*	you
VCC words *(all)*	all, ask(ed)
CVCC words *(fish)*	with, soft, long, down, back, purr, will, yuck(y)
CVVC words *(soap, foot)*	look, said, bear, roar(ed)

Appendix

continues

201

CVCe words **Regular pattern** *(make)* **Other** *(have)*	1. home, like 2. live(d), have, sure
CCVC words *(then)*	that, then
CCVCC words *(black)*	skunk, black, short, stink(y), smell
CCVCe words *(white)*	white
Sentence length	4–12
Sentences per page	2–5
Number of words	333

Lesson	82
Book Title	*THE TREE HOUSE*
Feature	**Examples from the Text**
Labels/Names	Bear, Mouse, Rabbit, Squirrel, Raccoon, Owl
Content words	making, tree, house, help, cut, wood, busy, himself, carry, rabbit, carried, squirrel, lift, lifted, raccoon, hammer, nails, hammered, owl, paint, much, painted, last, heard, noise, chair, coming, helping
High-frequency words	saw, I, am, a, said, will, you, me, the, can't, too, all, by, so, into, the, asked, at, had, his, but, he, was, then, looked, down, up, we, have, for, your, were
Pronouns	I, you, me, himself, his, he, we, your
Prepositions	by, into, at, up, for
Words with inflectional endings	making, carried, lifted, hammered, asked, painted, heard, looked, coming, helping
Compound words	himself, into
Contractions	can't
Plurals	chairs, nails
Difficult word patterns	house, mouse, busy, squirrel, asked, paint, heard, noise,
Difficult multisyllable words	busy, himself, rabbit, carry, raccoon, hammer, hammered, painted, coming, helping
Words ending in *y* **Sounding like (1) *i* or (2) *e***	1. by 2. busy, carry
Words with vowel and *r*	squirrel, hammer, for, were
Vowel patterns *ow, ay, ey*	owl
CVC words **Regular pattern** *(run)* **Other** *(how)*	1. cut, had, his, but 2. saw, was, for
CVV words *(see)*	too
VCC words *(all)*	all, owl, ask(ed)
CVCC words *(fish)*	will, help, lift, much, last
CVVC words *(soap, foot)*	said, wood, your, look(ed)
CCVVC words *(cream)*	chair

continues

CVCe words Regular pattern *(make)*	1.
Other *(have)*	2. have, were
CCVC words *(then)*	then
Sentence length	3–12
Sentences per page	1–5
Number of words	198

Lesson	83
Book Title	**THE GINGERBREAD MAN**
Feature	**Examples from the Text**

Labels/Names	Gingerbread Man
Content words	once, upon, time, old, woman, lived, deep, woods, cut, gave, eyes, nose, mouth, inside, oven, bake, hungry, ready, I'll, peeked, jumped, cried, laughed, fast, catch, road, met, pig, cow, river, across, fox, take, sly, jump, tail, won't, fox's, getting, wet, stay, dry, right, yum, end
High-frequency words	a, little, and, man*, in, the, one, day, said, let's, make, so, they, made, out, then, she, two, put, him, to, I'm. is, eat, look, out, you, can't, me, he, ran, away, come, back, after, run, as, can, down, stop, want, but, from, I, good, came, oh, no, how, will, get, saw, on, my, will, up, am, there, into, that, was, of
Pronouns	they, she, him, you, me, he, I, my,
Prepositions	in, out, inside, to, from, on, up, of
Words with inflectional endings	lived, peeked, jumped, laughed, getting
Compound words	upon, inside
Contractions	let's, I'm, I'll, can't, won't
Plurals	woods, eyes, characters
Difficult word patterns	once, eyes, mouth, ready, laughed, catch
Difficult multisyllable words	gingerbread, woman, hungry, ready, away, after, river, across, characters, narrator
Words with *a* as *schwa*	away, across
Words ending in *y* **Sounding like (1) *i* or (2) *e***	1. sly, my, dry 2. hungry, ready
Words with vowel and *r*	gingerbread, after, river
Vowel patterns *ow, ay, ey*	day, they, away, down, cow, how, stay, play
CVC words **Regular pattern** *(run)* **Other** *(how)*	1. man, let('s), cut, him, ran, run, can, met, pig, but, get, fox, wet, yum 2. put, cow, how, saw, was
CVV words *(see)*	you
VVC words *(out)*	eat, out
VCC words *(all)*	old, and, end
CVCC words *(fish)*	jump, back, fast, down, want, will

continues

Appendix

CVVC words *(soap, foot)*	deep, said, look, peek(ed), road, good, tail
CVCe words **Regular pattern** *(make)*	1. time, make, made, gave, nose, bake, came, take
Other *(have)*	2. live(d), come
CCVC words *(then)*	they, then, stop, from, that
CCVCe words *(white)*	there
Sentence length	1–14
Sentences per page	1–8
Number of words	447

Lesson	84
Book Title	***OUT FOR LUNCH***
Feature	**Examples from the Text**

Labels/Names	Mom
Content words	mom, grandma, brother, pizza, think, I'll, cheese, soup, chicken, hot, dog(s), bun, peanut, butter, jelly, home, food, smelled, may, try, sure, slice, plate, gave, cup, okay, thanks
High-frequency words	let's, go, out, to, eat, said, my, so, and, I, went, for, too, like, have, a, some, on, they, don't, do, you, want, or, no, just, at, we, got, the, it, good, your, asked, she, put, of, yes, me, in, he, then, his, that, was, give, had, little, big
Pronouns	my, I, they, we, your, she, me, he, you
Prepositions	out, for, to, on, at, of, in
Words with inflectional endings	smelled, asked, thanks
Compound words	grandma, peanut
Contractions	let's, I'll, don't
Plurals	dogs
Difficult word patterns	lunch, pizza, peanut, asked
Difficult multisyllable words	grandma, brother, pizza, chicken, peanut, butter, jelly
Words with *a* as *schwa*	grandma, pizza
Words ending in *y* Sounding like (1) *i* or (2) *e*	1. my, try 2. jelly
Words with vowel and *r*	for, brother, butter, sure
Vowel patterns *ow, ay, ey*	they, may, okay
CVC words Regular pattern *(run)* Other *(how)*	1. let('s), mom, hot, dog, bun, got, yes, cup, had, big 2. for, may, put, was
CVV words *(see)*	too, you
VVC words *(out)*	eat, out
VCC words *(all)*	and, ask(ed)
CVCC words *(fish)*	went, want, just
CVVC words *(soap, foot)*	said, soup, food, good, your

continues

Appendix

CVCe words **Regular pattern** *(make)* **Other** *(have)*	1. like, home, gave 2. have, some, sure, give
CCVC words *(then)*	they, then, that
CCVCC words *(black)*	think, smell(ed), thank(s)
CCVCe words *(white)*	slice, plate
CCVVCe words *(cheese)*	cheese
Sentence length	3–14
Sentences per page	1–4
Number of words	235

Lesson	85
Book Title	***DINNER FOR MAISY***
Feature	**Examples from the Text**

Labels/Names	Maisy, Dana, Nate, Dad, Dr. Green
Content words	every, dinner, dish, ate, food, begged, more, until, didn't, bite, wouldn't, next, still, sniffed, upset, why, won't, must, sick, worry, we'll, take, vet, wagged, tail, what's, matter, know, checked, gained, pounds, doctor, eating, something, took, home, maybe, old, bags, bag, dog, basement, smiled, called
High-frequency words	loved, to, eat, day, at, she, ran, her, all, and, for, was, the, same, one, put, in, just, looked, your, said, but, walked, away, were, asked, be, don't, when, saw, you, know, loves, has, three, they, this, is, too, there, are, some, new, went, get, oh, no, look, that, came, out, of, I, who, did, it, me
Pronouns	she, her, your, you, they, this, that, I, it, me
Prepositions	for, to, at, in, of
Words with inflectional endings	loved, begged, looked, sniffed, walked, asked, wagged, loved, checked, gained, eating, smiled, called,
Compound words	something, maybe
Contractions	didn't, wouldn't, won't, we'll, what's
Plurals	pounds, bags
Difficult word patterns	asked, three, pounds
Difficult multisyllable words	dinner, until, upset, worry, doctor, eating, basement, something, maybe
Words with *a* as *schwa*	away
Words ending in *y* Sounding like (1) *i* or (2) *e*	1. why 2. every, worry
Words with vowel and *r*	dinner, for, every, her, more, were, doctor, are
Vowel patterns *ow, ay, ey*	day, away, they
CVC words Regular pattern *(run)* Other *(how)*	1. ran, beg (begged) but, dad, vet, wag (wagged) has, bag, dog, get, did 2. day, for, her, was, put, saw, new
CVV words *(see)*	you, too
VVC words *(out)*	eat, out
VCC words *(all)*	all, and, old, ask(ed)

continues

Appendix

CVCC words *(fish)*	dish, just, next, walk(ed), must, sick, went, call(ed)
CVVC words *(soap, foot)*	food, look, your, said, tail, took, gain(ed)
CVCe words **Regular pattern** *(make)* **Other** *(have)*	1. same, bite, take, home, came 2. more, love(d), were
CCVC words *(then)*	when, know, they, this, that
CCVCC words *(black)*	still, sniff(ed), check(ed)
CCVCe words *(white)*	smile (smiled)
Sentence length	2–12
Sentences per page	1–5
Number of words	239

Lesson	86
Book Title	***JUST WAIT AND SEE***
Feature	**Examples from the Text**
Labels/Names	Father Beaver, Little Beaver, Baby Beaver, Mother Beaver
Content words	yard, wood, wait, house, tell, close, eyes, open, color, paint
High-frequency words	was, working*, in, the, he, making*, something*, out, of, said, what, are, you, is, it, for, me, and, just, worked*, asked, see, came, out, will, not, us, then, your, some, more,* look, at, this, little, them
Pronouns	he, you, it, me, us, your, this, them
Prepositions	in, of, for, out, at
Words with inflectional endings	working, making, worked, asked
Compound words	something
Plurals	eyes
Difficult word patterns	Father, Beaver, house, asked, baby, paint
Difficult multisyllable words	Father, Beaver, working, making, something, little, Mother, Baby, open, color
Words with vowel and *r*	Father, yard, are, for, Mother, working, worked, more, color
CVC words **Regular pattern** *(run)* **Other** *(how)*	1. not 2. was, for
CVV words *(see)*	see, you
VVC words *(out)*	out
VCC words *(all)*	and, ask(ed)
CVCC words *(fish)*	just, work (working) (worked), yard, will, tell
CVVC words *(soap, foot)*	wait, said, your, look, wood
CVCe words **Regular pattern** *(make)* **Other** *(have)*	1. make (making), came 2. some, more
CCVC words *(then)*	what, then, this, them
Sentence length	4–11
Sentences per page	1–5
Number of words	185

continues

Lesson	87
Book Title	***IN WINTER***
Feature	**Examples from the Text**
Content words	winter, bird, cold, fly, warm, sunny, place, snowy, bat, snow, nap, cave, long, friends, frog, icy, mud, ice, sleep, chilly, time, squirrel, snuggle, keep, beaver, covers, pond, mind, swim, den, keeps, nice, cozy, white, rabbit, grow, fur, hide, feet, hop, animals, coat, hat, scarf, mittens, outside
High-frequency words	what, do, you, in, asked, the, girl*, said, is, here, I, don't, like, to, be, fly*, away, for, go, a, and, stay*, out, of, my, all, there, too, it's, me, under, with, we, each*, other*, it, go, into, lets*, big, help*, on, put, they, then, play
Pronouns	you, I, my, me, we
Prepositions	in, to, for, out, of, with, under, it, into, on
Words with inflectional endings	asked, sunny, snowy, chilly, covers, keeps, lets
Compound words	into, outside, away
Contractions	don't, it's
Plurals	friends, animals, mittens
Difficult word patterns	asked, icy, squirrel, each, beaver
Difficult multisyllable words	winter, sunny, snowy, under, chilly, snuggle, other, beaver, into, cozy, rabbit, animals, mittens, outside, away
Words with *a* as *schwa*	away
Words ending in *y* Sounding like (1) *i* or (2) *e*	1. fly, my 2. sunny, snowy, icy, chilly, cozy
Words with vowel and *r*	winter, girl, bird, for, warm, under, squirrel, other, beaver, covers, fur, scarf
Vowel patterns *ow, ay, ey*	away, snowy, snow, stay, grow, play, they
CVC words Regular pattern *(run)* Other *(how)*	1. sun (sunny), bat, nap, mud, den, let(s), big, hop, hat 2. for, fur, put
CVV words *(see)*	you, too
VVC words *(out)*	out
VCC words *(all)*	and, all, ask(ed)
CVCC words *(fish)*	girl, bird, cold, warm, long, with, pond, mind, help
CVVC words *(soap, foot)*	said, keep, feet, coat

CCVVC words *(cream)*	sleep
CVCe words **Regular pattern** *(make)*	1. here, like, cave, time, nice, hide
Other *(have)*	2.
CCVC words *(then)*	what, snow, stay, frog, swim, grow, they, then, play
CCVCC words *(black)*	scarf, chill(y)
CCVCe words *(white)*	place, there, white
CCVVCC words *(friend)*	friend(s)
Sentence length	4–9
Sentences per page	1–5
Number of words	263

continues

Lesson	88
Book Title	***ALL ABOUT ANIMAL BABIES***
Feature	**Examples from the Text**
Content words	animal, moms, care, babies, robin, feeds, baby, birds, worms, kangaroo, carries, rides, pouch, hippo, teaches, shows, swim, lion, cleans, licks, keep, clean, bear, catch, fish, whale, swims, air, chimp, bugs, dad, penguin, keeps, warm, holds, feet
High-frequency words	take*, of, their, this, mother, her, the, eat, a, in, she, how, to, it, with, up, get, can, too, father*, his, he, on
Pronouns	their, this, her, she, it, his, he
Prepositions	in, to, with, up, on
Words with inflectional endings	babies, eats, carries, rides, teaches, shows, cleans, licks, swims, keeps, holds
Plurals	moms, babies, birds, worms, bugs
Difficult word patterns	babies, carries, pouch, teaches, catch, father, penguin
Difficult multisyllable words	animal, babies, robin, kangaroo, carries, hippo, teaches, penguin
Words with *a* as *schwa*	kangaroo
Words ending in *y* Sounding like (1) *i* or (2) *e*	1. 2. baby
Words with vowel and *r*	mother, her, bird, worm, father, warm
Vowel patterns *ow, ay, ey*	shows, how
CVC words Regular pattern *(run)* Other *(how)*	1. mom(s), get, bug(s), dad, can, his 2. her, how
CVV words *(see)*	too
VVC words *(out)*	eat(s), air
CVCC words *(fish)*	bird, worm, lick(s), fish, with, warm, hold(s)
CVVC words *(soap, foot)*	feed(s), lion, keep, bear, keep(s), feet
CCVVC words *(cream)*	their, clean
CVCe words Regular pattern *(make)* Other *(have)*	1. take, care, ride(s) 2.
CCVC words *(then)*	this, show(s), swim

CCVCC words *(black)*	chimp
CCVCe words *(white)*	whale
Sentence length	6–12
Sentences per page	2–3
Number of words	135

continues

Lesson	89
Book Title	***THE GECKO THAT CAME TO SCHOOL***
Feature	**Examples from the Text**
Labels/Names	Annie, Tess, Jen, David, Mrs. Peck, Mrs. Wells
Content words	peeking, pocket, pet, gecko, cute, school, mad, bring, best, ever, really, fast, showed, arm, leg, across, floor, yelled, kids, tried, catch, room, friends, cried, grabbed, fell, raced, lunchroom, screamed, chairs, crashed, milk, spilled, dropped, glasses, mashed, potatoes, art, room, teacher, screamed, papers, flew, paint, cans, hall, back, tumbled, top, sorry, giggling, that's
High-frequency words	was, into, her, what, is, in, your, asked, come, and, see, said, looked, too, it's, my, new, he, but, you, can't, have, a, will, get, I, just, had, to, him, so, much*, fun*, can, run, then, the, them, how, could, ran, down, stop, that, little, was, out, of, after, there, for, over, all, goes*, on, wanted, off, I'm, now, look, at, us, not, where, did, go
Pronouns	her, he, you, my I, him, them, us
Prepositions	to, into, in, down, of, for, over, on, off, at, out
Words with inflectional endings	peeking, asked, looked, really, showed, tried, yelled, cried, grabbed, raced, screamed, crashed, spilled, dropped, mashed, goes, yelled, screamed, wanted, giggling
Compound words	into, across, lunchroom
Contractions	it's, can't, I'm, that's
Plurals	kids, friends, chairs, glasses, potatoes, papers, cans
Difficult word patterns	school, your, asked, could, across, catch, little, screamed, potatoes, goes, teacher, screamed, paint, tumbled, giggling
Difficult multisyllable words	gecko, pocket, really, after, lunchroom, little, glasses, potatoes, teacher, papers, tumbled, sorry, giggling
Words with *a* as *schwa*	across
Words ending in *y* **Sounding like (1) *i* or (2) *e***	1. my 2. sorry
Words with vowel and *r*	ever, after, for, over, art, papers
Vowel patterns *ow, ay, ey*	showed, show, how, down, now, okay
CVC words **Regular pattern** *(run)* **Other** *(how)*	1. pet, but, get, mad, had, him, fun, can, run, ran, leg, kid(s), for, can(s), top, not, did 2. was, her, new, how, now

CVV words *(see)*	see, too, you
VVC words *(out)*	out
VCC words *(all)*	ask(ed), and, all, art, off
CVCC words *(fish)*	will, just, much, best, fast, down, yell(ed), fell, milk, mash(ed), yell(ed), hall, back, want(ed)
CVVC words *(soap, foot)*	peek(ing), your, said, look, room, goes, room, real(ly)
CCVVC words *(cream)*	floor, tried, cried, chair(s)
CVCe words **Regular pattern** *(make)* **Other** *(have)*	1. came, race(d) 2. come, cute, have,
CCVC words *(then)*	that, what, then, show, them, stop, grab(grabbed), drop(dropped), flew
CCVCC words *(black)*	bring, crash(ed), spill(ed), glass(es)
CCVCe words *(white)*	there, where
CCVVCC words *(friend)*	friend(s)
Sentence length	2–11
Sentences per page	3–6
Number of words	302

continues

Lesson	90
Book Title	***GRANDMA'S GLASSES***
Feature	**Examples from the Text**

Labels/Names	Grandma
Content words	grandma, lots, flower, seeds, plant, glasses, need, read, garden, hat, sunflower, deep, check, pack, must, table, inside, chairs, long, time, couldn't, find, Grandma's, yet, anywhere, took, found
High-frequency words	my, had, of, let's, the, she, said, where, are, asked, I, them, to, about*, how, here, your, put, on, her, then, go, you, can, help, me, got, and, all, will, we, get, they, be, went, inside*, looked, for, a, but, came, back, did, not, I'll, look, with, just, could, sat, down, off
Pronouns	my, she, I, them, your, her, you, me, we, they
Prepositions	of, to, on, for, with
Words with inflectional endings	asked, looked, Grandma's
Compound words	sunflower, inside, anywhere, grandma
Contractions	let's, I'll
Plurals	lots, seeds, glasses, chairs
Difficult word patterns	flower, asked, read, about, chairs, couldn't, anywhere, took, found, said, where, your, how, could
Difficult multisyllable words	grandma, flower, sunflower, inside, couldn't, anywhere
Words with *a* as *schwa*	grandma, about
Words ending in *y* Sounding like (1) *i* or (2) *e*	1. my 2. any (anywhere)
Words with vowel and *r*	flower, garden, sunflower, for
Vowel patterns *ow, ay, ey*	flower, sunflower, down, how
CVC words Regular pattern *(run)* Other *(how)*	1. lot(s), let('s), hat, sun (sunflower), yet, sat, had, can, got, get, but, did, not 2. put, her, how, for
CVV words *(see)*	you
VCC words *(all)*	ask(ed), any (anywhere), off, and, all
CVCC words *(fish)*	help, pack, must, long, find, down, will, went, back, with, just
CVVC words *(soap, foot)*	seed(s), need, read, deep, look, took, said, your

CCVVC words *(cream)*	chair(s)
CVCe words **Regular pattern** *(make)*	1. side (inside), time, here, came
Other *(have)*	2.
CCVC words *(then)*	them, then, they
CCVCC words *(black)*	grand(ma), plant, glass(es), check
CCVCe words *(white)*	where
CVCCe words *(table, taste)*	table
Sentence length	3–9
Sentences per page	2–3 (1 page with 1)
Number of words	193

Appendix

continues

Lesson	91
Book Title	*FUN FOR HUGS*
Feature	**Examples from the Text**
Labels/Names	Meg, Hugs, Gram, Gramps
Content words	scarf, yarn, rolled, puzzle, pushed, pieces, watched, floor, top, okay, forget, piano, plan, plunk, PLONK, reading, paper, time, turned, page, ripped, bits, needs, raining, well, toy, watch, movie, together, old, mouse, tied, lots, added, bell, beautiful, popcorn, started, gave, didn't, television
High-frequency words	was, making a, for, liked, the, he, jumped*, on, it, then, over, and, having*, fun, but, wasn't, any, at, all, stop, said, go, see, what, is, doing*, working, so, worked, too, some, them, fall, to, I, can't, make, this, with, you, of, much, I'll, play, that, played, no, get, off, wanted, every*, soon, something, do, it's, outside*, yes, know, just, look, let's, new, can, his, we, have, all, they, got, an, made, come, your, want
Pronouns	he, them, this, you, we, his, they, your, what
Prepositions	for, on, over, at, to, with, of
Words with inflectional endings	making, Hugs, liked, jumped, rolled, having, doing, working, worked, pushed, watched, played, Gramps, reading, wanted, turned, ripped, needs, raining, tied, added, started
Compound words	forget, something, outside, popcorn
Contractions	wasn't, can't, I'll, it's, let's, didn't
Plurals	pieces, lots
Difficult word patterns	making, scarf, having, wasn't, any, puzzle, pieces, watch, floor, know, new, toy, tied
Difficult multisyllable words	making, having, puzzle, pieces, piano, reading, paper, something, raining, outside, movie, together, beautiful, popcorn, television
Words ending in *y* Sounding like (1) *i* or (2) *e*	1. 2. any, every
Words with vowel and *r*	scarf, yarn, working, forget, paper, every, turned, together, popcorn, started, for, over
Vowel patterns *ow, ay, ey*	know, okay, play, they
CVC words **Regular pattern** *(run)* **Other** *(how)*	1. Meg, Hug(s), fun, top, rip(ped), bit(s), let('s), lot(s), pop (popcorn), did(n't), but, get, yes, can, his, got 2. was, for, new, toy
Onomatopoetic words	plunk, PLONK

CVV words *(see)*	see, too, you
VVC words *(out)*	out (outside)
VCC words *(all)*	off, old, add(ed), and, all
CVCC words *(fish)*	yarn, jump(ed), roll(ed), work(ing), push(ed), fall, much, want, turn(ed), well, bell, corn (popcorn), with, want, just
CVVC words *(soap, foot)*	read(ing), soon, need(s), rain(ing), tied, said, look, your
CCVVC words *(cream)*	floor
CVCe words **Regular pattern** *(make)* **Other** *(have)*	1. like(d), time, page, side (outside), gave, make, made 2. have, some, come
CCVC words *(then)*	Gram, stop, plan, play, know, then, what, them, this, play, that, they
CCVCC words *(black)*	plunk, PLONK, Gramp(s), thing (something), start(ed)
Sentence length	1–14
Sentences per page	1–8
Number of words	307

Appendix

continues

Lesson	92
Book Title	*HOME SWEET HOME*
Feature	**Examples from the Text**

Labels/Names	Hen, Cow, Pig, Duck
Content words	nice, white, color, paint, red, thought, along, hello, today, need, ladder, find, wait, waited, tired, waiting, grabbed, blue, sky, bright, cans, must, painting, yellow, sun, lots, green, grass, fine, tall, morning, smiled, rainbow, needs, door, rose
High-frequency words	had, a, house*, she, liked, her, but, wanted, new, for, I, will, my, came, said, do, you, want, to, play, with, me, not, going, help, we, a, go, one, here, and, got, of, so, can, use, this, is, as, the, good, did, look, at, all, be, out, he, has, your, hi*, oh, no, looked, then, it, I'll
Pronouns	she, her, I, my, you, me, we, this, your, it
Prepositions	for, along, to, with, of, at, all
Words with inflectional endings	liked, wanted, going, waited, tired, waiting, grabbed, painting, looked, smiled, needs
Compound words	along, today, rainbow
Contractions	I'm, I'll
Plurals	cans
Difficult word patterns	house, paint, thought, along, blue, use, bright
Difficult multisyllable words	color, along, hello, today, going, ladder, waited, tired, waiting, painting, yellow, morning, rainbow
Words with *a* as *schwa*	along
Words ending in *y* Sounding like (1) *i* or (2) *e*	1. my, sky 2.
Words with vowel and *r*	her, color, for
Vowel patterns *ow, ay, ey*	cow, play, today
CVC words Regular pattern *(run)* Other *(how)*	1. hen, had, but, for, red, not, got, can, did, pig, sun, has, lot(s) 2. her, new, cow
CVV words *(see)*	you
VCC words *(all)*	and, all
CVCC words *(fish)*	want, will, with, help, find, must, duck, tall
CVVC words *(soap, foot)*	said, need, wait, good, look, your, door

CCVVC words *(cream)*	sweet, green
CVCe words **Regular pattern** *(make)*	1. home, nice, like(d), came, here, fine, rose, tire(d)
Other *(have)*	2.
CCVC words *(then)*	grab (grabbed), this, then
CCVCC words *(black)*	grass
CCVCe words *(white)*	white, smile(d)
Sentence length	3–10
Sentences per page	2–6
Number of words	299

continues

Lesson	93
Book Title	***BEAR'S BIRTHDAY***
Feature	**Examples from the Text**

Labels/Names	Bear, Rabbit, Beaver, Fox
Content words	woke, smiled, beautiful, birthday, party, cake, eggs, hello, bake, party, thanked, sadly, hats, paper, blow, balloons, blew, table, finished, wait, friends, waited, sad, told, because, planned, forgot, surprise
High-frequency words	up, he, looked, outside, and, what, a, day, for, my, said, I, will, have, a, make, but, don't, any, so, went, to, house, do, you, want, some, is, the, for, it's, I'm, having, took, then, home*, why, didn't*, ask, me, his, asked, when, got, made, now, are, these*, good, up, they, put, on, am, no, came, it, was, where, were, there, come, we, did, not, us, oh, all, this, yes, is
Pronouns	he, my, I, you, me, his, these, they, it, them, we, us, this
Prepositions	up, for, to, on
Words with inflectional endings	looked, smiled, thanked, sadly, finished, waited, planned
Compound words	birthday, outside, because, forgot
Contractions	don't, it's, I'm, didn't
Plurals	eggs, hats, balloons, friends
Difficult word patterns	beautiful, house, asked, Beaver, balloons, finished, because, surprise
Difficult multisyllable words	birthday, outside, beautiful, Rabbit's, hello, having, party, sadly, paper, Beaver, balloons, table, finished, waited, because, forgot, surprise
Words ending in *y* **Sounding like (1) *i* or (2) *e***	1. my, why 2. any, party
Words with vowel and *r*	birthday, for, now, paper, Beaver, are, were, surprise
Vowel patterns *ow, ay, ey*	birthday, day, blow, they
CVC words **Regular pattern *(run)*** **Other *(how)***	1. for, but, his, sad, got, hat(s), did, not, yes 2. day, now, put, was
CVV words *(see)*	you
VCC words *(all)*	and, egg(s), ask, all
CVCC words *(fish)*	will, went, want, told
CVVC words *(soap, foot)*	bear, look(ed), said, took, good, wait

CVCe words **Regular pattern** *(make)* **Other** *(have)*	1. woke, make, cake, bake, home, made, came 2. have, some, were, come
CCVC words *(then)*	what, then, when, blow, they, blew, them, plan(planned), this
CCVCC words *(black)*	thank(ed)
CCVCe words *(white)*	smile(d), these, where, there
CVCCe words *(table, taste)*	table
CCVVCC words *(friend)*	friend(s)
Sentence length	3–13
Sentences per page	4–11
Number of words	432

continues

Appendix

Lesson	94
Book Title	*THE BOSSY PIG*
Feature	**Examples from the Text**

Labels/Names	Mrs. Pig, Mrs. Sheep, Mrs. Goat, Mrs. Cow, Mr. Horse, Mrs. Owl
Content words	picnic, Saturday, told, friends, list, table, six, chairs, juice, plates, bossy, pig, bring, blanket, right, milk, such, again, need, anything, everything, else, animals, games, flew, kite, tree, set, last, time, that's, please, food, dear, forgot, smiled, wise
High-frequency words	we, will, have, a, on, her, you, must*, come, made, I, want, and, said, some, she, was, very, can, is, not, my, the, all, looked, at, what, don't, know, but, something, came, to, they, played, stop, playing, put, under, that, big, help, up, one, it, now, sit, down, where, asked, oh, didn't, are, let's, eat
Pronouns	we, her, you, I, she, my, they, that, it, where
Prepositions	on, at, to, under, up
Words with inflectional endings	looked, played, playing, asked, smiled
Compound words	anything, everything, something, forgot
Contractions	don't, that's, didn't, let's
Plurals	friends, chairs, plates, animals, games
Difficult word patterns	juice, bring, right, again, else
Difficult multisyllable words	bossy, picnic, Saturday, table, very, blanket, again, anything, everything, something, animals, playing, under, forgot
Words with *a* as *schwa*	again
Words ending in *y* **Sounding like (1) *i* or (2) *e***	1. my 2. bossy, very
Words with vowel and *r*	her, Saturday, everything, under, forgot, are
Vowel patterns *ow, ay, ey*	Saturday, know, they, played, down
CVC words **Regular pattern** *(run)* **Other** *(how)*	1. pig, her, six, can, not, but, big, set, sit, let('s) 2. was, cow, put, now
CVV words *(see)*	you
VVC words *(out)*	eat
VCC words *(all)*	and, all, owl, ask(ed)
CVCC words *(fish)*	told, must, list, want, milk, such, help, last, down

CVVC words *(soap, foot)*	said, goat, need, food, dear, look(ed)
CCVVC words *(cream)*	chair(s), sheep
CVCe words **Regular pattern** *(make)*	1. made, came, game(s), kite, time, wise
Other *(have)*	2. have, come, some
CCVC words *(then)*	will, know, what, they, play(ed), flew, stop, that
CCVCC words *(black)*	bring
CCVCe words *(white)*	plate(s), where, smile(d)
CVCCe words *(table, taste)*	table, horse
CCVVCe words *(cheese)*	please
CCVVCC words *(friend)*	friend(s)
Sentence length	3–13
Sentences per page	2–6
Number of words	240

continues

Lesson	95
Book Title	***STONE SOUP***
Feature	**Examples from the Text**

Content words	long, ago, young, poor, town, soup, pot, spoon, hungry, stopped, knocked, door, cold, bit, food, woman, sorry, beans, enough, share, until, another, old, meat, people, gave, still, plan, first, fire, right, middle, filled, water, next, set, last, picked, nice, round, stone, steam, rose, stirred, loudly, ready, people, plenty, easy, need, would, better, few, dropped, mmm, thank, getting, carrots, potato, boy, corn, bowls, men, women, children, never, again, smiled
High-frequency words	a, man, came, into, little, all, he, had, was, and, very, the, at, house, I, am, said, may, have, of, this, is, we, don't, any, I'm, now, some, but, not, to, went, on, from, they, were, no, one, him, so, up, with, made, in, then, his, put, it, with, this, looks, good, soon, will, be, eat, out, see, what, doing, are, you, they, asked, making, I'll, give, when, there, for, us, how, do, make, girl, it's, much, off, got, them, our, want, yes, ran, get, your, know, can, just, way
Pronouns	he, I, this, we, they, him, his, it, this, you, us, them, our, your
Prepositions	into, at, of, to, on, from, up, with, in, with, for, off
Words with inflectional endings	stopped, knocked, filled, picked, stirred, looks, loudly, doing, asked, making, dropped, getting, smiled
Compound words	into, another
Contractions	don't, I'm, I'll, it's
Plurals	beans, carrots, bowls
Difficult word patterns	young, little, spoon, very, hungry, house, enough, people, first, right, middle, round, ready, people, plenty, easy, would, children, again
Difficult multisyllable words	little, very, hungry, woman, enough, until, people, middle, water, ready, people, doing, making, plenty, easy, better, carrots, potato, women, children, never, again
Words with *a* as *schwa*	again
Words ending in *y* **Sounding like (1) *i* or (2) *e***	1. 2. very, hungry, any, sorry, ready, plenty, easy
Words with vowel and *r*	very, another, were, first, are, for, girl, better, carrots, corn, never
Vowel patterns *ow, ay, ey*	town, may, now, they, how, bowls, know, way
CVC words **Regular pattern *(run)*** **Other *(how)***	1. man, had, pot, bit, not, but, set, for, got, get, yes, ran, can, men 2. was, may, now, put, how, few

Onomatopoetic words	mmm
CVV words *(see)*	see, you
VVC words *(out)*	eat, out, our
VCC words *(all)*	all, and, old, ask(ed)
CVCC words *(fish)*	long, town, cold, went, with, fill(ed), next, last, pick(ed), with, will, girl, much, want, corn, salt, bowl(s), just
CVVC words *(soap, foot)*	soup, poor, door, said, food, bean(s), meat, look(s), good, loud(ly), soon, need, your
CCVVC words *(cream)*	spoon, steam
CVCe words **Regular pattern *(make)*** **Other *(have)***	1. came, gave, made, nice, rose, make 2. have, some, were, fire, give
CCVC words *(then)* drop(dropped), them, know	stop(stopped), this, from, they, plan, then, stir(stirred), this, what, when,
CCVCC words *(black)*	still, thank, knock(ed)
CCVCe words *(white)*	stone, share, there, smile(d)
Sentence length	2–14
Sentences per page	3–6
Number of words	555

continues

Appendix

Lesson	96
Book Title	***BEST NEW FRIENDS***
Feature	**Examples from the Text**

Labels/Names	Brian, Paul, dad, Jake, Luke
Content words	best, friends, school, together, lived, next, door, ball, told, sad, news, family, moving, move, you're, best, friend, sale, talked, worry, send, letters, phone, felt, thought, van, good-bye, gave, baseball, keep, sure, drove, alone, tossed, hand, catch, thanks, feel, playing, another, car, along, boy(s,) jumped, we're
High-frequency words	and, were, they, went, to, each, other, played, every, day, one, some, my, is, can't, said, you, for, his, I, don't, want, away, can, call, him, on, the, but, he, who, will, play, with, me, be, soon, a, came, house, went, say*, have, something, it, are, then, was, all, in, outside, asked, do, no, like, two, jumped, out, of, make, I'm, going, could, make
Pronouns	they, my, you, his, I, want, him, he, me, it
Prepositions	to, for, on, with, in, out, of
Words with inflectional endings	lived, played, moving, talked, tossed, asked, thanks, playing, jumped, going
Compound words	away, good-bye, something, baseball, alone, outside, another, along
Contractions	can't, you're, don't, I'm, we're
Plurals	friends, letters, boys
Difficult word patterns	school, together, each, every, moving, said, phone, thought, house, good-bye, catch, two, going, could
Difficult multisyllable words	together, other, every, family, moving, worry, letters, good-bye, something, baseball, alone, outside, playing, another, along, going, away
Words with *a* as *schwa*	away
Words ending in *y* **Sounding like (1) *i* or** **(2) *e***	1. my 2. every, family, worry
Words with vowel and *r*	were, together, other, every, for, letters, are, sure, another
Vowel patterns *ow, ay, ey*	they, played, day, away, play, say,
CVC words **Regular pattern *(run)*** **Other *(how)***	1. sad, can, his, dad, him, but, van, boy 2. for, new, day, say, was, car
CVV words *(see)*	you
VVC words *(out)*	out

VCC words (*all*)	and, all, ask(ed)
CVCC words *(fish)*	best, went, next, ball, told, news, best, talk(ed), want, send, call, felt, will, with, next, toss(ed), hand, jump(ed)
CVVC words *(soap, foot)*	door, said, soon, keep, feel
CVCe words Regular pattern *(make)* Other *(have)*	1. sale, came, gave, like, make 2. were, live, some, move, have, sure
CCVC words *(then)*	they, play, then
CCVCC words *(black)*	thank(s)
CCVCe words *(white)*	phone, drove
CCVVCC words *(friend)*	friend
Sentence length	4–11
Sentences per page	2–6
Number of words	257

Appendix

continues

Lesson	97
Book Title	***THE MISSING CAT***
Feature	**Examples from the Text**
Labels/Names	Meg, Hugs, Gram, Dr. Jan, Gramps
Content words	time, dinner, gave, cat, food, sniffed, turned, head, chicken, today, still, won't, beef, doesn't, turkey, cheese, even, tuna, never, leaves, bit, dish, feel, sick, poor, okay, vet, kitchen, gone, seen, think, read, paper, lap, took, meatballs, freezer, thaw, watched, haven't, since, closets, beds, tables, behind, curtains, basement, didn't, maybe, hide, hours, oven, around, house, found, bathroom, asleep, tub, silly, that's, you're, hungry, ate
High-frequency words	come, on, said, it's, for, your, she, some, at, then, he, his, away, you, don't, want, that, do, new, can, of, but, did, not, eat, to, or, the, with, I, see, loves, a, in, must, oh, no, will, be, let's, call*, she, know, what, went, they, came, back, get, and, take, him, was, have, asked, let, me, sat, my, out, here, called*, her, I'll, look, under, all, help, looked, find*, where, is, just, don't, knows, like, go, may, from, us, put, wanted, one, more, soon, something, too, why, has, our
Pronouns	your, she, he, his, you, that, she, they, him, me, my, her, us, our
Prepositions	on, for, at, of, to, with, in, out, from
Words with inflectional endings	sniffed, turned, loves, leaves, asked, watched, called, looked, knows, wanted, Hugs, Gramps
Compound words	meatballs, something, bathroom, asleep, away, around, maybe
Contractions	it's, won't, doesn't, let's, I'll, didn't, that's, you're, don't
Plurals	meatballs, closets, tables, curtains, hours
Difficult word patterns	it's, head, new, won't, doesn't, even, leaves, gone, read, thaw, haven't, since, around, found, house, hours, want, where, you're, said, one, our
Difficult multisyllable words	chicken, turkey, even, okay, kitchen, paper, meatballs, freezer, closets, behind, curtains, basement, around, something, bathroom, asleep, hungry
Words with *a* as *schwa*	around, asleep, away
Words ending in *y* Sounding like (1) *i* or (2) *e*	1. my, why 2. silly, hungry
Words with vowel and *r*	dinner, turned, turkey, never, paper, freezer, under, curtains, more, for, her
Vowel patterns *ow, ay, ey*	know, today, okay, may, away, turkey, they

Word Analysis Charts, *continued*

CVC words **Regular pattern** *(run)* **Other** *(how)*	1. Hug(s), Meg, cat, bit, Jan, vet, let, sat, lap, bed(s), tub, his, can, but, did, not, get, him, has 2. day (today), new, for, way (away), was, may, put, her
CVV words *(see)*	you, see, too
VVC words *(out)*	eat, out, our
VCC words *(all)*	ask(ed), and, all
CVCC words *(fish)*	turn(ed), dish, must, sick, call, ball (meatballs), help, find, bath (bathroom), want, with, will, went, back, just
CVVC words *(soap, foot)*	food, head, beef, feel, poor, seen, read, took, meat (meatballs), look, hour(s), soon, room (bathroom), said, your, look
CCVVC words *(cream)*	sleep (asleep)
CVCe words **Regular pattern** *(make)* **Other** *(have)*	1. time, gave, take, hide, came, here, like 2. love(s), gone, more, come, some, have
CCVC words *(then)*	Gram, know, thaw, then, that, what, they, from
CCVCC words *(black)*	sniff(ed), still, Gramp(s), think, thing (something)
CCVCe words *(white)*	where
CVCCe words *(table, taste)*	since, table(s)
CCVVCe words *(cheese)*	cheese, freeze(r)
Sentence length	1–16
Sentences per page	2–7 (1 page with 1)
Number of words	414

continues

Appendix

Lesson	98
Book Title	*THE LUCKY PENNY*
Feature	**Examples from the Text**

Labels/Names	Mom, Max, Ben, Deena
Content words	gave, shiny, penny, lose, lucky, won't, pocket, school, hole, fell, couldn't, ground, picked, bag, round, found, still
High-frequency words	a, new, don't, it, said, this, is, I, put, in, his, then, he, walked, to, but, had, out, looked, for, oh, no, where, my, find, so, went, on, was, walking*, too, saw, something, up, at, playing, into, after, she, her, home, and, down, here, how, do, you, your, yes
Pronouns	it, this, his, he, my, is, she, her, you
Prepositions	I, in, to, for, on, up, at, out, into,
Words with inflectional endings	lucky, walked, looked, walking, playing
Compound words	something, into
Contractions	don't, lose, won't, couldn't
Difficult word patterns	school, couldn't, picked, ground, round, found
Difficult multisyllable words	lucky, penny, shiny, pocket, walking, something, playing, after
Words ending in *y* **Sounding like (1)** *i* **or** **(2)** *e*	1. my 2. lucky, penny, shiny
Words with vowel and *r*	for, after, her
Vowel patterns *ow, ay, ey*	down, how
CVC words **Regular pattern** *(run)* **Other** *(how)*	1. mom, his, but, had, for, bag, yes 2. new, put, was, saw, how, her
CVV words *(see)*	too, you
VVC words *(out)*	out
VCC words *(all)*	and
CVCC words *(fish)*	luck(y), walk(ed), fell, find, went, pick(ed), down
CVVC words *(soap, foot)*	said, look(ed), your
CVCe words **Regular pattern** *(make)* **Other** *(have)*	1. gave, hole, home, here 2. lose

CCVC words *(then)*	this, then, play(ing)
CCVCC words *(black)*	still
CCVCe words *(white)*	where
Sentence length	3–9
Sentences per page	2–6
Number of words	259

continues

Appendix

Lesson	99
Book Title	***ALL ABOUT HONEYBEES***
Feature	**Examples from the Text**

Labels/Names	honeybees, nectar, hive, cells, beekeepers
Content words	garden, flowers, bloom, warm, summer, hear, sound, bees, buzz, honeybees, around, sweet, nectar, worker, sip, carry, hive, live, boxes, cells, flap, wings, fast, dries, turns, honey, food, bears, animals, bear, sting, save, beekeepers, people, keep, bring, hives, cover, cannot, bottles, jars, sticky, treat
High-frequency words	in, the, on, a, day, you, can, of, little, fly, these, are, working, something, is, inside, it, called, from, then, they, home, many*, looks, like, lot*, put, into, lots, their, very, this, out, and, for, but, other, too, wants, take, up, so, them
Pronouns	it, they, this, them
Prepositions	in, on, of, from, into, for, up,
Words with inflectional endings	working, called, worker, looks, dries, turns, wants, sticky
Compound words	honeybees, around, something, inside, beekeepers, cannot
Plurals	honeybees, flowers, bees, boxes, cells, wings, animals, hives, bottles, jars
Difficult word patterns	about, honeybees, flowers, bloom, sound, little, around, honey, people, bottles
Difficult multisyllable words	about, honeybees, garden, flowers, summer, little, around, working, something, inside, nectar, worker, carry, many, inside, into, very, honey, other, animals, beekeepers, people, cover, cannot, bottles, sticky
Words with *a* as *schwa*	about
Words ending in *y* Sounding like (1) *i* or (2) *e*	1. fly 2. carry, many, very, honey, sticky
Words with vowel and *r*	garden, flowers, warm, summer, are, turns, for, other, beekeepers, cover
Vowel patterns *ow, ay, ey*	flowers, day, they
CVC words Regular pattern *(run)* Other *(how)*	1. can, sip, lot, box(es), for, but 2. day, put, jar(s)
Onomatopoetic words	buzz
CVV words *(see)*	you, bee(s), too
VVC words *(out)*	out

VCC words *(all)*	all, and
CVCC words *(fish)*	warm, work(ing), call(ed), cell(s), wing(s), fast, turn(s), want(s)
CVVC words *(soap, foot)*	hear, look(s), food, bear, keep
CCVVC words *(cream)*	bloom, sweet, their, dries, treat
CVCe words **Regular pattern** *(make)* **Other** *(have)*	1. home, hive, like, take, save 2. live
CCVC words *(then)*	then, they, flap, this
CCVCC words *(black)*	sting, bring, stick(y)
CCVCe words *(white)*	these
Sentence length	3–12
Sentences per page	2–3
Number of words	194

Appendix

continues

Lesson	100
Book Title	***A WALK AT NIGHT***
Feature	**Examples from the Text**
Labels/Names	Dad
Content words	night, woods, most, animals, sleep, waking, listen, moon, bright, moonlight, hoot, owl, tree, owl's, yellow, eyes, shine, sky, bats, flying, wake, bugs, red, fox, hiding, bush, raccoon, black, fur, around, its, mask, hear, crunching, sound, deer, behind, trees, time
High-frequency words	it, is, in, the, go, to, at, but, some, are, just, up, I, for, a, walk, with, we, look, and, that, come, out, very, will, help, us, see, of, an, there, now, here, they, eat, jumps*, runs, away, big, has, looks, like, what, from, off, into, love, home
Pronouns	it,, I, we, that, us, they, into
Prepositions	at, in, to, up, for, with, of, from, around, behind
Words with inflectional endings	waking, flying, hiding, jumps, runs, looks, crunching
Compound words	moonlight, around, into, away
Plurals	animals, eyes, bats, bugs, trees
Difficult word patterns	night, are, waking bright, moonlight, listen, eyes, flying, raccoon, around, hear, crunching, sound, behind
Difficult multisyllable words	animal(s), waking, listen, very, moonlight, listen, yellow, flying, away, raccoon, around, crunching, behind
Words with *a* as *schwa*	away, around
Words ending in *y* Sounding like (1) *i* or (2) *e*	1. sky 2. very
Words with vowel and *r*	are, for, fur
Vowel patterns *ow, ay, ey*	yellow, now, they, away
CVC words Regular pattern *(run)* Other *(how)*	1. but, dad, bat(s), bug(s), red, fox, run(s), big, has 2. now, for, fur
Onomatopoetic words	hoot
CVV words *(see)*	see
VVC words *(out)*	out, eat

Word Analysis Charts, *continued*

VCC words *(all)*	and, owl, off
CVCC words *(fish)*	walk, most, just, with, will, help, jump(s), bush, mask
CVVC words *(soap, foot)*	look, moon, hoot, hear, deer, wood(s)
CCVVC words *(cream)*	sleep
CVCe words **Regular pattern** *(make)* **Other** *(have)*	1. here, wake, hide(hiding), like, time, home 2. some, come, love
CCVC words *(then)*	that, they, what, from
CCVCC words *(black)*	black
CCVCe words *(white)*	there, shine
Sentence length	3–11
Sentences per page	1–4
Number of words	198

continues

Appendix

Lesson	101
Book Title	*TOO TALL*
Feature	**Examples from the Text**
Labels/Names	Lola, Monday, Tuesday, volleyball, softball, Wednesday, track, Thursday, Friday, bowling, Saturday, Jill, Mindy, Sunday, basketball
Content words	team, try, volleyball, team, sorry, coach, you're, net, tall, sad, pick, told, still, decided, another, Tuesday, softball, pitch, ball, hung, head, you'll, that's, right, Wednesday, track, wouldn't, fair, you'd, race, those, long, legs, cried, ever, swim, shook, head, pool, only, four, feet, deep, anyway, wasn't, quite, bowling, well, tried, couldn't, even, fit, through, door, alley, shouted, Saturday, friends, need, player, won't, please, change, mind, picked, thought, okay, basketball, time, perfect
High-frequency words	wanted, to, play, on, a, she, went, out, for, the, said, up, there, and, is, down, here, just, too, was, they, didn't, me, her, mother, father, but, I, want, no, one, can, you, again*, find, it, be, every, with, will, their, don't, give, his, I'm, much, like, so, inside, can't, came, over, come, our, we, more, your, know, get, about, help, did, let's, go, this, away, not, asked, all
Pronouns	she, they, me, her, I, you, it, his, our, we, your
Prepositions	to, on, out, for, up, with, over
Words with inflectional endings	wanted, decided, cried, bowling, tried, shouted, picked, asked
Compound words	volleyball, another, softball, anyway, inside, basketball, away
Contractions	you're, didn't, you'll, wouldn't, you'd, I'm, don't, wasn't, couldn't, can't, won't, let's, that's
Plurals	legs, friends
Difficult word patterns	coach, decided, another, Tuesday, pitch, again, right, Wednesday, wouldn't, anyway, quite, bowling, couldn't, even, through, alley, change, thought, about, perfect
Difficult multisyllable words	Monday, volleyball, sorry, mother, father, decided, another, Tuesday, Wednesday, every, ever, Thursday, anyway, Friday, bowling, alley, shouted, inside, Saturday, Sunday, okay, basketball, perfect, away
Words with *a* as *schwa*	again, about, away,
Words ending in *y* Sounding like (1) *i* or (2) *e*	1. try 2. sorry, every
Words with vowel and *r*	for, her, mother, father, ever, Thursday, Saturday, over, more, player, perfect

Vowel patterns *ow, ay, ey*	play, Monday, down, they, Tuesday, Wednesday, Thursday, anyway, Friday, Saturday, Sunday, know, okay, away
CVC words **Regular pattern *(run)***	1. net, sad, her, but, leg(s), fit, get, not
Other *(how)*	2. for, was, her
CVV words *(see)*	too, you
VVC words *(out)*	out, our
VCC words *(all)*	and, ask(ed), all
CVCC words *(fish)*	tall, want, went, down, just, pick, told, ball, hung, find, with, long, will, well, mind, help
CVVC words *(soap, foot)*	team, said, head, fair, pool, four, feet, deep, door, need, your
CCVVC words *(cream)*	cried, their, shook, tried, shout(ed)
CVCe words **Regular pattern *(make)***	1. here, race, like, came, more, time
Other *(have)*	2. give, come
CCVC words *(then)*	play, they, that('s), swim, know, this
CCVCC words *(black)*	still, track
CCVCe words *(white)*	there, those
CCVVCe words *(cheese)*	please
CCVVCC words *(friend)*	friend(s)
Sentence length	3–11
Sentences per page	2–5
Number of words	423

Appendix

continues

241

Lesson	102
Book Title	***TWO TEAMS***
Feature	**Examples from the Text**
Content words	sports, team, football, players, soccer, hold, ball, hands, throw, catch, kick, kicker, hit, heads, goalie, playing, win
High-frequency words	this, is, a, the, plays, love, to, play, game*, can, with, their, they, and, run, too, some, on, one, of, called, not, it, just
Pronouns	this, they, it, with, on
Prepositions	to, with, of
Words with inflectional endings	plays, called, player, kicker, playing
Compound words	football
Plurals	teams, sports, players, hands, heads
Difficult word patterns	throw, catch, goalie
Difficult multisyllable words	football, soccer, goalie
Words with vowel and *r*	soccer
Vowel patterns *ow, ay, ey*	play, they, throw
CVC words **Regular pattern *(run)*** **Other *(how)***	1. can, run, not, hit, win 2.
CVV words *(see)*	too
VCC words *(all)*	and
CVCC words *(fish)*	hold, ball, with, hand(s), kick, call(ed), hold, with, just
CVVC words *(soap, foot)*	team, head(s)
CCVVC words *(cream)*	their
CVCe words **Regular pattern *(make)*** **Other *(have)***	1. game 2. love, some
CCVC words *(then)*	this, they
CCVCC words *(black)*	sport(s)
Sentence length	4–11
Sentences per page	2–3
Number of words	146

Lesson	103
Book Title	***ALL ABOUT DOLPHINS***
Feature	**Examples from the Text**

Content words	dolphin, dolphins, sea, fish, need, breathe, air, breathes, blowhole, top, head, flipper, side, fin, tail, swim, fast, 25, miles, hour, together, groups, pods, pod, baby, grown-up, calf, years, kinds, drink, water, hunting, food, noisy, animals, slap, fins, top, click, squeak, even, whistle, sounds, babies, chase, ride, waves, high, smart, learn, tricks, learned, shake, hands, trick, job, pink, swallow, whole, 20, feet
High-frequency words	this, is, a, live, in, the, but, they, are, not, to, through*, on, of, its, has, one, each, it, its, back, and, helps*, some, can, up, an, called, stays*, with, mother, for, two, or, three, eat, many, do, get, from, their, make, call, find, love, play, other, jump*, out, just, fun, very, do, this, how, when, does, gets, good
Pronouns	this, they, his, it,
Prepositions	in, to, on, of, up, with, for, from, out
Words with inflectional endings	breathes, helps, called, stays, hunting, gets
Plurals	dolphins, miles, flippers, groups, pods, years, kinds, animals, fins, sounds, waves, hands, facts
Difficult word patterns	about, dolphin, breathe, breathes, through, each, grown-up, two, three, noisy, squeak, even, whistle, sounds, babies, learn, does, swallow
Difficult multisyllable words	about, dolphin, flipper, together, baby, mother, many, water, noisy, animals, even, whistle, babies, other, very, swallow
Words with *a* as *schwa*	about
Words ending in *y* **Sounding like (1) *i* or** **(2) *e***	1. 2. baby, many, noisy, very
Words with vowel and *r*	are, flipper, together, mother, for, water, other, smart
Vowel patterns *ow, ay, ey*	they, stays, stay, play, how, swallow
CVC words **Regular pattern *(run)*** **Other *(how)***	1. but, not, top, his, has, fin, can, pod(s), get, top, fun, job 2. how, for
CVV words *(see)*	sea
VVC words *(out)*	eat, out, air
VCC words *(all)*	all, and

continues

CVCC words *(fish)*	fish, back, help, call(ed), calf, with, kind(s), hunt(ing), find, jump, high, just, hand(s), fact(s), pink
CVVC words *(soap, foot)*	need, head, tail, hour, year(s), food, does, good, feet
CCVVC words *(cream)*	group(s), their
CVCe words **Regular pattern** *(make)* **Other** *(have)*	1. hole, side, make, safe, ride, wave(s) 2. live, some, mile(s), love
CCVC words *(then)*	this, they, swim, fast, stay, from, slap, play, when
CCVCC words *(black)*	grown, drink, click, smart, trick
CCVCe words *(white)*	chase, shake, whole
Sentence length	3–12
Sentences per page	1–3
Number of words	242

Lesson	104
Book Title	***THE CHERRIES***
Feature	**Examples from the Text**

Labels/Names	Froggy, Turtle, Duck, Otter
Content words	picking, cherries, yum, yummy, tummy, picked, until, basket, full, time, hop, hopped, road, sorry, need, surprised, share, o'clock, tag, better, bugs, told, frog, cook, beautiful, cherry, pie, happy, song, sang, couldn't, wait, smell, that's, why, needed, took, slice, pan, left, friends
High-frequency words	was, some, he, said, are, so, good, for, my, his, then, it, to, go, home, down, the, out, a, walk, I, love, may, have, one, or, two, all, didn't, want, but, come, house, at, and, were, playing, they, than, we, you, lot, of, got, work, that, very, soon, big, made, up, new, it's, wanted, with, looked, in, don't, lots
Pronouns	he, my, his, it, I, they, we, you
Prepositions	for, to, at, of, on, up, in
Words with inflectional endings	picking, yummy, picked, hopped, surprised, playing, needed, wanted, looked
Contractions	didn't, couldn't, that's, it's, don't
Plurals	cherries, bugs, friends
Difficult word patterns	Turtle, two, surprised, house, Otter, o'clock, beautiful, cherry, couldn't
Difficult multisyllable words	Froggy, picking, yummy, tummy, until, basket, Turtle, sorry, surprised, Otter, better, very, beautiful, cherry, happy, until
Words ending in *y* **Sounding like (1) *i* or** **(2) *e***	1. my, why 2. Froggy, yummy, tummy, sorry, very, cherry, happy
Words with vowel and *r*	are, for, Turtle, Otter, better, her, work
Vowel patterns *ow, ay, ey*	down, may, they, may
CVC words **Regular pattern *(run)*** **Other *(how)***	1. yum, his, hop, but, tag, bug(s), lot, got, had, big, pan 2. was, for, new, her
CVV words *(see)*	you, pie
VVC words *(out)*	out
VCC words *(all)*	all, and
CVCC words *(fish)*	pick(ing), full, down, walk, want, Duck, told, work, song, sang, left

continues

Appendix

CVVC words *(soap, foot)*	good, road, said, need, cook, soon, wait, took, look(ed)
CVCe words **Regular pattern** *(make)* **Other** *(have)*	1. time, home, made, make 2. some, love, have, come, were
CCVC words *(then)*	then, play(ing), they, than, frog, that('s)
CCVCC words *(black)*	(o')clock, smell
CCVCe words *(white)*	share, slice
CCVVCC words *(friend)*	friend(s)
Sentence length	4–11
Sentences per page	1–8
Number of words	286

Lesson	105
Book Title	*THE LION AND THE MOUSE*
Feature	**Examples from the Text**

Labels/Names	Lion, Mouse
Content words	taking, nap, running, hurry, right, nose, woke, loud, roar, grabbed, paw, roared, opened, jaws, dear, please, mean, wake, kept, talking, begging, maybe, laughed, hard, think, ever, funny, hungry, anyway, happy, thank, hear, still, laughing, few, days, later, suddenly, hunter's, net, trapped, caught, tried, free, close, heard, needs, silly, bit, ropes, teeth, chewed, took, long, time, last, well, thing, friend, became, best, friends, learned, lesson
High-frequency words	one, day, a, was, soon, little, came, by, he, in, to, get, home, did, not, see, ran, so, over, up, with, his, big, I'm, going, to, eat, you, me, do, said, I, let, go, and, if, will, help, at, that, could, stop, asked, how, what, are, am, off, called, but, too, out, walking, him, when, my, went, find, saw, can, work, more, now, some, there, is, want, be, your, this, all
Pronouns	he, his, you, me, I, him, my
Prepositions	by, in, to, up, with, at, off, out
Words with inflectional endings	taking, running, grabbed, going, roared, opened, talking, laughed, called, asked laughing, walking, trapped, tried, heard, needs, chewed, learned
Compound words	maybe, anyway, became
Contractions	I'm
Plurals	jaws, days, ropes, friends, characters
Difficult word patterns	Mouse, right, laughed, could, asked, caught, heard, learned, characters
Difficult multisyllable words	taking, running, hurry, going, opened, maybe, ever, funny, hungry, anyway, happy, laughing, later, walking, suddenly, hunter's, silly, became, lesson
Words ending in *y* Sounding like (1) *i* or (2) *e*	1. by, my 2. hurry, funny, hungry, happy, suddenly, silly
Words with vowel and *r*	over, hard, ever, are, later, more
Vowel patterns *ow, ay, ey*	day, how, anyway, days, play
CVC words **Regular pattern *(run)* Other *(how)***	1. nap, run(running), get, did, not, ran, his, big, let, beg(begging), but, net, him, can, bit 2. was, how, few, paw, jaw(s), saw, now

continues

Appendix

CVV words *(see)*	see, you, too
VVC words *(out)*	eat, out
VCC words *(all)*	and, ask(ed), off, all
CVCC words *(fish)*	with, kept, talk(ing), will, help, hard, call(ed), walk(ing), went, find, work, long, last, well, want, best
CVVC words *(soap, foot)*	Lion, soon, loud, roar, dear, said, mean, hear, need(s), took, your
CCVVC words *(cream)*	tried
CVCe words **Regular pattern** *(make)* **Other** *(have)*	1. take(taking), came, home, nose, woke, wake, rope(s), more, time 2. some
CCVC words *(then)*	grab(grabbed), that, stop, what, trap(trapped), when, chew(ed), this, play
CCVCC words *(black)*	think, thank, still, thing
CCVCe words *(white)*	close, there
CCVVCe words *(cheese)*	please
CCVVCC words *(friend)*	friend
Sentence length	3–10
Sentences per page	2–5
Number of words	427

Lesson	106
Book Title	***ALL ABOUT BOATS***
Feature	**Examples from the Text**
Labels/Names	tugboat, fishing boat, ferryboat, fireboat, barge, houseboat
Content words	boats, water, small, kind, job, tugboat, tugboats, strong, pulling, ship, sea, fishing, boat, catch, fish, nets, deep, full, ferryboat, ferryboats, carry, people, across, cars, trucks, fireboat, fires, ships, sprays, fire, barge, long, flat, carries, loads, carrying, coal, pushing, houseboat, floating, rooms, sleeping, family, lives, kinds
High-frequency words	look, at, these, in, the, some, are, big, and, all, do, of, this, is, a, but, they, very, out, to, it, goes, has, that, go, into, comes, back, with, here, take, work, them, home, again, can, too, helps, put, on, little, for, eating*, many, play
Pronouns	some, this, they, it, them
Prepositions	at, in, of, to, into, with, on, for
Words with inflectional endings	pulling, fishing, goes, comes, helps, sprays, carries, carrying, pushing, floating, eating, sleeping, lives
Compound words	tugboat, ferryboat, fireboat, houseboat, into
Plurals	boats, tugboats, fish, nets, ferryboats, people, cars, trucks, fires, ships, rooms
Difficult word patterns	these, kind, boat, strong, pulling, sea, goes, catch, comes, full, carry, people, work, again, sprays, barge, carries, loads, coal, pushing, houseboat, floating, many, they, very, out, too, little
Difficult multisyllable words	water, tugboat, pulling, ferryboat, carry, people, again, fireboat, carries, carrying, pushing, houseboat, floating, eating, family, many, very
Words with *a* as *schwa*	again
Words ending in *y* Sounding like (1) *i* or (2) *e*	1. 2. ferry (ferryboat), carry, family, many, very
Words with vowel and *r*	water, work, cars, barge, are, for
Vowel patterns *ow, ay, ey*	sprays, play, they
CVC words Regular pattern *(run)* Other *(how)*	1. job, tug (tugboat), net(s), big, but, has, can 2. car(s), put, for
CVV words *(see)*	sea, too
VVC words *(out)*	eat(ing), out
VCC words *(all)*	and, all

continues

CVCC words *(fish)*	kind, pull(ing), fish, full, work, help(s), long, push(ing), kind(s), back, with
CVVC words *(soap, foot)*	boat, goes, deep, load(s), coal, room(s), look
CCVVC words *(cream)*	float(ing), sleep(ing)
CVCe words **Regular pattern** *(make)* **Other** *(have)*	1. take, home, here 2. come(s), fire, live(s), some
CCVC words *(then)*	ship, flat, this, they, that, them, play
CCVCC words *(black)*	small, truck(s)
CCVCe words *(white)*	these
CVCCe words *(table, taste)*	barge
Sentence length	4–12
Sentences per page	3–5
Number of words	199

Lesson	107
Book Title	***THE THREE BILLY GOATS***
Feature	**Examples from the Text**

Labels/Names	Billy Goats, Big, Little, Small
Content words	goats, long, ago, named, small, grass, always, hungry, across, river, green, hill, covered, tasty, grass, fine, lunch, reached, edge, sign, warning, troll, bridge, cross, neither, worry, pointed, smart, only, first, trotted, feet, sound, trip-trap, woke, crossing, yelled, fresh, please, cried, try, gobble, stopped, think, thin, wait, sister, bigger, well, right, before, change, mind, next, middle-sized, brother, tastier, meal, climbed, nice, won't, throw, head, began, pushed, fell, crossed, joined, felt, smart, lovely
High-frequency words	the, there, were, three, big, little, and, like, all, they, loved, for, more, one, day, said, look, over, looked, saw, a, that, is, so, it, must, be, with, will, make, let's, go, now, of, do, not, don't, he, under, we, are, I, see, can, get, went, as, his, made, up, who, my, it's, me, want, some, to, eat, let, no, may, if, am, very, she, you, find, her, much, more, then, run, away, ran, came, this, just, had, than, I'm, going, into, put, down, off
Pronouns	they, there, that, it, we, he, his, my, me, she, you, her, I, this
Prepositions	for, over, with, of, under, to, up, into
Words with inflectional endings	named, loved, looked, covered, tasty, reached, warning, pointed, trotted, crossing, yelled, cried, stopped, bigger, middle-sized, tastier, climbed, going, crossed
Compound words	across, away, into
Contractions	let's, don't, it's, won't
Plurals	goats, trolls, characters
Difficult word patterns	three, tasty, lunch, reached, edge, bridge, neither, pointed, only, first, sound, gobble, right, change, middle-sized, tastier, throw, characters, narrator
Difficult multisyllable words	always, hungry, across, river, covered, tasty, neither, worry, pointed, under, only, gobble, sister, bigger, away, before, middle-sized, brother, tastier, going, river, lovely, characters, narrator
Words with *a* as *schwa*	across, away
Words ending in *y* Sounding like (1) *i* or (2) *e*	1. my, try 2. hungry, tasty, worry, only, very
Words with vowel and *r*	for, over, river, under, smart, first, sister, bigger, her, before, brother, river, smart
Vowel patterns *ow, ay, ey*	always, they, day, now, may, away, throw, play

continues

CVC words **Regular pattern** *(run)* **Other** *(how)*	1. big, not, can, get, his, let, run, ran, had 2. for, saw, now, her
Onomatopoetic words	trip-trap
CVV words *(see)*	see, you
VVC words *(out)*	eat
VCC words *(all)*	and, all
CVCC words *(fish)*	long, hill, must, with, will, warn(ing), went, yell(ed), want, find, much, well, next, mind, just, fell, felt, sign
CVVC words *(soap, foot)*	goats, said, look, feet, wait, meal, join(ed)
CCVVC words *(cream)*	green, cried
CVCe words **Regular pattern** *(make)* **Other** *(have)*	1. name(d), like, more, make, fine, made, woke, came, nice 2. were, love(d), some
CCVC words *(then)*	they, that, trot(trotted), trip, trap, stop(stopped), thin, then, this, than, play
CCVCC words *(black)*	small, grass, troll, cross, smart, cross(ing), fresh, think, climb(ed)
CCVCe words *(white)*	there
CCVVCe words *(cheese)*	please
Sentence length	3–15
Sentences per page	2–8
Number of words	532

Lesson	108
Book Title	***ALL ABOUT CHIMPS***
Feature	**Examples from the Text**
Content words	chimp, chimps, dark, hair, ears, hands, most, live, forest, spend, time, tree, trees, long, arms, strong, swing, foot, toe, climb, groups, sounds, talk, food, clean, other's, hair, fingers, bugs, dirt, bug, fruit, leaves, flowers, seeds, also, eggs, team, share, tools, stick, catch, pokes, hole, crawl, pulls, sleep, nests, branches, night, baby, rides, mother's, twins
High-frequency words	this, is, a, have, they, big, and, in, the, lot, of, their, are, very, can, from, to, this, look, at, it, helps, what, do, make, each, other, help, find, with, looks, for, if, he, finds*, eats, eat, some, work, use, uses*, as, into, out, how, new, every, she, her, mother, on, back, mothers*, one, but, had
Pronouns	this, they, it, he, she, her
Prepositions	in, of, at, to, with, for, into, up, on
Words with inflectional endings	helps, looks, finds, eats, uses, pokes, pulls, rides
Plurals	chimps, ears, hands, trees, groups, sounds, fingers, bugs, leaves, seeds, eggs, tools, nests, branches, mothers, twins
Difficult word patterns	sounds, each, fingers, leaves, use, uses, catch, branches, every, night
Difficult multisyllable words	forest, other, fingers, also, branches, every, baby, mother
Words ending in *y* **Sounding like (1) *i* or (2) *e***	1. 2. very, every, baby
Words with vowel and *r*	dark, arms, other, for, dirt, work, every, her, mother
Vowel patterns *ow, ay, ey*	they, how
CVC words **Regular pattern *(run)*** **Other *(how)***	1. big, lot, can, bug, but, had 2. how, new, for, her
CVV words *(see)*	toe
VVC words *(out)*	ear(s), eat, out
VCC words *(all)*	and, arm(s), egg(s)
CVCC words *(fish)*	dark, hand(s), most, long, help, talk, find, with, dirt, work, pull(s), nest(s), back
CVVC words *(soap, foot)*	hair, foot, look, food, hair, seed(s), team, tool(s)
CCVVC words *(cream)*	their, group(s), clean, fruit, sleep

Appendix

continues

CVCe words Regular pattern *(make)* **Other** *(have)*	1. time, make, poke(s), hole, ride(s) 2. have, live, some
CCVC words *(then)*	this, they, from, what, twin(s)
CCVCC words *(black)*	chimp, spend, swing, climb, stick, crawl
Sentence length	4–10
Sentences per page	1–3 (one page with 5)
Number of words	218

Lesson	109
Book Title	***BAD-LUCK DAY***
Feature	**Examples from the Text**

Labels/Names	Tia, Gracie, Tony, Benny
Content words	would, never, forget, matter, hard, tried, everyone, family, getting, ready, school, alarm, clock, gone, later, enjoying, breakfast, dog, bumped, table, most, cereal, ended, lap, changed, clothes, stepped, time, bus, driving, great, whispered, turning, real, bad-luck, bothering, forgotten, opened, backpack, lunch, homework, missing, kids, turned, math, row, cups, window, wind, blew, cup, side, name, friend, felt, sorry, you're, such, lucky, charm, bring, thanks, someone, principal's, office, class, bag, grinned, think, stopped, wash, hands, fell, neck, sink, I'd, better, keep, nervously, almost, drain, lunchroom, puddle, milk, floor, slipped, crash, sandwich, right, everyone, enjoying, offered, half, tuna, brother, surprised, started, bite, noticed, bug, shrieked, dropping, leaned, plastic, worm, knew, else, reading, stomach, rumbled, searched, found, old, candy, bar, finally, shadow, across, desk, teacher, allowed, sure, sighed, room, shut, door, stay, rest, told, nothing, bad, happen, friend, things, happened, feel, better, talking, think, finally, stopped, hello
High-frequency words	was, about, to, have, a, day, she, no, how, in, her, for, work, or, but, not, had, off, the, up, and, outside, just, see, away, this, into, walking, something, when, got, were, all, their, sat, by, one, over, of, having, here, take, my, will, you, good, said, from, came, into, with, your, is, working, way, went, down, didn't, me, he, made, this, big, then, it's, back, eat, an, some, I, that, you, know, do, home, ran, I'll, can, called, him, about, what
Pronouns	she, her, your, my, me, he, this, that, you, him
Prepositions	to, in, up, for, off, on, by, into
Words with inflectional endings	getting, enjoying, bumped, ended, changed, stepped, driving, whispered, turning, walking, bothering, forgotten, opened, missing, turned, having, thanks, grinned, working, stopped, nervously, slipped, enjoying, offered, surprised, started, shrieked, dropping, leaned, reading, rumbled, searched, finally, allowed, sighed, called, happened, talking, stopped
Compound words	forget, everyone, breakfast, outside, away, into, something, backpack, homework, someone, into, lunchroom, everyone, across, nothing
Contractions	you're, I'd, didn't, it's, I'll
Plurals	clothes, kids, cups, hands, things
Difficult word patterns	about, would, ready, school, cereal, clothes, lunch, right, shrieked, else, searched, found
Difficult multisyllable words	about, never, matter, family, ready, alarm, later, table, cereal, driving, whispered, window, principal's, office, better, almost, puddle, sandwich, offered, surprised, noticed, plastic, stomach, rumbled, finally, shadow, teacher, happen, happened, better, hello

Appendix

continues

Words with *a* as *schwa*	alarm, across, away, about
Words ending in *y* **Sounding like (1) *i* or** **(2) *e***	1. by, my 2. family, ready, sorry, lucky, nervously, candy
Words with vowel and *r* surprised, worm, sure, better	never, hard, her, for, work, later, bothering, were, over, charm, better, brother,
Vowel patterns *ow, ay, ey*	day, how, away, row, window, way, down, allowed, know, stay, way
CVC words **Regular pattern** *(run)* **Other** *(how)*	1. bad, get(getting), but, not, had, dog, lap, bus, got, kid(s), cup, sat, bag, big, bug, bar, ran, him 2. her, for, was, how, row
CVV words *(see)*	see, you
VVC words *(out)*	eat
VCC words *(all)*	off, end(ed), and, all, old
CVCC words *(fish)*	luck, hard, work, bump(ed), most, just, turn(ing), walk(ing), miss(ing), turn(ed), math, wind, felt, such, will, with, work(ing), wash, hand(s), fell, neck, sink, went, down, milk, half, worm, back, desk, rest, told, sigh(ed), call(ed), told, talk(ing)
CVVC words *(soap, foot)*	real, good, said, your, keep, read(ing), room, door, feel, leaned
CCVVC words *(cream)*	tried, great, their, drain, floor
CVCe words **Regular pattern** *(make)* **Other** *(have)*	1. time, side, name, here, take, came, made, bite, home 2. have, gone, were, some, sure
CCVC words *(then)*	step(stepped), this, when, blew, from, grin(grinned), slip(slipped), this, then, drop(dropping), knew, that, know, shut, stay, stop(stopped), what
CCVCC words *(black)*	clock, charm, thank(s), class, think, crash, start(ed), thing(s), think, bring
CCVCe words *(white)*	drive(driving)
CVCCe words *(table, taste)*	
CCVVCe words *(cheese)*	change(d)
CCVVCC words *(friend)*	friend
Sentence length	3–17
Sentences per page	3–7
Number of words	466

Lesson	110
Book Title	***A TRIP TO THE LAUNDROMUTT***
Feature	**Examples from the Text**
Labels/Names	laundromutt, Orson, Taco, Jack, Mom
Content words	looked, needs, bath, really, tubs, dogs, those, wash, first, pushed, pulled, tub, turned, water, wet, dog, shook, gave, scrub-a-dub-dub, next, hair, dryer, fur, blew, time, around, floor, walls, hates, barked, woof, last, need
High-frequency words	at, a, said, looked, let's, go, to, the, had, big, for, did, not, like, look, of, she, and, got, into, on, soon, was, then, too, is, in, here, there, up, down, very, good, it, give, put, that, little, jumped, out, no, ran, we, you, all, he, but, us, now
Pronouns	she, that, we, you, it, he, us
Prepositions	to, at, of, for, into, on, in, up
Words with inflectional endings	looked, needs, really, pushed, pulled, turned, dryer, jumped, hates, barked
Contractions	let's
Plurals	tubs, dogs, walls
Difficult word patterns	laundromutt, first, dryer, little, around
Difficult multisyllable words	laundromutt, really, water, scrub-a-dub-dub, dryer, very, little, around
Words with *a* as *schwa*	around
Words ending in *y* Sounding like (1) *i* or (2) *e*	1. 2. very
Words with vowel and *r*	for, fur
Vowel patterns *ow, ay, ey*	down, now
CVC words Regular pattern *(run)* Other *(how)*	1. mom, let('s), had, big, tub, dog, did, not, got, wet, ran, but 2. was, for, put, fur, now
Onomatopoetic words	woof
CVV words *(see)*	too, you
VVC words *(out)*	out
VCC words *(all)*	and, all
CVCC words *(fish)*	bath, wash, push(ed), pull(ed**)**, turn(ed), next, down, jump(ed), wall(s), last, bark(ed)

continues

Appendix

CVVC words *(soap, foot)*	look(ed), need, said, real(ly), look, soon, hair, good, woof
CCVVC words *(cream)*	shook, floor
CVCe words **Regular pattern** *(make)* **Other** *(have)*	1. like, gave, here, time, hate(s) 2. give
CCVC words *(then)*	trip, then, blew, that
CCVCe words *(white)*	those, there
Sentence length	4–11
Sentences per page	1–3
Number of words	229

▶ Record-Keeping Forms

The LLI system provides a number of record-keeping forms that you can print out from the *Lesson Resources CD*. You can use these forms to take Reading Records and monitor the children in terms of their lesson and reading progress.

Recording Form: a form to use to take the Reading Record on each child. You will code the reading behavior using a standardized system for coding (see Coding a Reading Record, page 82, and the *Professional Development and Tutorial DVDs*). You will also score and analyze the record (see Scoring and Analyzing a Reading Record, page 83, and the *Professional Development and Tutorial DVDs*) to get important information on how the reader is using sources of information, initiating strategic actions, and comprehending the book.

Lesson Record: a tool to record your specific observations of the reading and writing behaviors of the children in every lesson. Write notes about what is significant in your observations.

Letter/Word Record: a tool to keep track of each child's specific letter learning as well as the specific high-frequency words the group almost knows or controls consistently. When the children are learning letters, you may want to note for each child whether he knows the name of the letter, its sound, or how to form it.

Reading Graph: a tool that allows you to record information on each child over time. You can enter the child's instructional level, resulting in a graph that shows the child's progress throughout the course of the intervention.

Intervention Record: a tool used to monitor the amount of leveled literacy intervention and the amount of small group instruction in the classroom each week.

Student Achievement Log: a tool to document a child's performance as she enters or exits the LLI system.

Individual Communication Sheet: a tool used to communicate with the classroom teacher regarding an individual's weekly progress.

Group Communication Sheet: a tool used to communicate with the classroom teacher about a group's weekly progress.

▶ Glossary

The following is a glossary of the terms, materials, and Instructional Routines used in the LLI system and described briefly in this guide. Often, a particular routine will be briefly described within a lesson also. You can refer to Instructional Routines for LLI, page 62, to learn more about the routines. In addition, you will find more information on these routines in *When Readers Struggle: Teaching that Works*, in the chapters titled "Learning about Print: Early Reading Behaviors" and "Building and Using a Repertoire of Words." You can use any or all of these routines to enrich your instruction and make it more powerful.

accuracy (as in oral reading) or **accuracy rate**
The percentage of words the child reads aloud correctly.

adjust (as a strategic action)
To read in different ways as appropriate to the purpose for reading and type of text.

affix
A part added to the beginning or ending of a base or root word to change its meaning or function (a prefix or a suffix).

alphabet book (*My ABC Book*)
A book that helps children develop the concept and sequence of the alphabet by pairing alphabet letters with pictures of people, animals, or objects with labels related to the letters.

Alphabet Linking Chart
A chart containing upper- and lowercase letters of the alphabet paired with pictures representing words beginning with each letter (*a, apple*).

alphabetic principle
The concept that there is a relationship between the spoken sounds in oral language and the graphic forms in written language.

analogy
The resemblance of a known word to an unknown word that helps to solve the unknown word's meaning.

analyze (as a strategic action)
To examine the elements of a text in order to know more about how it is constructed and to notice aspects of the writer's craft.

analyzing a Reading Record
Looking at errors, self-corrections, and sources of information and strategic actions to plan instruction.

animal fantasy
A make-believe story in which personified animals are the main characters.

assessment
A means for gathering information or data that reveals what learners control, partially control, or do not yet control consistently.

automaticity
Rapid, accurate, fluent word decoding without conscious effort or attention.

base word
A whole word to which affixes can be added to create new word forms (for example, *wash* plus *-ing* becomes *washing*).

behaviors
Actions that are observable as children read or write.

blend
To combine sounds or word parts.

bold (boldface)
Type that is heavier and darker than usual, often used for emphasis.

book and print features (as text characteristics)
The physical attributes of a text (for example, font, layout, and length).

capitalization
The use of capital letters, usually the first letter in a word, as a convention of written language (for example, for proper names and to begin sentences).

choral reading
To read aloud in unison with a group.

code (a Reading Record)
To record a child's oral reading errors, self-corrections, and other behaviors.

Coding and Scoring Errors at-a-Glance
A chart containing a brief summary of how to code and score oral reading errors.

compound word
A word made up of two or more words or morphemes (for example, *playground*). The meaning of a compound word can be a combination of the meanings of the words it contains or can be unrelated to the meanings of the combined units.

comprehension (as in reading)
The process of constructing meaning while reading text.

comprehension conversation
The conversation that takes place in the Rereading and Assessment section of the lesson, in which the child shares his understanding of the text.

concept words
Words that represent abstract ideas or names. Categories of concept words include colors, numbers, months, days of the week, position words, and so on.

connecting strategies
Ways of solving words by using connections or analogies with similar known words (for example, knowing *she* and *out* helps with *shout*).

consonant-vowel-consonant (CVC)
A common sequence of sounds in a single syllable (for example, *hat*).

consonant
A speech sound made by partial or complete closure of the airflow that causes friction at one or more points in the breath channel. The consonant sounds are represented by the letters *b, c, d, f, g, h, j, k, l, m, n, p, q, r, s, t, v, w* (in most uses), *x, y* (in most uses), and *z*.

consonant blend
Two or more consonant letters that often appear together in words and represent sounds that are smoothly joined, although each of the sounds can be heard in the word (for example, *tr* in *trim*).

consonant cluster
A sequence of two or three consonant letters that appear together in words (for example, *tr*im, *ch*air).

Consonant Cluster Linking Chart
A chart of common consonant clusters paired with pictures representing words beginning with each cluster (for example, *bl, block*).

consonant digraph
Two consonant letters that appear together and represent a single sound that is different from the sound of either letter (for example, *sh*ell).

content (as a text characteristic)
The subject matter of a text.

contraction
A shortening of a syllable, word, or word groups, usually by the omission of a sound or letters (for example, *didn't*).

conventions (in writing)
Formal usage that has become customary in written language. Grammar, capitalization, and punctuation are three categories of conventions in writing.

critique (as a strategic action)
To evaluate a text using one's personal, world, or text knowledge, and to think critically about the ideas in the text.

cumulative tale
A story with many details repeated until the climax.

Data Management CD
A resource that enables the teacher to track and print reports on entry/exit data and progress-monitoring data for individuals or groups of children.

decoding
Using letter-sound relationships to translate a word from a series of symbols to a unit of meaning.

dialect
A regional variety of language. In most languages, including English and Spanish, dialects are mutually intelligible; the differences are actually minor.

dialogue
Spoken words, usually set off with quotation marks in text.

dictated writing
The teacher reads aloud a sentence, and children write it in *My Writing Book* to learn how to go from oral to written language. The teacher provides support as needed.

directionality
The orientation of print. In the English language, directionality is from left to right.

distinctive letter features
Visual features that make every letter of the alphabet different from every other letter.

early literacy concepts
Very early understandings related to how written language or print is organized and used.

English language learners
People whose native language is not English and who are acquiring English as an additional language.

error
A reader's response that is not consistent with the text and that is *not* self-corrected.

expository text
A composition that explains a concept, using information and description.

F&P Calculator Stopwatch
A device that will calculate the reading time, reading rate, accuracy rate, and self-correction ratio for a reading.

factual text
(See **informational text**.)

fantasy
An imaginative, fictional text containing elements that are highly unreal.

fiction
An invented story, usually narrative.

figurative language
Language that is filled with word images and metaphorical language to express more than a literal meaning.

fluency (as in oral reading)
The way an oral reading sounds, including phrasing, intonation, pausing, stress, rate, and integration of the first five factors.

fluency in reading
To read continuous text with good momentum, phrasing, appropriate pausing, intonation, and stress.

fluency in word solving
Speed, accuracy, and flexibility in solving words.

fold sheet
A tool for classroom and home practice that involves having children work with letters or words by writing and illustrating, folding the sheet if necessary, and writing their name on the cover.

folktale
A traditional story, originally passed down orally.

font
In printed text, the collection of type (letters) in a particular style.

form (as a text characteristic)
A kind of text that is characterized by particular elements. Mystery, for example, is a form of writing within the narrative fiction genre.

genre
A category of written text that is characterized by a particular style, form, or content.

gradient of reading difficulty
(See **text gradient**.)

grammar
Complex rules by which people can generate an unlimited number of phrases, sentences, and longer texts in a language. Conventional grammar reflects the accepted conventions in a society.

grapheme
A letter or cluster of letters representing a single sound or phoneme (for example, *a, eigh, ay*).

Guide for Observing and Noting Reading Behaviors
Lists questions a teacher should ask himself or herself about the ways a child is processing or problem solving texts.

hard reading level
The level at which the child reads the text aloud with less than 90% accuracy (Levels A–K) or less than 95% accuracy (Levels L–Z).

high-frequency words
Words that occur often in the spoken and written language (for example, *the*).

historical fiction
An imagined story set in the realistically (and often factually) portrayed setting of a past era.

illustrations (as a text characteristic)
Graphic representations of important content (for example, art, photos, maps, graphs, charts).

independent reading level
The level at which the child reads the text with 95% or higher accuracy and excellent or satisfactory comprehension (Levels A–K) or 98% or higher accuracy with excellent or satisfactory comprehension (Levels L–Z).

independent writing
Children write a text independently with teacher support as needed.

interactive writing
The teacher and children compose and construct a text on chart paper for everyone to see and reread.

individual instruction
The teacher working with one child.

infer (as a strategic action)
To go beyond the literal meaning of a text; to think about what is not stated but is implied by the writer.

inflectional ending
A suffix added to a base word to show tense, plurality, possession, or comparison (for example, *-er* in *darker*).

informational text
A category of texts in which the purpose is to inform or to give facts about a topic. Nonfiction articles and essays are examples of informational text.

insertion (as an error in reading)
A word added during oral reading that is not in the text.

instructional reading level
At Levels A–K, the level at which the child reads the text with 90–94% accuracy and excellent or satisfactory comprehension; or 95% or higher accuracy and limited comprehension. At Levels L–Z, the level at which the child reads the text with 95–97% accuracy and excellent or satisfactory comprehension; or 98% or higher accuracy and limited comprehension.

interactive read-aloud
The teacher reading aloud to a group of children and inviting them to think and talk about the text before, during, and after reading.

interactive writing
A teaching context in which children cooperatively plan, compose, and write a group text; both teacher and children act as scribes (in turn).

intervention
Intensive additional instruction for children not progressing as rapidly as expected; usually one-on-one tutoring or small group (one-on-three) teaching.

intonation
The rise and fall in pitch of the voice in speech to convey meaning.

italic (italics)
A type style that is characterized by slanted letters.

key understandings
Important ideas within (literal), beyond (implied), or about (determined through critical analysis) the text that are necessary to comprehension.

label (in writing)
Written word or phrase that names the content of an illustration.

label book
A picture book consisting of illustrations with brief identifying text.

language and literary features (as text characteristics)
Qualities particular to written language that are qualitatively different from spoken language (for example, dialogue; figurative language; and literary elements such as character, setting, and plot in fiction or description and technical language in nonfiction).

language use (in writing)
The craft of using sentences, phrases, and expressions to describe events, actions, or information.

layout
The way the print is arranged on a page.

Lesson Resources CD
A resource that provides the specific materials for each lesson. It includes Recording Forms for taking Reading Records on instructional books, word and picture cards, Letter Minibooks, Alphabet Linking Chart, *My Poetry Book*, Parent Letters, and other record-keeping and observation forms and resources used in LLI.

letter and word games (Lotto, Follow the Path, and so on)
Games that require children to look carefully at words, letters, and parts of words.

Letter Minibooks
Short books, each of which is focused on a particular letter and its relation to a sound.

letter-sound correspondence
Recognizing the corresponding sound of a specific letter when that letter is seen or heard.

letter-sound relationships
(See **letter-sound correspondence**.)

letter knowledge
The ability to recognize and label the graphic symbols of language.

letters
Graphic symbols representing the sounds in a language. Each letter has particular distinctive features and may be identified by letter name or sound.

leveled books
Texts designated along a gradient from Level A (easiest) to Level Z (hardest).

lexicon
Words that make up language.

long vowel
The elongated vowel sound that is the same as the name of the vowel; it is sometimes represented by two or more letters (for example, c*a*ke, *eigh*t, m*ai*l).

lowercase letter
A small-letter form that is usually different from its corresponding capital or uppercase form.

M (meaning)
One of the sources of information that readers use (MSV: meaning, language structure, visual information). Meaning, the semantic system of language, refers to meaning derived from words, meaning across a text or texts, and meaning from personal experience or knowledge.

magnetic letters
Multicolored upper- and lowercase letters that children manipulate to learn to read and form words.

maintain fluency (as a strategic action)
To integrate sources of information in a smoothly operating process that results in expressive, phrased reading.

make connections (as a strategic action)
To search for and use connections to knowledge gained through personal experiences, learning about the world, and reading other texts.

memoir
An account of something important, usually part of a person's life. A memoir is a kind of biography, autobiography, or personal narrative.

monitor and correct (as a strategic action)
To check whether the reading sounds right, looks right, and makes sense, and to solve problems when it doesn't.

My ABC Book
A book containing upper- and lowercase letters on each page, along with a key word and a picture to develop children's knowledge of the alphabet, upper- and lower-case letters, features of letters, and letter/sound relationships.

My Poetry Book
A book containing all of the poems used in lessons in the particular system in which you are working.

My Vowel Book
A book containing just the vowels. On each page, you have the upper and lowercase vowel and one picture that can be either the short or long sound of the

vowel. You can print books for children that feature only the short or the long sound. Or, you can print pages back to back so that the left page has the short sound and the right page has the long sound.

My Writing Book
A consumable blank book that children can use for all of their writing needs. The books are filled as children write and draw for activities in LLI lessons. When all pages of a book are filled, the child takes it home and begins a new book for subsequent lessons. Completed pages of *My Writing Book* are excellent for reading practice either in school or at home.

name chart
A tool for helping children learn about letters, sounds, and words. It is a list of names, usually in alphabetical order by the first letter. Some teachers write the first letter of each name in red and the rest of the name in black. The print should be clear, and names should not be jammed together.

name puzzle
Using a set of letters, each child forms a puzzle of his or her own name in order to notice letters and their distinguishing characteristics.

narrative text
A category of texts in which the purpose is to tell a story. Stories and biographies are kinds of narrative.

new word learning
A variety of ways children learn new words, including looking at the first letter and then running their finger left to right as they scan the word with their eyes.

nonfiction
A text whose primary purpose is to convey accurate information and facts.

omission (as in error)
A word left out or skipped during oral reading.

onset-rime segmentation
The identification and separation of onsets (first part) and rimes (last part, containing the vowel) in words (for example, *dr-ip*).

onset
In a syllable, the part (consonant, consonant cluster, or consonant digraph) that comes before the vowel (for example, *cr*-eam).

oral games
Games teachers can play with children to help them learn how to listen for and identify words in sentences, syllables, onsets and rimes, and individual phonemes.

oral reading
In even-numbered lessons, the section called Rereading Books and Assessment, during which the child reads a text aloud and the teacher codes his or her reading behavior using the Recording Form, has a brief comprehension conversation, and makes a teaching point that will be helpful to the reader.

orthographic awareness
The knowledge of the visual features of written language, including distinctive features of letters, as well as spelling patterns in words.

orthography
The representation of the sounds of a language with the proper letters according to standard usage (spelling).

phoneme
The smallest unit of sound in spoken language. There are approximately forty-four units of speech sounds in English.

phoneme-grapheme correspondence
The relationship between the sounds (phonemes) and letters (graphemes) of a language.

phoneme addition
To add a beginning or ending sound to a word (for example, *h + and, an + t*).

phoneme blending
To identify individual sounds and then to put them together smoothly to make a word (for example, *c-a-t = cat*).

phoneme deletion
To omit a beginning, middle, or ending sound of a word (for example, *cart – c = art*).

phoneme isolation
The identification of an individual sound (beginning, middle, or end) in a word.

phoneme manipulation
To move sounds from one place in a word to another place in the word.

phoneme reversal
The exchange of the first and last sounds of a word to make a different sound.

phoneme substitution
The replacement of the beginning, middle, or ending sound of a word with a new sound.

phonemic (or phoneme) awareness
The ability to hear individual sounds in words and to identify individual sounds.

phonemic strategies
Ways of solving words that use how words sound and relationships between letters and letter clusters and phonemes in those words (for example, *cat, hat*).

phonetics
The scientific study of speech sounds—how the sounds are made vocally and the relation of speech sounds to the total language process.

phonics
The knowledge of letter-sound relationships and how they are used in reading and writing. Teaching phonics refers to helping children acquire this body of knowledge about the oral and written language systems; additionally, teaching phonics helps children use phonics knowledge as part of a reading and writing

process. Phonics instruction uses a small portion of the body of knowledge that makes up phonetics.

phonogram
A phonetic element represented by graphic characters or symbols. In word recognition, a graphic sequence composed of a vowel grapheme and an ending consonant grapheme (such as *-an* or *-it*) is sometimes called a word family.

phonological awareness The awareness of words, rhyming words, onsets and rimes, syllables, and individual sounds (phonemes).

phonological system
The sounds of the language and how they work together in ways that are meaningful to the speakers of the language.

picture book
A highly illustrated fiction or nonfiction text in which pictures work with the text to tell a story or provide information.

plural
Of, relating to, or constituting more than one.

possessive
Grammatical constructions used to show ownership (for example, *John's, his*).

predict (as a strategic action)
To use what is known to think about what will follow while reading continuous text.

principle (in phonics)
A generalization or a sound-spelling relationship that is predictable.

processing (as in reading)
The mental operations involved in constructing meaning from written language.

prompt
A question, direction, or statement designed to encourage the child to say more about a topic.

Prompting Guide 1
A tool you can use in each lesson as a quick reference for specific language to teach for, prompt for, or reinforce effective reading and writing behaviors. The guide is organized in categories and color-coded so that you can turn quickly to the area needed and refer to it as you teach.

Professional Development and Tutorial DVDs
You can use the *Professional Development and Tutorial DVDs* to support your work individually or with a study group of professionals. There are two disks for each system (Orange, Green, and Blue). The first disk provides an overview of the program and presents model lessons. The second disk contains a tutorial on coding, scoring, and analyzing Reading Records and information on using the data to inform your teaching.

punctuation
Marks used in written text to clarify meaning and separate structural units. The comma and the period are common punctuation marks.

reading graph
A graph that charts individual or group progress through leveled books.

reading rate (words per minute, or WPM)
The number of words a child reads per minute, either orally or silently.

Reading Record
The transcript of the text on which oral reading is coded.

Recording Form
The form on which oral reading, the comprehension conversation, and the "writing about reading" assessment for a text are coded and scored. There is a Recording Form for each book in the Leveled Literacy Intervention System. All are located on the *Data Management CD-ROM*.

repetition (in oral reading)
The reader saying a word, phrase, or section of the text more than once.

rhyme
The ending part (rime) of a word that sounds like the ending part (rime) of another word (for example, m-*ail*, t-*ale*).

rime
The ending part of a word containing the vowel; the letters that represent the vowel sound and the consonant letters following it in a syllable (for example, dr-*eam*).

rubric
A scoring tool that relies on descriptions of response categories for evaluation.

running words
The number of words read aloud and coded during the Rereading Books and Assessment part of even-numbered lessons.

S (structure)
One of the sources of information that readers use (MSV: meaning, language structure, visual information). Language structure refers to the way words are put together in phrases and sentences (syntax or grammar).

scoring a Reading Record
Counting coded errors and self-corrections, which allows you to calculate *accuracy rate* and *self-correction ratio* on the Recording Form. The form also provides space for a *fluency score* (Levels C–N) and *reading rate* (Levels J–N).

Scoring and Coding At-a-Glance
A summary of the steps for scoring the three parts of a running record: oral reading, comprehension conversation, and writing about reading.

search for and use information (as a strategic action)
To look for and to think about all kinds of content in order to make sense of text while reading.

searching
The reader looking for information in order to read accurately, self-correct, or understand a text.

segment (as a strategic action)
To divide into parts (for example, c-*at*).

self-correction ratio
The proportion of errors the reader corrects himself.

semantic system
The system by which speakers of a language communicate meaning though language.

sentence complexity (as a text characteristic)
The complexity of the structure or syntax of a sentence. Addition of phrases and clauses to simple sentences increases complexity.

sentence strips
Strips of oak tag on which sentences have been written and then cut up and mixed up so that children put the sentences back together.

series book
One of a collection of books about the same character or characters and the different events or situations they encounter.

shared reading
Teacher and children read a large-print text together after the teacher has read it aloud once to the children. The teacher points under each word and later places the pointer at the start of each line.

short vowel
A brief-duration sound represented by a vowel letter (for example, c*a*t).

silent *e*
The final *e* in a spelling pattern that usually signals a long vowel sound in the word and does not represent a sound itself (for example, mak*e*).

silent reading
The reader reading the text to herself.

sketching and drawing (in writing)
To create a rough (sketch) or finished (drawing) image of a person, a place, a thing, or an idea to capture, work with, and render the writer's ideas.

small books

In the Leveled Literacy Intervention, learning takes place with the foundational support of seventy children's books, called small books.

small-group reading instruction

The teacher working with children brought together because they are similar enough in reading development to teach in a small group; guided reading.

solve words (as a strategic action)

To use a range of strategies to take words apart and understand their meaning.

sound boxes and letter boxes (Elkonin Boxes)

A tool for helping children to learn about the sounds and letters in words.

sounding out

Pronouncing the sounds of the letters in a word as a step in reading the word.

sources of information

The various cues in a written text that combine to make meaning (for example, syntax, meaning, and the physical shape and arrangement of type).

spelling aloud

Naming the letters in a word rather than reading the word.

spelling patterns

Beginning letters (onsets) and common phonograms (rimes) form the basis for the English syllable; knowing these patterns, a child can build countless words.

split dialogue

Written dialogue in which a "said" phrase divides the speaker's words: for example, "Come on," said Mom, "let's go home."

standardized

Remaining essentially the same across multiple instances.

strategic action

Any one of many simultaneous, coordinated thinking activities that go on in a reader's head. See **thinking within, beyond, and about the text**.

stress

The emphasis given to some syllables or words.

student folders

A set of folders to keep Reading Records and other data for each child. These folders can be passed on each year as part of children's records. The inside of the folder includes a graph for tracking a child's initial level, progress throughout LLI, and exit information.

substitution (as in error in reading)

The reader reading aloud one (incorrect) word for another.

suffix

An affix or group of letters added at the end of a base word or root word to change its function or meaning (for example, hand*ful*, hope*less*).

summarize (as a strategic action)

To put together and remember important information, while disregarding irrelevant information, during or after reading.

syllabication

The division of words into syllables (for example, *pen-cil*).

synonym

One of two or more words that have different sounds but the same meaning (for example, *chair, seat*).

syntactic awareness

The knowledge of grammatical patterns or structures.

syntactic system

Rules that govern the ways in which morphemes and words work together in sentence patterns. Not the same as proper grammar, which refers to the accepted grammatical conventions.

syntax
The study of how sentences are formed and of the grammatical rules that govern their formation.

synthesize (as a strategic action)
To combine new information or ideas from reading text with existing knowledge to create new understandings.

table charts
Charts the teacher constructs with the children, based on activities in the lessons, that are large enough for all the children in a group to see across a table.

take-home bags
Bags in which children take home items such as word bags, sentence strips, Take-Home Books, or other materials for classroom and home connection activities.

Take-Home Books
Black-and-white versions of the books children read in their lessons.

text gradient
A twenty-six point (A–Z) text-rating scale of difficulty, in which each text level, from the easiest at Level A to the most challenging at Level Z, represents a small but significant increase in difficulty over the previous level. The gradient correlates these levels to grade levels.

text structure
The overall architecture or organization of a piece of writing. Chronology (sequence) and description are two common text structures.

theme
The central idea or concept in a story or the message that the author is conveying.

thinking within, beyond, and about the text
Three ways of thinking about a text while reading. Thinking *within* the text involves efficiently and effectively understanding what is on the page, the author's literal message. Thinking *beyond* the text requires making inferences and putting text ideas together in different ways to construct the text's meaning. In thinking *about* the text, readers analyze and critique the author's craft.

told
The teacher telling the reader a word he cannot read.

topic
The subject of a piece of writing.

understandings
Basic concepts that are crucial to comprehending a particular area.

V (visual information)
One of three sources of information that readers use (MSV: meaning, language structure, visual information). Visual information refers to the letters that represent the sounds of language and the way they are combined (spelling patterns) to create words; visual information at the sentence level includes punctuation.

Verbal Path
Language used to help children get the hand moving the right way to form letters efficiently.

vocabulary (as a text characteristic)
Words and their meanings.

voice-print match
Usually applied to a beginning reader's ability to match one spoken word with one printed word while reading and pointing. In experienced readers, the eyes take over the process.

vowel
A speech sound or phoneme made without stoppage of or friction in the airflow. The vowel sounds are represented by *a, e, i, o, u,* and sometimes *y* and *w.*

ways to sort and match letters

Using magnetic letters or letter cards, children sort letters to learn their distinctive features.

word

A unit of meaning in language.

word analysis

To break apart words into parts or individual sounds in order to read and understand them.

word bags

A collection of high-frequency word cards that are kept in a sealable, one-quart plastic bag.

word boundaries

The white space that defines a word; the white space before the first letter and after the last letter of a word. It is important for beginning readers to learn to recognize word boundaries.

word family

A term often used to designate words that are connected by phonograms or rimes (for example, *hot, not, pot, shot*). A word family can also be a series of words connected by meaning (affixes added to a base word; for example: *base, baseball, basement, baseman, basal, basis, baseless, baseline, baseboard, abase, abasement, off base, home base; precise, précis, precisely, precision*).

word ladders

A technique for helping children learn how to manipulate letters and word parts to construct new words. You start with a word, then change, add, or remove one or more letters to make a new word.

word-solving actions

(See **solve words**.)

words (as a text characteristic)

The decodability of words in a text; phonetic and structural features of words.

words in text

Children use their eyes to locate known and unknown words in text.

writing

Children engaging in the writing process and producing pieces of their own writing in many genres.

writing about reading

Children responding to reading a text by writing and sometimes drawing.

writing words fluently

Children learning to write words fast by writing a word several times.

"You Try It"

A prompt given by the teacher that directs a child to make an attempt at reading a word during oral reading.

▶ Using the Fountas and Pinnell Calculator/Stopwatch

Using the Fountas and Pinnell Calculator/Stopwatch will facilitate taking a Reading Record on each child. This device is easy to use in conjunction with the Recording Form, which can be printed out from the *Lesson Resources CD*. The following are the instructions for using the calculator/stopwatch in abbreviated form. In this guide on page 89 and 90, you can see how to integrate this tool into the administration of the Reading Record.

1. Press **RW** and enter the number of running words (RW) in the text on the calculator/stopwatch.

2. Press **Start Time** on the calculator as the child begins oral reading. Press **End Time** when the reading is complete.

3. Press **#Errors** and enter the number of errors on the calculator.

4. Press **#SC** and enter the number of self-corrections on the calculator.

5. Press **Time** to get **Elapsed Minutes or Seconds**.

6. Press **WPM** to see **Words per Minute**.

7. Press **Accur.%** for **Percentage of Accuracy**.

8. Press **SC** to get the **Self-Correction Ratio**.

▶ LLI as a Complement to Reading Recovery

Reading Recovery is a one-to-one tutoring program for grade 1 children who are the lowest achieving readers in their age cohorts. Selected using multiple assessments, Reading Recovery children receive attention at the developmental moment when one-to-one intervention can make the most difference in learning to read. A large body of research shows that children who receive one-to-one tutoring in Reading Recovery make accelerated progress, catch up with their peers, and become readers in a very short period of time. No other program has ever achieved the results of Reading Recovery. For some children, one-to-one instruction at a particular point in time is the only option that will have successful results. (See the What Works Clearinghouse Web site at www.whatworks.ed.gov.) Group instruction can not replace Reading Recovery.

A single solution to reading difficulties, however, is seldom enough, even in schools with strong, broad-based, school-wide literacy initiatives. There is a need for a series of interventions so that many more children can benefit. Inevitably, schools will provide small-group instruction to address this need. Leveled Literacy Intervention seeks to make small-group interventions more effective.

Ideally, where Reading Recovery exists, LLI will complement one-to-one tutoring in the following ways:

❑ Children who are having difficulty engaging with reading and writing at mid- and late-kindergarten before they are can have some very specific attention in the form of daily lessons. In our experience, many will develop basic competencies that will enable them to succeed in first grade. Those who do not can enter Reading Recovery immediately in the fall. They will likely enter with a greater level of competence.

❑ Children who are not the lowest achievers in reading but still need extra help can receive intensive instruction beginning in fall of grade one. Some children will not need extra help after the group intervention. If they still need extra help, they can enter Reading Recovery in the second round of children. Reading Recovery is a short term intervention designed to provide 12–20 weeks of intensive individual tutoring, making room for at least 2 "rounds" of children in the available teaching slots over the school year.

❑ Children who are not at discontinuing status at the end of about 20 weeks of Reading Recovery can receive small group support for the rest of the grade one year. Many, with this extended support, will reach expected grade levels.

❑ Children in grades 2 and 3 can receive supplemental instruction of a systematic nature to help them benefit from ongoing class instruction.

The above-described system, combining Reading Recovery and Leveled Literacy Intervention, represents a coherent, multi-layered approach to helping struggling readers. For schools that have Reading Recovery in place, we seek to extend the impact of those expert teachers over the entire school day to serve children in both one-to-one tutoring and small group instruction. For schools that do not have Reading Recovery in place, LLI offers a more effective alternative to many current practices.

▶ Leveled Literacy Intervention Within Comprehensive Educational Systems

LLI is available to schools that want to make it a part of a comprehensive system. It is a streamlined and easy-to-implement group intervention that is effective and works with the one-to-one system. The LLI system includes small books created especially for this purpose. Districts and schools can incorporate LLI into their present system, with these goals:

- ❑ Helping a large number of young children enter the world of literacy.

- ❑ Helping teachers learn the value of a well-selected sequence of texts.

- ❑ Helping teachers learn to plan and implement small group lessons that are very efficient and effective.

- ❑ Creating a system within which multiple needs, at many levels, can be met.

Ultimately, we expect coherent, many-layered systems that embrace highly effective classroom teaching and multiple interventions—some highly individualized and others supportive in systematic ways—to help all children who are having difficulty learning to read and write (see Figure 59 below). We strongly recommend the Leveled Literacy Intervention to prevent long-term difficulties and for identifying children who may need longer term services such as special education. The diagnostic information from LLI can be provided to the SPED teacher. The child who has been in LLI will have made some progress and can enter SPED at a higher level. For a more detailed discussion of a comprehensive literacy system with multiple levels of intervention, see Chapter 21 of *When Readers Struggle: Teaching that Works*.

A Many-Layered System for Early Intervention (K–2)

Grade Level	All Children	Children Who Need Extra Help	
K	Good Classroom Teaching	LLI	
1	Good Classroom Teaching	Reading Recovery if available	For Lowest Achieving
		LLI	For Lowest Achieving not in Reading Recovery
2	Good Classroom Teaching	LLI for lowest achieving	Special Education for children identified for long-term help
3+	Good Classroom Teaching	LLI to Level N	Special Education

FIGURE 59 A Many-Layered System for Early Intervention (K–2)

▶ Bibliography

Armbruster, B.B. F. Lehr, and J. Osborn. *Put Reading First: The Research Building Blocks for Teaching Children to Read*, Jessup, MD: Center for the Improvement of Early Learning Achievement, 2003.

Armbruster, B. B., F. Lehr, and J. Osborn. *Put Reading First: The Research Building Blocks for Teaching Children to Read: Kindergarten through Grade 1.* Jessup, MD: National Institute for Literacy, 2001.

Clay, Marie. *Becoming Literate: the Construction of Inner Control.* Portsmouth, NH, 1991.

Clay, Marie. *Change Over Time in Children's Literacy Development.* Portsmouth, NH: Heinemann, 2001.

Clay, Marie. *By Different Paths to Common Outcomes.* York, ME: Stenhouse, 1998.

Clay, Marie. *The Observation Survey of Early Literary Achievement.* Chicago, IL: Heinemann Library, 2005.

Fountas, Irene C., and Gay Su **Pinnell**. *Fountas and Pinnell Benchmark Assessment System 1: Grades K–2, Levels A–N.* Portsmouth, NH: Heinemann, 2007.

Fountas, Irene C., and Gay Su **Pinnell**. *Guided Reading: Good Teaching for All Children.* Foreword by Mary Ellen Giacobbe, Portsmouth, NH: Heinemann, 1996.

Fountas, Irene C., and Gay Su **Pinnell**. *Fountas and Pinnell Benchmark Assessment System 2: Grades 3–8, Levels L–Z.* Portsmouth, NH: Heinemann, 2007.

Fountas, Irene C., and Gay Su **Pinnell**. *Teaching for Comprehending and Fluency: Thinking, Talking, and Writing About Reading, K–8.* Portsmouth, NH: Heinemann, 2003.

Goldenberg, C. N. "Promoting Early Literacy Achievement Among Spanish-Speaking Children: Lessons from Two Studies." *Getting Ready Right from the Start: Effective Early Literacy Interventions.* Needham, MA: Allyn & Bacon, 1994.

Hiebert, E. H., and B. M. Taylor (Eds.). "Promoting Early Literacy Achievement Among Spanish-Speaking Children: Lessons from Two Studies."

Getting Ready Right from the Start: Effective Early Literacy Interventions. Needham, MA: Allyn & Bacon, 1994.

Juel, C. "Learning to Read and Write: A Longitudinal Study of 54 Children from First Through Fourth Grades." *Journal of Educational Psychology*, Vol. 80, No. 4 (1988), pp. 437-447.

McCarrier, A., I.C. Fountas, and G.S. Pinnell. *Interactive Writing: How Language & Literacy Come Together.* Portsmouth, NH, 1999.

Pikulsky, John J. *Factors Common to Successful Early Intervention Programs.* Boston: Houghton Mifflin, 1997.

Pinnell, Gay Su and Irene C. **Fountas**. *The Continuum of Literacy Learning, Grades K–2: A Guide to Teaching.* Portsmouth, NH: Heinemann, 2007.

Pinnell, Gay Su and Irene C. **Fountas**. *The Continuum of Literacy Learning, Grades 3–8; A Guide to Teaching.* Portsmouth, NH: Heinemann, 2007.

Pinnell, Gay Su and Irene C. **Fountas**. *Phonics Lessons with CD-ROM, Grade K: Letters, Words, and How They Work.* Portsmouth, NH: Heinemann, 2003.

Pinnell, Gay Su and Irene C. **Fountas**. *Phonics Lessons with CD-ROM, Grade 1: Letters, Words, and How They Work.* Portsmouth, NH: Heinemann, 2003.

Pinnell, Gay Su and Irene C. **Fountas**. *Phonics Lessons with CD-ROM, Grade 2: Letters, Words, and How They Work.* Portsmouth, NH: Heinemann, 2003.

Pinnell, Gay Su and Irene C. **Fountas**. *Sing a Song of Poetry, K: A Teaching Resource for Phonemic Awareness, Phonics and Fluency.* Portsmouth, NH: Heinemann, 2004.

Pinnell, Gay Su and Irene C. **Fountas**. *Sing a Song of Poetry, Grade 1: A Teaching Resource for Phonemic Awareness, Phonics and Fluency.* Portsmouth, NH: Heinemann, 2004.

Pinnell, Gay Su and Irene C. **Fountas**. *Sing a Song of Poetry, Grade 2: A Teaching Resource for Phonemic Awareness, Phonics and Fluency.* Portsmouth, NH: Heinemann, 2003.

Pinnell, Gay Su and Irene C. **Fountas**. *When Readers Struggle: Teaching that Works*. Portsmouth, NH: Heinemann, 2008.

Pinnell, Gay Su and Irene C. **Fountas**. *Word Matters: Teaching Phonics and Spelling in the Reading/ Writing Classroom*. Portsmouth, NH: Heinemann, 1998.

Report of the National Reading Panel: Teaching Children to Read: An Evidence-Based Assessment of the Scientific Research Literature on Reading and Its Implications for Reading Instruction. Reports of the Subgroups. Washington, DC: National Institutes of Health and Human Development, 2001.

Snow, C.E., M.S. Burns and P. Griffin (Eds.). *Committee on the Prevention of Reading Difficulties in Young Children, National Research Council* Washington, DC: National Academy Press, 1998.

Stanovich, K. E. "Matthew Effects in Reading: Some Consequences of Individual Differences in the Acquisition of Literacy." *Reading Research Quarterly*, Vol. 21 (1986), pp. 301-406.

Vygotsky, L.S. *Mind in Society: The Development of Higher Psychological Processes*. Cambridge, MA: Harvard University Press, 1978.